Eric Knowles
ANTIQUES

A Beginner's Guide with over 1,400 Illustrations

Eric Knowles
ANTIQUES

A Beginner's Guide with over 1,400 Illustrations

MITCHELL BEAZLEY

ANTIQUES
by Eric Knowles

First published in Great Britain in 2006 by Mitchell Beazley,
an imprint of Octopus Publishing Group Limited,
2–4 Heron Quays, London E14 4JP.

A CIP catalogue record for this book is available
from the British Library.

ISBN-13: 978 1 84533 234 1
ISBN-10: 1 84533 234 2

Senior executive editor Anna Sanderson
Executive art editors Rhonda Summerbell, Christine Keilty
Senior editors Suzanne Arnold, Emily Anderson
Editor Theresa Bebbington
Proofreader Howard Watson
Design Peter Gerrish
Picture research Nick Wheldon
Indexer Alan Thatcher
Production Jane Rogers

Set in Vectora and Versailles

Colour reproduction by Fine Arts, Hong Kong
Printed and bound in China by Toppan Printing Company Ltd

Contents

Foreword

Some of us are natural-born collectors, while others gravitate to the condition at a later stage in life, started by a chance purchase of an object that catches the eye – then before you know it there are a dozen more in your display cabinet. You realize that you are well and truly hooked as a collector when you begin to drag yourself out of bed at some unearthly hour in the morning in order to be one of the first at some distant antique fair or sale.

So why do we do it? Is it really a distant throwback to our ancestors' past and an innate hunter-gatherer instinct, which has been conditioned by modern living to otherwise remain dormant? Personally, I believe we become collectors with the hope of experiencing the pleasurable adrenalin rush that comes with discovering an unrecognized treasure at a bargain price lurking at the bottom of a cardboard box.

Even as a young boy I collected – and not just the obligatory stamps and coins. For some reason I became fascinated with the beautifully decorated tissue paper in which fruit was individually wrapped during the early 1960s. I gathered a hundred plus and soon became the bane of most of our local greengrocers. Fossils soon followed, but the weight involved made a large collection impractical and they, along with my prize stalactite, were banished from the house. As a child of the space age I was never short of a ray gun and a robot or two – how I wish I'd kept them, especially after checking the recent auction prices for the robot section of my book.

This book follows and will hopefully complement several others I have written with my own two fingers (God bless the laptop computer), and it endeavours to provide an image-led scenario of the many different subjects awaiting to fascinate and thrill. Having started out in the antique business 35 years ago, I am pleased to announce that I still retain my fascination and am constantly enthralled.

Writing this book has been a pure indulgence on my part and I have tried to concentrate on those areas where I have had the opportunity to see and handle the goods illustrated. The prices shown against each image are the actual auction hammer prices, and it is wise to accept them as a guide rather than as a definitive value.

Virtually all the illustrations in my book are courtesy of Bonhams, the auctioneers, and I am grateful to all my colleagues in Britain and the United States for their much valued advice and support. I am especially grateful to my Chairman Robert Brooks, without whose permission to allow me access to the company's marvellous image library this book would have never have been written.

At an editorial level I have benefited from splendid support by the team at Mitchell Beazley, especially Anna Sanderson, the commissioning editor, and Suzanne Arnold, my senior editor who made such a sterling effort to ensure this finished result.

I can only hope that you enjoy what waits between the pages. Happy hunting!

Eric Knowles *F.R.S.A*

Introduction

If you find the world of antiques more than a little daunting, let me reassure you that even the great experts started out with only their enthusiasm and a thirst for knowledge. For any new collector, rule number one is don't be tempted to spend money, except for purchasing one or two good reference books. Without any "feel" for objects, it is only too easy to make expensive mistakes, but a good range of books will earn their keep – however costly the initial outlay may seem. For those entering the antiques and collectables arena, what follows are the other basic ground rules.

Dealers and antiques shops

Although books provide essential information, no matter how well-read you become, they can never compensate for hands-on experience. The more you can handle objects and study their distinguishing features, the more of an instinct you will develop for knowing when something is good, bad, or indifferent. You should also pick up a knowledge of styles and periods, which will help you to date pieces and set the appropriate alarm bells ringing. For example, a porcelain trinket box painted with a female figure wearing a costume that features a bustle cannot be from the 18th century because the bustle had not been invented until the 19th century.

Get to know one or two dealers who run either antiques shops or galleries. Those worth their salt will be happy for you to examine the stock if they feel reassured that you will handle items with care, and they are usually a fountain of useful information. It's amazing how much more attentive they become should you decide to make a purchase.

There are many collectors who only buy pieces through one or two dealers whom they trust and respect and who, in many cases, become valued friends. Once you build up a good relationship with a dealer, he or she will go to endless trouble to find the pieces they know you are looking for, and buying in this way is usually a relaxed process involving none of the pressures bidding at auction can hold.

If you have never bought or sold from an antiques shop, contact the professional organizations to which the best dealers belong; they carry out a strict selection procedure before admitting members. These include the BADA (British Antiques Dealers' Association) and LAPADA (London and Provincial Antiques Dealers' Association) in Great Britain and NAADAAI (National Antique and Art Dealers' Association of America Incorporated) in the United States. Once you have the members' list, you can select those who seem to hold the type of stock that interests you. Check their opening times before you make a visit because dealers are often out buying early in the morning or may spend part of the day attending auction views or sales.

If you make a purchase, make sure you get a written receipt stating exactly what the object is, its date,

authenticity, and any known history (called its provenance). If it is in pristine condition, ask the dealer to note this down too, so that you are covered if you later find that areas have been restored, or even that the piece is not genuine.

The auction

You will find that auction houses are another great "hands-on" learning environment. They are in the business of buying and selling, and could not survive without maintaining a good relationship with their clients. There is usually a viewing of goods before a sale, and experts will be available to answer questions. You can browse and touch, and any advice will be a good mixture of history and common sense. If any aspect of an auction sale seems intimidating to you, sit in on several sales until you feel comfortable enough to become a potential buyer. A good sale with an experienced auctioneer who knows how to handle the room can be as entertaining as a trip to the theatre. It won't be long before the atmosphere rubs off on you and you become smitten by the auction bug!

A catalogue is produced for each sale with each item or group of items (known as lots) allocated a number and a description. At some small, weekly auctions, such as those held in farm outbuildings or hired halls, this can consist simply of a photocopied sheet handed out as you arrive,

but at the larger auction houses, you should expect to pay from £10/$17 to £30/$55 for an illustrated catalogue. The catalogue will state the viewing time for the sale and when the items are displayed for potential buyers to look at and handle. Check the times carefully and confirm them by telephone, particularly if a journey is involved. Printing errors do slip through occasionally!

Allow yourself plenty of time to view, which should be relaxed and unhurried. Examine pieces carefully for damage or restoration and don't be afraid to ask questions. If you cannot get to the view, the larger houses will supply condition reports over the telephone, but there is no real substitute for handling the goods yourself. Read the wording relating to the objects you are interested in carefully, and satisfy yourself completely that the pieces are exactly what you want before you set yourself a limit on how high you are prepared to bid to secure them.

Bidding at auction

If you can't face bidding yourself, or if you can't get to the sale, most auction houses provide a free and confidential bidding service where a commission clerk will act for you. If you are bidding and the lots you are interested in are at the end of the sale, ask how many lots per hour the auctioneer expects to sell. The average number is 80 to 140, so you can

time your arrival, but remember that you have to register, giving your personal and bank details, before being issued with a numbered card or "paddle" and entering the saleroom.

If you intend to spend a significant amount, it is advisable to let the accounts department know at least 24 hours before the sale so that they can get the necessary guarantees from your bank that the funds are in place. Don't forget to add 10 to 20 percent for commission onto the hammer price, plus tax on the commission, to arrive at the final price you will have to pay per item. If you want to be able to walk away with your pieces, cash or card are the best methods of payment. The terms and conditions of sale are usually explained in the catalogue, including a clause stating that you can return any object you have bought within a certain time limit if you can prove without doubt that it is a forgery.

Bidding techniques vary enormously, from the slightest nod of the head to the firm raising of the paddle, but it is a complete myth that a slight gesture will result in you becoming the unwitting owner of a valuable and unwanted object. An auctioneer will always confirm that the final bid is definite, often by pointing to where the last bid came from or announcing that the bid is "on my left" or "at the back" before bringing down the hammer. Initially, it is best to make your bid absolutely clear by raising your card or paddle. Remember, too, that the auctioneer is there to achieve the best prices possible for the sellers, so set

yourself a top limit before you make a single bid and try not to get carried away by making that extra bid, which can so easily turn into two or three.

If you are successful, you may be able to "clear" your item or items while the sale is still in progress, or you may have to wait until the final lot has been offered. Most auction houses offer at least seven days free storage if you are waiting for a cheque to clear. After that, you will find yourself paying storage charges on a per lot, per day basis. If you are buying furniture, find out if it should be collected from the saleroom or from storage elsewhere.

Selling an antique or collectable

If you have a piece you want to sell and you don't know its value, taking it to an auction house is the best policy. Not only will your item be valued free of charge, but it is in the saleroom's interest to get the best price for it at auction: the higher the price realized, the more commission they earn.

It is often a good idea initially to send photographs or e-mail images of your object to several houses, asking for an indication of its value, but the estimates they give should always be confirmed by an expert who is able to examine the piece properly. If you are selling a substantial amount of property, or a collection that the experts think may be worth a good deal of money, they will make the journey to you to

give a valuation. The service is usually free, although if you live at a distance, the saleroom may charge the expert's travelling expenses. The expert will give you a potential auction value for your object and also recommend a price under which it cannot be sold: the protective reserve.

Before you allow your property to be "taken in" for sale, ask exactly what charges you will be paying and write them down so that you can work out how much money you should have once you have paid seller's commission (15–20 percent), insurance costs while the object is waiting to come up for sale (usually 1 to 1.5 percent of the hammer price, levied after the sale), and illustration costs, which are always agreed prior to production of the catalogue.

In return for entering into a contract with the saleroom, it is obliged to present a true and fair description of your property in a catalogue, along with an estimate of its value. It should also announce the auction in all the relevant local, national, or trade publications. The top houses will also have access to an international network of dealers, collectors, and museums, who will be alerted to any objects or collections of great interest. Should your piece sell, how quickly you receive your money depends on how long it takes the saleroom to receive payment from the buyer, but expect to wait an average of one week to a month.

When selling at an auction, a reserve price can safeguard your object from selling below a certain price, but it may not sell for the valuation price, or if you are lucky, it can acheive a higher price than the valuation. If you sell to a dealer, you won't have to worry about the deductions an auction house makes for commission and other charges, but you should have a good idea of what your property is worth before selling to a dealer. The price you agree on will be the sum you receive. Once the dealer has handed you the money and a receipt for your object, it belongs to him. Most pay cash when buying and will ask you to sign a book that can be checked by the police. They need some assurance that the piece is legally yours to sell. Dealers must protect their credibility and minimize any risk of prosecution.

The internet

Finally, there is the internet market that some folk swear by and others avoid at all costs. I personally prefer being able to handle an object before parting with hard-earned cash. However, I know plenty of people in the antiques business who both buy and sell well online. The premier selling and auction sites police their marketplace and sellers are graded as a result of feedback from buyers so there is a real attempt to foster confidence. It may well be part of modern-day shopping and it might save on petrol, but for yours truly it is a positively soul-less exercise – call me old-fashioned; after all, in my business there's no greater compliment.

Artistic Styles and Periods

British Periods

French Periods

Styles	AD	British Periods	French Periods
Gothic	1450	**Late Medieval** (c.1400–85)	**Gothic** (1140–1500)
	1500		
	1510		
	1520		
	1530	**Tudor** (Henry VII, 1485–1509)	**Renaissance** (1500–1610)
	1540	(Henry VIII, 1509–47)	
	1550	(Edward VI, 1547–53)	
	1560	(Mary I, 1553–58)	
	1570	(Elizabeth I, 1558–1603)	
Renaissance	1580		
	1590		
	1600		
	1610	**Jacobean** (James I, 1603–25)	
	1620		**Louis XIII** (1610–43)
	1630	**Carolean** (Charles I, 1625–49)	
	1640		
	1650	**Cromwellian** (Commonwealth, 1649–60)	
	1660		
Baroque	1670	**Restoration** (Charles II, 1660–85)	**Louis XIV** (1643–1715)
	1680	(James II, 1685–88)	
	1690	(William III and Mary II, 1688–94)	
	1700	(William III, 1694–1702)	
	1710	(Anne, 1702–14)	
Rococo	1720	**Early Georgian** (George I, 1714–27)	**Regence** (1715–23)
	1730		
	1740	**Mid Georgian** (George II, 1727–60)	**Louis XV** (1723–74)
	1750		
	1760		
	1770		
Neoclassicism	1780	**Late Georgian** (George III, 1760–1820)	**Louis XVI** (1774–93)
	1790		
	1800		**Directoire** (1793–99)
Empire	1810		**Empire** (1799–1815)
Regency	1820	**Regency** (George, Prince Regent, 1811–20)	**Restauration** (1815–30)
	1830	**George IV** (1820–30) / **William IV** (1830–37)	**Louis-Philippe** (1830–48)
	1840		
Revival	1850		
	1860	**Victorian** (Victoria 1837–1901)	**Second Empire** (1848–70)
	1870		
Aesthetic	1880		
Art Nouveau	1890		**Third Republic** (1870–1945)
	1900		
Arts and Crafts	1910	**Edwardian** (Edward VII (1901–10)	
	1920	**George V** (1910–36)	
Art Deco	1930	**Edward VIII** (1936: abdicated same year)	
	1940	**George VI** (1936–52)	
Post-modernism	1950		**Postwar Design** (1945–)
	1960	**Elizabeth II** (1952–)	

German Periods

Gothic
(1140–1500)

Renaissance
(1500–1650)

Baroque
(1650–1730)

Rococo
(1730–60)

Neoclassicism
(1760–1800)

Empire (1800–15)

Biedermeier
(1815–48)

Revivale
(1830–90)

Jugendstil (1890–1915)

Moderne/Bauhaus (1915–33)

Fascist Idealism (1933–45)

Postwar Design (1945–)

How to use this table

The timelines on these pages show general artistic styles or movements in the blue columns down the sides, and more specific information in the country-by-country columns. Design practices do not usually have definite start and end dates because some people continue to use an old style even after new ideas have become popular. The most extreme of these overlaps are indicated by the dotted lines in the blue columns.

The terms given are a combination of artistic styles and names of kings or types of government. This is because these are the terms used by antiques experts to refer to design trends throughout time; sometimes they do not match the terms used by historians. For instance, the timeline for the United States allocates the years 1700 to 1730 to William and Mary, yet the British reign of those monarchs was from 1688 to 1694. This difference in dating arises from the fact that what is known as the "William and Mary" style is used by American design historians to categorize the style prevalent between 1700 and 1730.

American Periods

Pre-Colonial
(To 1625)

Early Colonial (Pilgrim)
(1625–1700)

William and Mary
(1700–30)

Queen Anne
(1725–55)

Chippendale
(1755–90)

Federal (1790–1815)

Empire (1815–40)

Restauration (1830–40)

Revival
(1840–70)

Aesthetic (1870–80)

Arts and Crafts (1880–1930)
Art Nouveau (1890–1910)

Art Deco/Moderne (1920–45)

Postwar Design (1945–)

1610	
1620	
1630	
1640	
1650	
1660	**Baroque**
1670	
1680	
1690	
1700	
1710	
1720	**Rococo**
1730	
1740	
1750	
1760	
1770	
1780	**Neoclassicism**
1790	
1800	
1810	**Empire**
1820	**Regency**
1830	
1840	
1850	**Revival**
1860	
1870	
1880	**Aesthetic**
1890	**Art Nouveau**
1900	
1910	**Arts and Crafts**
1920	
1930	**Art Deco**
1940	
1950	**Post-modernism**
1960	

Furniture

1

2

3

4

1 Dutch bombé-shaped marquetry bureau, *c*.1800
2 Regency mahogany sideboard, *c*.1820
3 Charles II walnut stool, *c*.1680
4 Regency rosewood chiffonier, *c*.1820

Most people during the Middle Ages had few items of furniture. A typical house might contain a stool or two, a simple table, and a wooden box in which to store a few possessions.

In the early 18th century, furniture began to appear with details that were for purely decorative purposes, and as customs and habits changed, new types of furniture were made. The bureau (a writing desk with a sloping front and drawers) came into being as more people learned to write, and bureau bookcases began to appear as mass printing made books less expensive and more readily available.

Formal dining rooms were established in Europe and the United States by the end of the 18th century. The sideboard was invented so that food could be served from its surface and table linen stored beneath. Dumb waiters for displaying foods, wine coolers, and knife boxes took care of other aspects of dining.

The rapidly expanding and prosperous middle class wanted to spend their increased leisure time in luxury and comfort. As a result, more upholstered furniture was produced. Glass became less expensive, enabling decorative mirrors to be made in great quantity, and they were used to reflect light in a room. Boudoir furniture was constructed for the bedroom of the lady of the house and solid library pieces for the master.

Where to begin

Buying a piece of antique furniture is a big purchase, so when deciding on your first piece take your time. Learn to be systematic and don't be afraid of handling objects, looking inside and underneath them, and pulling out drawers to examine them more carefully.

5

6

7

8

5 William IV oak window seat, *c*.1835
6 Regency mahogany drum table, *c*.1820
7 William IV carved giltwood Baroque sofa, *c*.1830
8 French kingwood commode, *c*.1790

Wood

Learning to differentiate between the wide variety of wood takes time. The more you look at and handle antique furniture, the shorter will be your apprenticeship. Wood can be transformed in colour by insensitive restoration or by applying a dark varnish. Inspect the areas where the wood is unfinished and in its natural state to identify it.

Amaranth A dense wood with a purplish colour, maturing to a dark brown and whitish grain. Also known as "purpleheart". Imported from Central America and used in Holland and France from the late 17th century, initially as a veneer on cabinets.

Amboyna Imported from the Moluccas, a wood with an orange-brown colour and tightly curled, iridescent grain. Used in Europe and the United States as a veneer in the first half the 19th century.

Birch A lustrous, cream-white to biscuit-coloured wood indigenous to Europe, with straight grain and fine texture. It has good properties for steam bending. First used as a veneer in the 18th century.

Bird's-eye maple Imported from Canada and United States. A creamy white colour when felled. Rotary cut to produce a "bird's-eye" figure.

Calamander A dense hardwood, also known as zebrawood, with strong yellow streaks alternating with dull brown to blackish stripes. Imported from the Coromandel Coast of India and later from West Africa. Used in the solid form in American Colonial furniture but as a veneer in Europe.

Elm Light brown wood from the temperate regions, similar in appearance to oak but without the medullary rays and a more noticeable grain

Types of wood

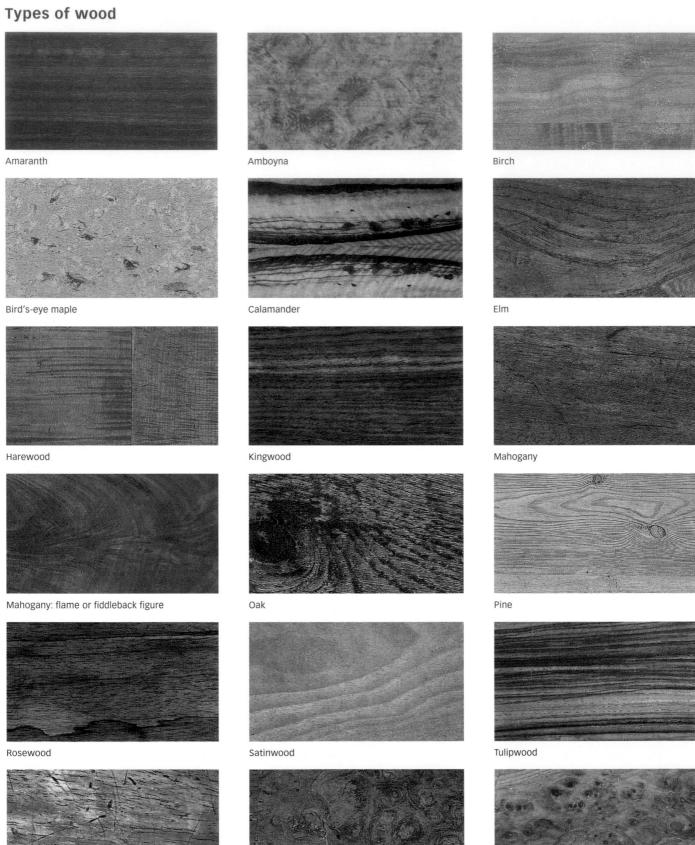

Amaranth

Amboyna

Birch

Bird's-eye maple

Calamander

Elm

Harewood

Kingwood

Mahogany

Mahogany: flame or fiddleback figure

Oak

Pine

Rosewood

Satinwood

Tulipwood

Walnut

Walnut: burr figure

Yew: burr figure

due to its faster growth. Used for Windsor chair seats in Britain and provincial chests of drawers.

Harewood A term used for stained sycamore, a light coloured softwood displaying strong parallel lines on a speckled ground. Favoured in the early 18th century by French cabinet-makers and used in parquetry and cross-banding.

Kingwood West Indian wood with fine, purple streaks, fading quickly to greyish brown when exposed to air and light. Used as cross-banding due to being available in only small blocks.

Mahogany A variety of hardwoods from Honduras, the West Indies, and other tropical areas with a hard, dense, reddish colour and straight grain to finely figured veneers. The most popular wood from the early 18th century due to its strength and its ease of importation. Modern mahogany is coarse and open-grained and bears little resemblance to its 18th-century counterpart.

Oak Hard, strong wood available in good plank widths and used throughout history in Europe and the United States. Identifiable by the medullary rays (iridescent flecks) that can be accentuated by the way it is cut. It is resistant to woodworm.

Pine and deal A large group of wood used in Britain and the United States that is soft and pale, but darkens with age. It is inexpensive wood often used for the unseen parts of furniture. Provincial English and American furniture was made in solid pine, but little has survived with its original painted or waxed finish.

Rosewood Highly figured reddish wood with almost black streaks imported from Brazil, where the best specimens were available, and the Far East. When first cut, it is dark and purplish. The decorative figuring only becomes apparent after exposure to air. Rosewood pieces are difficult to repolish because the purplish colour comes through again if the surface is removed. Used mainly during the late 18th and early 19th centuries in Europe.

Satinwood Two main varieties of this yellow, iridescent wood come from the East and the West Indies. The East Indies' variety, paler and with more subtle figuring, was used at the end of the 18th century for English Sheraton-style furniture. The more vibrant West Indies' variety was used in Europe and the United States at the end of the 19th century.

Tulipwood A hard dense wood with a reddish pink grain. Imported from Brazil and Peru and known in France as *bois de rose*. The strongly figured grain and smooth texture made it suitable for parquetry and marquetry, but it was mainly used for cross-banding from the late 18th century.

Walnut The most predominantly used cabinet-makers' wood until the mid-18th century, when mahogany began to be imported. It enjoyed a revival from the mid-19th century as a veneer in Europe and the United States. It was used in many forms, from plain, straight planks used in the solid form for tabletops and chair frames, to highly figured burrs.

Yew Reddish brown hardwood used in solid or veneered form for much British provincial furniture, with the choicest burr veneers reserved for making tea caddies and other small items.

Construction

Before the late 15th century, medieval chests with drop lids consisted of planks of wood simply nailed together, with iron hinges and bands supplied by the blacksmith. The development of the mortise-and-tenon joint in the 16th century enabled a "joiner" to create a strong frame to support panels of wood. Rectangular holes were cut into the vertical sections, known as stiles, to make mortises. The tenons, similarly shaped pieces of wood jutting out from the horizontal sections, known as rails, fitted into them and were held together by pegs or dowels.

As furniture became more sophisticated, the cabinet-maker carried out any work beyond the capabilities of the joiner. A strong, smooth carcass was constructed as the framework for a piece of case furniture, usually in pine or oak, with dovetail joints used to hold together the sides, the top, and the base of the carcass. Dovetail joints comprise two interlocking fan-shaped tenons that make a right-angled joint. The carcass was then veneered, usually by a different craftsman, but the areas that would remain unseen – for example, because the piece was intended to be placed against a wall – were not finely finished. Panelled construction was used for the backs of late 18th-century furniture. Bow-fronted chests were constructed using small pieces of timber, "block built" in the same way as laying bricks and then smoothed to the required shape. This technique, developed in the later 18th century, was less wasteful than cutting a curve from solid wood and created finer, more delicate lines.

The earliest drawers were usually made with two dovetails to a side, pinned for greater strength. The number of dovetails increased, and they became finer as the 18th century progressed. Check that each drawer of a piece has the same number of dovetails and has not had replacement pieces added because this affects value. Early drawers had channels cut in their sides, which ran on runners set into the carcass. After *c.*1702, runners went underneath the drawers and ran on bearers along the inside of the carcass. Runners are prone to wear but replacements are acceptable. Drawer linings from the 17th century are often 2cm (¾in) thick, but they became finer, thinning down to 0.5cm (¼in) by the 18th century. Drawer fronts from the 17th century have

Types of joints and screws

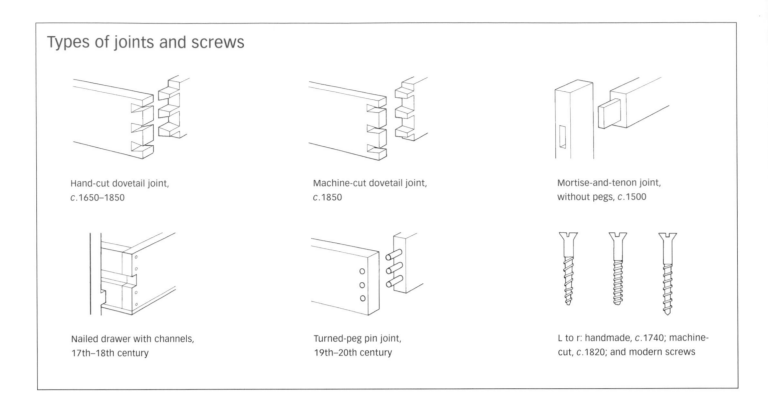

Hand-cut dovetail joint,
c.1650–1850

Machine-cut dovetail joint,
c.1850

Mortise-and-tenon joint,
without pegs, *c*.1500

Nailed drawer with channels,
17th–18th century

Turned-peg pin joint,
19th–20th century

L to r: handmade, *c*.1740; machine-
cut, *c*.1820; and modern screws

either simple, raised decoration or mouldings fixed to them, but they became flat by the 18th century and were finished off with quarter-round moulding or cock beading (a slip of rounded wood).

Nails and screws should be treated with scepticism. Do not use them to judge the age of a piece because they often fell out and were replaced. Old nails were hand cut until *c*.1790. You may find old nails in fakes and alterations, because they can be recovered from timbers from demolished houses and sold on. The earliest screws were made *c*.1675 with hand-filed threads. The spiral is shallow, and they have almost no taper or point. The slots in the top are usually slightly off-centre. If you are looking at a piece supposedly made prior to this date and it contains screws, either the piece is not genuine or the screws have been added during repair.

The metal mounts on a piece of furniture can be useful guides to dating. These include hinges, handles, locks, and escutcheons. However, handles are often replaced to update an item to make it more fashionable. Replacement handles are acceptable if they are in keeping with the piece. Feet are another guide to dates, but because they are susceptible to wear, they are also often replaced. The bun feet on late 17th- and early 18th-century furniture are almost always replacements and are acceptable.

Decoration

Carving A natural development from whittling, paring, and shaping wood with sharp tools, which became increasingly sophisticated as time went on. Close-grained woods are more suitable for carving than open-grained ones, such as oak. Original carving on a solid piece of wood protrudes from it because a generous amount of timber was allowed for it before work began. However, carving added later to "improve" a piece has to eat into the existing timber of, for instance, a cabriole leg. Looking at good, original examples will help you to spot the difference. Later carving reduces the value of a piece considerably.

Veneer Applying thin sheets of fine wood to a carcass of cheaper, coarser wood is an ideal way of using expensive timber sparingly. The figure of the wood, the pattern made by the grain, can make a piece more desirable. Certain woods such as satinwood, kingwood, and calamander were used only for veneers either because the timber was scarce and expensive, or because the size of the trunks produced planks too small to be used in any other way. Walnut and mahogany were used both for veneer and for solid pieces. Hand-cut veneer from the 17th and 18th centuries is often up to 0.3cm (⅛in) thick. Modern machine-cut veneer is almost paper thin.

Cutting along the length of a log produces "straight cut" veneer, across the grain produces "cross cut" veneer, and slices cut transversely from branches produce circular-patterned, "oyster" veneer. Successive slices can be opened out so that one is the mirror image of the other, and four successive slices at the top and bottom of a panel are known as "quarter" veneer. Cutting through the irregular growths from trunks or roots of trees such as walnut, ash, elm, and yew produces decorative "burr" veneers.

Small sections or strips of veneer known as banding are used around the edges of drawer fronts and surfaces to complement the principal veneer. Cross-banding is laid in short sections at right angles to the main veneer; straight banding is applied in one long strip; and feather- or herringbone-banding consists of two strips of diagonally banded veneers, creating a featherlike appearance.

Marquetry A type of ornamental veneer made up of interlocking pieces of wood to form a pattern. Different, contrasting colours of veneer can create stunning effects of perspective and illusion. When the pattern is geometric, it is referred to as parquetry.

Inlay Where small pieces of ivory, mother-of-pearl, precious metals, or wood are fitted into indentations chiselled into the furniture to create patterns or pictures. Stringing involves laying narrow strips of inlay of contrasting colour.

Gilding Since ancient times, wood has been decorated with gold leaf, wafer thin layers of the precious metal. Once several layers of gesso (a mixture of whiting, linseed oil, and size) are applied to the surface of the piece, it is treated with a "mordant" to help the gold leaf adhere. On water-gilded pieces, the mordant is a mixture of red clay, or "bole", with egg white and hot water. Water is used to moisten the surface before the gold leaf is applied, often in two layers, which is then burnished. The mordant for the cheaper oil-gilding is cooked linseed oil mixed with ground raw sienna. Gold leaf is applied to this much stickier surface as a single layer.

Lacquering and japanning True lacquer, painstakingly applied to furniture and smaller objects in as many as 200 layers in China and Japan, uses the refined sap of the *Rhus vernicifera* tree. Europeans, anxious to copy the technique as early as the late 17th century, were unable to discover this essential ingredient and began to use shellac (a resinlike substance produced by certain insects) as an imitation. Good quality Japanese lacquer was imported to Europe at this time, so the process was referred to in England as "japanning" and this term remains. In England, japanned sheet-iron made into useful and decorative objects is known as Pontypool ware (the first factory was at Pontypool in Wales). Excellent imitations of Oriental lacquer were also produced in the Low Countries and in France.

Painting Painted and stencilled furniture is fashionable today, but the modern equivalent is reviving a style in favour as long ago as the 14th and 15th centuries, when oak furniture was first painted. At this time, the favoured medium was tempera (powdered pigment mixed with size, varnish, or egg white) applied over gesso. In the 18th century, satinwood and beech-veneered furniture was painted with borders and medallions in the Neoclassical style, and then varnished. During the 19th century, wood was painted to simulate marble, and the leaders of the Arts and Crafts Movement decorated cabinets and cupboards.

Types of furniture decoration

Carving

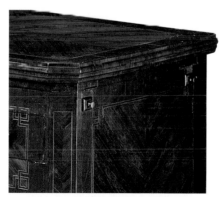

Veneer

Marquetry

Gilding

Lacquering

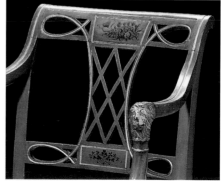

Painting

Oak and Country Furniture

The amount of medieval oak furniture available to the collector today is extremely limited and usually expensive, whereas a surprising number of 17th-century pieces regularly appear on the market. The value for one of these pieces generally depends upon its original condition, the quality of the carving, and whether or not a piece is dated. It is still possible to find relatively plain late 17th-century oak coffers selling at auction for less than £300/$500. However, it is far more likely that you will find oak furniture produced during the 18th and early 19th centuries. There is a much wider variety of pieces available and these are sold at more affordable prices.

In the towns and cities, 18th-century cabinet-makers catered to the prevailing fashion. Walnut was in the greatest demand, followed by mahogany. Although oak and country furniture followed the forms popularized by the city dwellers, country cabinet-makers were more occupied with providing their clientele with sturdy, practical furniture, which was sometimes custom made for a particular situation. These pieces often lagged a few years behind the styles favoured in the cities, but they were – and still remain – both serviceable and affordable. For those that appreciate rustic furniture more than the sophisticated pieces made by city cabinet-makers, such criteria add to its enduring charm.

Oak court cupboard. 1670–1700, 175cm (69in) high, £2,700/$4,600

Oak open armchair. 1670–1700, size unavailable, £3,200/$5,450

Oak side table. 1670–1700, 73cm (29in) high, £480/$815

Oak wainscot chair, made in Yorkshire, England. 1660–90, size unavailable, £1,450/$2,465

Oak side chair. 1670–90, size unavailable, £400/$680

Oak court cupboard. Dated 1693, 158cm (62in) high, £2,500/$4,250

Oak court cupboard

In the 17th century, the court cupboard (a type of sideboard) was a status symbol. Most had two sections, not three (as in this one). Regional differences often indicate the place of origin. This example does not bear a date; treat dated pieces – especially those with early 18thC dates – with suspicion. *1600–50, 154cm (61in) high, £3,600/$6,100*

The carving is original and has none of the stiffness or sharp edges of a Victorian copy. Learning about period construction will help you assess whether carving was added long after a piece was made.

The piece should display a deep surface patination, often of a colour akin to molasses, due to centuries of beeswax and accidental dirt being rubbed into the grain.

The shelves were intended for displaying the family pewter – or the silver tableware of a rich mercantile family.

The legs are often replaced. This is usually expected and is considered acceptable.

Oak centre table. 1670–1700, 64cm (25in) high, £1,000/$1,700

Oak lowboy with integral press. 1740–60, 73cm (29in) high, £900/$1,530

Oak dresser base. 1700–40, 82cm (32in) high, £6,000/$10,200

Oak dresser, with boarded rack (shelves). 1740–60, 213cm (84in) high, £3,000/$5,100

Oak and Country Furniture

Oak bureau-on-stand. 1740–60, 106cm (42in) high, £500/$850

Oak lowboy. 1740–60, 73cm (29in) high, £900/$1,530

Oak high dresser, with open rack (shelves) and central cupboard. 1760–90, 203cm (80in) high, £2,500/$4,250

Oak linen press. 1760–90, 206cm (81in) high, £2,000/$3,400

Elm box settle. 1750–90, 124cm (49in) high, £1,400/$2,400

Oak high dresser, with open rack. 1770–1800, 195cm (77in) high, £1,100/$1,870

Oak high dresser. 1770–1800, 200cm (79in) high, £1,500/$2,550

Oak and mahogany bureau, with cross-banding. 1760–90, 105cm (41in) high, £300/$510

Oak high dresser. 1770–1800, 218cm (86in) high, £3,000/$5,100

Oak low dresser. 1800–30, 88cm (35in) high, £1,500/$2,550

Sycamore and oak candle stand. 1800–30, 75cm (30in) high, £500/$850

Oak standing corner cupboard. 1800–30, 204cm (80in) high, £600/$1,020

Fruitwood occasional table. 1800–25, 67cm (26in) high, £550/$935

Oak dresser, with boarded back. 1800–30, 202cm (80in) high, £2,900/$4,900

"Harlequin" set of nine ash Windsor chairs. 1820–50, size unavailable, £1,000/$1,700

"Harlequin" set of ten ash ladderback chairs. 1800–30, size unavailable, £3,000/$5,100

Chests of Drawers and Commodes

A coffer with a lift-up top was a satisfactory box in which to store a few possessions, but it was impractical for storing a large number of personal effects – it was difficult to keep them in an organized manner, with everything within easy reach. Creating small sections for storage – drawers – within the box, which were accessible from the front, was one of the best design solutions in the history of furniture.

Chests of drawers were first made in the mid-17th century, and by the 18th century they were a common feature in the homes of the wealthy. In the 17th century, they were made mostly in walnut or oak, with small round "bun" feet. By the 18th century, mahogany was the favoured wood and feet were made in a bracket form; construction methods were also becoming increasingly finer. Variations evolved as the 18th century progressed, and new forms included chests-on-chests (tallboys), cabinets-on-chests, linen presses, and side cabinets – along with many elegant forms, such as the shallow double S-shape of a "serpentine" front and the bulbous "bombé" shape. The commode (a chest with drawers, cupboards, or both) with a convex "bow-front" was popular in the United States. During the 19th century the choice of woods increased: satinwood was popular in Britain; blonde woods such as ash and maple were popular in France and Germany; and walnut veneers were favoured throughout southern Europe.

British Chests

William and Mary walnut chest, with oyster veneer and boxwood cross-banding. 1680–1700, 86cm (34in) high, £2,200/$3,750

William and Mary princewood chest-on-stand, with cross-banding. 1680–1700, 94cm (37in) high, £2,200/$3,750

Walnut bachelor's chest, with cross- and feather-banding (and some restoration). 1720–40, 74cm (29in) high, £15,000/$25,500

George I walnut chest, with cross- and feather-banding. 1720–30, 79cm (31in) high, £10,000/$17,000

George I walnut chest-on-stand, with cross-banding. 1720–30, 117cm (46in) high, £3,800/$6,450

George III mahogany serpentine chest, with later carved details. 1760–80, 84cm (33in) high, £4,200/$7,150

Early George III mahogany serpentine chest.
1760–70, 89cm (35in) high, £6,000/$10,200

George III mahogany serpentine chest, with an enclosed hinged writing surface and carved detail. 1760–80, 89cm (35in) high, £9,500/$16,150

Regency mahogany serpentine chest, with a brushing slide and reeded carved details. 1800–20, 84cm (33in) high, £4,600/$7,800

Continental Commodes

Louis XIV commode, with palisander, amaranth, ebony, and brass marquetry, in the manner of Noel Gerard. 1710–35, 81cm (32in) high, £14,000/$23,800

French Régence kingwood and rosewood bombé commode, with gilt bronze mounts. 1750–70, 86cm (34in) high, £15,000/$25,500

Swedish kingwood and rosewood bombé commode, with parquetry, and gilt metal mounts. 1740–60, 84cm (33in) high, £2,800/$4,750

Early Italian Empire walnut commode.
1800–30, 92cm (36in) high, £1,600/$2,700

Chests, Tallboys, and Linen Presses

Originating in Europe, the chest-on-stand gained popularity in England in the 17th century. It was made in two sections – a chest and a stand – for ease of mobility. However, with the arrival of the 18th century, the more practical chest-on-chest, or tallboy, became popular. (It was referred to as a highboy in colonial America.) It was also made in two sections. The top chest usually incorporated three short drawers above three long drawers and the bottom chest was often fitted with three long graduated drawers.

Early examples were often rectangular and veneered in walnut. However, by the mid-18th century, solid mahogany became the most popular choice, along with the fashionable serpentine and bow-front shapes. As the century progressed cabinet-makers began using mahogany veneers, and they embellished their work with carved decoration, especially friezes of interlaced "blind" fretwork (the decoration was not pierced, or "open"). Tall pieces with flat tops were given pediments, which eventually developed into broken swan-neck types with a central carved urn, eagle, or other feature.

The linen, or clothes, press was also favoured during the second half of the 18th century. It consisted of a tall cupboard with two doors opening to reveal a series of shallow sliding drawers. It was normally found – but not exclusively – in mahogany, and was again made in two parts. The lower section contained a series of drawers. The sides sometimes incorporated brass handles for carrying the piece.

British Pieces

William and Mary cabinet-on-stand, with Japanese lacquered panels decorated in gilt, and a British giltwood stand and crest carved and pierced with Baroque scroll forms. *c.*1690, 180cm (71in) high, £8,000/$13,600

Black japanned chest-on-stand. 1705–15, 173cm (68in) high, £1,500/$2,550

George I walnut chest-on-chest, with cross- and feather-banding. 1720–30, 180cm (71in) high, £12,000/$20,400

Early George III mahogany chest-on-chest. 1760–70, 186cm (73in) high, £5,000/$8,500

George III mahogany linen press. 1770–1800, 190cm (75in) high, £4,000/$6,800

George III mahogany serpentine linen press, with shallow sliding drawers above two drawers. *c*.1780, 193cm (76in) high, £3,000/$5,100

Early George III mahogany mule chest. 1760–70, 104cm (41in) high, £2,800/$4,750

Continental Pieces

Antwerp cabinet-on-stand, with scarlet tortoiseshell and ebony ripple moulding, and drawers flanking a central cupboard between classical columns – the ebony stand with spiral twist legs is a later addition. 1640–70, size unavailable, £7,000/$11,900

Spanish walnut chest, with parcel gilding. 1620–90, 83cm (33in) high, £4,000/$6,800

Dutch Colonial chest. 1640–80, 72cm (28in) high, £1,500/$2,550

German walnut cabinet-on-chest, with marquetry and cross-banding. 1740–60, 206cm (81in) high, £6,000/$10,200

Chairs and Sofas

The stool had become commonplace in most homes by the 16th century, and new features were added to the stool in the 17th century. It had acquired a panel back and, in some cases, open arms – thus the chair, as we recognize it today, was created. The development of furniture design in the 18th century reflected the increase in British and other European wealth, which prompted the demand for more comfortable and stylish chairs. The legs took on the cabriole form (with an outward-curving knee), and upholstery become popular. By the 19th century, the straight leg gained in popularity, and chairs were designed to cater for specialist needs such as nursing chairs, reading chairs, and rocking chairs.

Few chairs produced in walnut in the early 18th century have managed to survive the ravages of woodworm, but 18th-century chairs produced in mahogany have fared much better and are widely available. Sets of chairs are rare and expensive, but pairs and single chairs are easy to find and affordable. You can purchase several single chairs or pairs of chairs in the same design to create a "harlequin" set.

The 18th-century sofa is a rarity when compared with those from the 19th century, especially the deep-buttoned types that were favoured in the latter part of the century. The almost ubiquitous chaise longue is often found at auction for £400/$680, depending on condition and the quality of the frame.

British Chairs and Sofas

Charles II walnut and ebonized armchair.
1660–80, size unavailable, £3,000/$5,100

Oak and elm armchair, in an unusual style.
1670–1700, size unavailable, £2,000/$3,400

Pair of William and Mary walnut side chairs,
with carved details and caning. 1680–1700, size
unavailable, £2,000/$3,400

George I walnut dining chair, with cabriole
legs, from a set of six. 1715–25, size unavailable,
£4,500/$7,650 (for the set)

Pair of George I mahogany side chairs.
1715–25, size unavailable, £3,800/$6,450

George III mahogany armchair, from
a set of 16. 1740–60, size unavailable,
£20,000/$34,000 (for the set)

The shaped moulded toprail exhibits a pagoda-type cresting that extends into the interlaced splat.

George II laburnum armchair

The overall composition of this chair displays an element of ambiguity. It is devoid of the purity that was featured in the "Chinese" furniture designs illustrated in Thomas Chippendale's *The Gentleman & Cabinet Maker's Director,* published a decade after this chair was made. *c.1740–60, size unavailable, £10,000/$17,000*

The outswept arms enclose fret carved Gothic arches. The arched pierced brackets below are purely decorative and many are missing.

The dark and light random mottle pattern in the wood indicates that this chair is of laburnum wood. This is more rare and valuable than mahogany examples.

The back legs continue as one piece to the toprail, which – with the outswept rake of the leg – provides strength to the construction.

George III mahogany dining chair, in the Chippendale Gothic style, from a matched set of 12. 1760–70, size unavailable, £20,000/$34,000 (for the set)

Pair of George III giltwood open armchairs, with carved details, after a design by Matthias Lock. 1755–65, size unavailable, £65,000/$110,500

George III mahogany wingback armchair. 1760–70, size unavailable, £3,500/$5,950

British Chairs and Sofas

George III mahogany side chair. 1760–80, size unavailable, £700/$1,190

George III giltwood open armchair, with carved details. 1780–1800, size unavailable, £2,800/$4,750

George III mahogany upholstered armchair. 1760–80, size unavailable, £7,000/$11,900

Pair of George III mahogany dining chairs, in the manner of Robert Mainwaring. 1760–80, size unavailable, £1,800/$3,050

George III mahogany open armchairs, with spindle backs, set of three. 1765–85, size unavailable, £2,500/$4,250

George III mahogany open armchair, in the French Hepplewhite style and in the manner of John Cobb. 1775–85, size unavailable, £1,000/$1,700

George III giltwood armchair, with carved details, in the manner of Gillows, from a set of six salon chairs. 1780–85, size unavailable, £8,000/$13,600 (for the set)

Pair of George III open armchairs, in the French Hepplewhite style. 1770–90, size unavailable, £8,000/$13,600 (for the pair)

Regency giltwood settee. 1800–20, 203cm (80in) wide, £4,000/$6,800

Geroge III giltwood bergère, with carved details. 1780–1800, size unavailable, £2,800/$4,750

Pair of Regency open armchairs, with later parcel-gilt and green painted decoration. 1800–20, size unavailable, £1,800/$3,050

Regency mahogany X-frame chair, in the manner of Thomas Hope. 1800–10, size unavailable, £6,000/$10,200

George III mahogany side chair, from a set of four. 1800–15, size unavailable, £3,800/$6,450 (for the set)

William IV walnut patent reclining chair, by J. Alderman, London. 1830–40, size unavailable, £1,800/$3,050

Regency rosewood library chair. 1810–30, size unavailable, £1,400/$2,400

Continental Chairs and Sofas

One of a pair of Spanish walnut open armchairs, with leather panel backs and seats. 1670–90, size unavailable, £1,200/$2,050 (for the pair)

Pair of north Italian walnut side armchairs, with carved details. 1740–70, size unavailable, £1,000/$1,700

Pair of Louis XV giltwood *fauteuils* (armchairs), in the manner of Nicolas-Quinibert Foliot (one of the creators of this style of chair).1735–45, size unavailable, £55,000/$93,500

Pair of Louis XVI walnut and beech chairs, with cabriole legs and carved details. 1770–90, size unavailable, £1,000/$1,700

Pair of Louis XIV beechwood chairs, with later decoration. 1690–1710, size unavailable, £3,000/$5,100

Rare pair of Indian export rosewood side chairs. 1760–70, size unavailable, £30,000/$51,000

Pair of Flemish walnut stand chairs, in the Louis XIII style, with inlaid decoration. 1670–1700, size unavailable, £3,000/$5,100

Tables and Lowboys

It was customary in the 18th century for furniture to be placed against a wall when not in use. The term "lowboy" was given to an early 18th-century table that was placed against the wall and used as a dressing or writing table. Tables that had a folding top were in demand. The demi-lune table opened into a circular tea table, and the card table – lined with green baize – followed a similar construction.

Other tables that were placed against the wall include the pier table, which was placed between two windows (the space between the windows is referred to as the pier), and the console table, which was often elaborately carved and gilt and had a heavy marble slab top. The console table was attached to the wall and supported by bracket-shaped legs.

The sofa table, as its name suggests, was made to be set before a sofa, where the lady of the house used it to write, read, or sew. Examples with a high single stretcher, which allows for more legroom when sitting at the table, are more desirable. Early 19th-century sofa tables were often raised on a central pedestal support. The drum table also had a pedestal support, with a round top that contained drawers.

There is a variety of drop-leaf tables, where hinged leaves can be lowered to save space, including the gate-leg table, where hinged "gate" legs swing out to support the leaves. The Pembroke table, a type of drop-leaf table, was made to be multifunctional and used for taking meals, writing, or playing cards.

William III walnut gate-legged table.
1690–1720, 74cm (29in) diameter, £2,000/$3,400

Parcel-gilt and faux-grained side table, in the manner of William Jones, 1740–50 in style. 19th century, size unavailable, £10,000/$17,000

George II giltwood console table, with marble top and carved details, in the manner of Matthias Lock. 1730–60, size unavailable, £20,000/$34,000

George II gilt gesso console table, with later decoration, in the manner of William Kent. 1730–50, size unavailable, £40,000/$68,000

George II mahogany tripod table, with a central column and tripod (three) legs ending with pad feet. 1730–60, size unavailable, £3,000/$5,100

Tables and Lowboys

Irish George II mahogany silver table, with carved details. 1740–60, size unavailable, £1,500/$2,550

George II giltwood console table, with carved details, in the manner of William Jones (one of a pair). 1737–57, size unavailable, £25,000/$42,500

George II mahogany candle stand. 1730–60, size unavailable, £7,000/$11,900

George III mahogany square-top tea table. *c.*1770, size unavailable, £1,300/$2,200

George II mahogany tea table, with a tripod support. 1740–60, size unavailable, £1,200/$2,050

George III mahogany lowboy. 1760–80, size unavailable, £2,500/$4,250

George III mahogany side table, with carved details, in the manner of Thomas Chippendale. 1760–80, size unavailable, £15,000/$25,500

George III mahogany supper table. 1760–80, size unavailable, £6,000/$10,200

Serpentine Pembroke table

The cabinetwork on this mahogany Pembroke table, attributable to Henry Hill of Marlborough, is of exceptional quality. Hill is recognized as a top provincial cabinet-maker. The records show that he was active in Marlborough from about 1740 until his death in 1778.
c.1770, 73cm (29in) high, £10,000/$17,000

The use of kingwood "lozenge" parquetry and tulipwood cross-banding on the shaped top is a highly desirable feature.

This table is more valuable because it was created by a known maker and is also in original condition.

The single sliding drawer has the advantage of being bow fronted and retaining the original brass handles.

The fluted legs have an interesting slender shape and are well carved with tapering acanthus leaves.

George III mahogany serpentine tea table, with hinged top. 1770–1800, size unavailable, £2,500/$4,250

German satinwood, sycamore, and calamander occasional table, with marquetry and cross-banding. *c.*1780, size unavailable, £1,800/$3,050

George III fiddleback mahogany and rosewood Pembroke table, with cross-branding and chequer-banding. 1775–95, size unavailable, £5,000/$8,500

Sycamore, tulipwood, and amaranth table, with floral marquetry, by Nicolas Petit. 1770–90, size unavailable, £5,000/$8,500

Louis XIV mahogany table ambulante (portable). 1770–90, size unavailable, £1,800/$3,050

Tables and Lowboys

George III mahogany Pembroke table, with cross-banding and boxwood inlay. 1780–1800, size unavailable, £6,500/$11,000

George III mahogany demi-lune card table. 1770–1800, size unavailable, £2,000/$3,400

George III mahogany Pembroke table, with painted decoration, in the manner of Seddon Sons and Shackleton. 1780–1800, size unavailable, £12,000/$20,400

Pair of scagliola (imitation marble) side tables, in the manner of Pietro Bossi. 1785–98, size unavailable, £15,000/$25,500

George III satinwood *demi-lune* card table. 1780–1800, size unavailable, £5,000/$8,500

George III mahogany Pembroke table. 1790–1810, size unavailable, £1,000/$1,700

Regency yew sofa table. 1800–20, size unavailable, £2,000/$3,400

Regency mahogany breakfast table, with satinwood cross-banding. 1800–20, size unavailable, £12,000/$20,400

Regency rosewood and tulipwood breakfast table. 1800–20, size unavailable, £4,000/$6,800

Regency mahogany sofa table, with crossbranding. 1800–20, size unavailable, £1,500/$2,550

Regency satinwood and tulipwood side table, with cross-banding, in the manner of Gillows. 1800–20, size unavailable, £1,000/$1,700

Regency rosewood card table, with brass inlay. 1810–30, size unavailable, £3,000/$5,100

Regency mahogany drum library table. 1820–30, size unavailable, £6,000/$10,200

George IV rosewood and parcel-gilt console table, with fossilitic marble top and mirrorback. 1820–30, size unavailable, £8,000/$13,600

Set of George IV rosewood quartetto tables, attributable to Gillows. 1820–30, size unavailable, £3,000/$5,100

Early Victorian black japanned centre table, with chinoiserie decoration. 1840–50, size unavailable, £1,800/$3,050

Victorian rosewood breakfast table. 1840–60, size unavailable, £3,000/$5,100

Dining Room Furniture

It was the custom in 17th-century Europe for those in positions of wealth to take their meals at an oak refectory table. By the mid-18th century, many of the mercantile classes had servants to set up a series of small drop-leaf dining tables in one room for serving food. These were multipurpose tables, as were the rooms, and they could be stored against a wall when not in use.

In both Europe and the United States, it became increasingly common by the end of the 18th century to reserve a room for the sole purpose of dining. This room contained a formal table surrounded by a set of chairs. By the 19th century, a dining room was an established part of every newly built house. Many dining tables were made with the ability to add one or more leaves to extend the size of the table, and some used ingenious mechanisms for this purpose.

A secondary parlour, or morning room, where members of the family gathered to eat breakfast and light meals, became the home for rosewood or mahogany breakfast tables. They were introduced at the end of the 18th century, and they were often rectangular. Round and oval versions made their appearance at the beginning of the 19th century.

Sideboards were a main feature of the dining room. These were used for serving food and storage, and some had built-in cellarette drawers for storing wine, which might also be stored in a separate wine cooler. Wooden boxes or urns displayed on the sideboard were used for storing cutlery.

George II mahogany side table, with calcarta marble top. 1740–60, size unavailable, £8,000/$13,600

George III mahogany wake table. 1780–1800, size unavailable, £4,200/$7,150

Regency mahogany three-section dining table, with inlaid decoration. 1810–20, size unavailable, £2,000/$3,400

Regency mahogany dining table, with three pedestals. 1800–20, size unavailable, £55,000/$93,500

Irish George III mahogany bottle carrier.
1760–90, size unavailable, £6,000/$10,200

George III-style mahogany kettle stand, in the manner of Mayhew and Ince. Late Victorian, size unavailable, £4,200/$7,150

George III mahogany and brass-bound cellarette on carved stand, in the manner of Thomas Chippendale. 1760–70, size unavailable, £10,000/$17,000

George III mahogany cellarette. 1800–20, size unavailable, £1,000/$1,700

Regency mahogany and ebonized cellarette. 1800–20, size unavailable, £4,000/$6,800

George III mahogany three-tiered dumb waiter. 1760–90, size unavailable, £4,500/$7,650

George III black-lacquered knife box. 1790–1810, size unavailable, £1,100/$1,870

Regency mahogany sideboard, with satinwood banding. 1800–20, size unavailable, £6,000/$10,200

William IV mahogany pedestal sideboard.
1835–37, size unavailable, £1,500/$2,550

Writing Furniture

Before the second half of the 17th century, few people (apart from some members of the nobility and a larger number of ecclesiastics) could read and write or had possessions to display. The pedestal desk, with a writing surface supported on pedestals containing drawers, was introduced in the late 17th century. During the 18th century, literacy increased dramatically, and with it the manufacture of desks and writing tables. It was during this time that the Carlton House desk appeared, a grand, D-shaped writing table, complete with a bank of drawers and compartments. The davenport, a small writing desk with a sloped top above a case of drawers, became popular in the late 18th century.

As more people began to own books, bookcases were increasingly added to desks to form bureau or secretaire bookcases, which had a flap that pulled forward to provide a writing surface. The earliest examples, built in walnut or oak, date from the late 17th century. The first mahogany examples appeared in the early 18th century.

The production of writing desks for both the home and office increased greatly during the Victorian period, and these tend to dominate the present-day antique trade. Smaller library furniture, such as revolving bookcases and library steps, made from the end of the 18th century, is collectable because it can fit easily into most smaller, modern homes.

William and Mary figured walnut bureau, with cross- and feather-banding. 1688–1700, size unavailable, £1,600/$2,700

Queen Anne walnut bureau cabinet, with cross- and feather-banding. 1700–20, size unavailable, £3,000/$5,100

George III mahogany secretaire bookcase. 1790–1810, size unavailable, £2,000/$3,400

George I kneehole writing desk, with cross- and chequer-banding. 1715–25, size unavailable, £4,000/$6,800

George II mahogany reading chair. 1730–60, size unavailable, £10,000/$17,000

George II fiddleback mahogany bureau cabinet. 1730–60, size unavailable, £19,000/$32,300

This example has a breakfront, with the central section protruding beyond the side sections. If a broken pediment had been added to the flat top, the bookcase would be more desirable and valuable.

George III secretaire bookcase

This mahogany piece would have been made for a wealthy gentleman of serious learning. It could only have been made in the 18th century, when bound books began to be published in greater numbers at more affordable prices and mahogany began to be imported in greater volume.
c.1770, 228cm (90in) high, £14,000/$35,560

Chinese-export black-lacquer bureau. *c.*1750, size unavailable, £4,800/$8,150

The use of the Vetruvian scroll and ebonized frieze is a Neoclassical detail that dates this piece to 1770 or later

The astragal ogee glazed panels use both the Gothic and chinoiserie styles popularized by Thomas Chippendale in the 1760s.

This internal cupboard is flanked by two secret compartments, four pigeonholes, and six short drawers.

George III secretaire cabinet. 1765–95, size unavailable, £8,000/$13,600

George III mahogany cylinder bureau, with satinwood and rosewood marquetry, in the French taste. 1780–90, size unavailable, £4,000/$6,800

Scottish George IV mahogany secretaire bookcase. 1820–30, size unavailable, £8,000/$13,600

Regency mahogany library bookcase. 1800–20, size unavailable, £10,000/$17,000

Writing Furniture

George III mahogany bow-front kneehole desk, with marquetry decoration. 1800–20, size unavailable, £3,000/$5,100

Regency mahogany patent writing desk, after a design by Morgan and Saunders. 1800–20, size unavailable, £6,000/$10,200

George III mahogany *bonheur du jour* (a lady's writing cabinet), with boxwood banding. 1800–20, size unavailable, £3,500/$5,950

Regency kingwood secretaire, with brass and ebony marquetry, in the manner of George Oakley. 1800–20, size unavailable, £8,000/$13,600

Regency rosewood writing desk, with brass inlay, in the manner of John Mclean. 1800–20, size unavailable, £6,000/$10,400

George III mahogany library table. 1800–20, size unavailable, £3,500/$5,950

George III mahogany library table, with satinwood banding. 1800–20, size unavailable, £12,000/$20,400

Regency writing table, by Gillows of Lancaster. 1800–20, size unavailable, £3,000/$5,100

Regency mahogany bow-front secretaire bookcase, with ebony and boxwood stringing. 1810–20, size unavailable, £5,500/$9,350

George IV mahogany breakfront library bookcase. 1820–30, size unavailable, £7,500/$12,750

George IV rosewood side cabinet, by Miles and Edwards. 1830–35, size unavailable, £4,000/$6,800

Victorian burr walnut, kidney-shaped pedestal desk, by Gillows of Lancaster. 1840–50, size unavailable, £26,000/$44,200

Victorian arbutus wood davenport, with Killarney marquetry, in the manner of Jeremiah O'Connor of Killarney. 1840–60, size unavailable, £2,500/$4,250

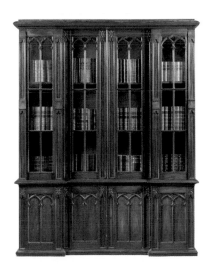

Regency mahogany library bookcase. 1800–10, size unavailable, £10,000/$17,000

Early Victorian fiddleback mahogany pedestal desk. 1840–60, size unavailable, £4,000/$6,800

Miscellaneous Furniture

Most basic antique furniture that might be available at auction or in the antique shop tends to be of a large size such as a dining table, chest of drawers, or a bookcase. However, there is a wide range of other useful and decorative furniture that by virtue of being smaller in size is better proportioned for those of us living in a modern-day home with small rooms. The present-day market is awash with plenty of late Georgian and Victorian furniture that is both modest in size and available at prices that might still be seen as bargains, especially when compared to their modern-day counterparts.

If given careful thought, most pieces of antique furniture can blend sympathetically into a modern-day interior by assigning them to another use. So even if your canterbury takes your newspapers and magazines in lieu of Victorian sheet music, your papier-mâché tray never plays host to a teacup and saucer while it is propped on display on a shelf, your work table no longer stores the essential accessories for sewing but is the keeper of your spare buttons, or your Regency bedside cabinet is unlikely to house a chamber pot, these items can still serve a useful purpose in your home.

The mirror, however, is something of an exception when it comes to still being fit for its original purpose. The most expensive tend to be those dating to the 18th century and carved in solid wood. Early large mirrors often had two or more pieces of mirrored glass because the glass, known as "Vauxhall Plate", did not come in large sizes. Georgian glass is much thinner than later Victorian glass. Victorian examples in moulded gesso are more readily available and affordable.

George III cabinet-on-stand, in the Chinese Chippendale taste, inset with Chinese reverse glass mirror panels (the stand is a later date). 1760–70, size unavailable, £6,000/$10,400

Baltic mahogany side table. 1830–60, size unavailable, £750/$1,275

Victorian rosewood Canterbury. 1850–70, size unavailable, £500/$850

Irish George III ribbed mahogany and brass-bound peat bucket (with later base). 1800–20, 40cm (16¾in) high, £2,800/$4,750

Irish George III ribbed mahogany and brass-bound peat bucket (later swing handle). 1800–20, 46cm (18in) high, £2,600/$4,400

Pair of George III mahogany dining room pedestals. 1790–1810, size unavailable, £4,400/$7,500

George III japanned tin tea tray, possibly made in Pontypool. 1800–20, size unavailable, £2,000/$3,400

Victorian papier-mâché tea tray, by Walton and Co. of Wolverhampton. 1842–47, size unavailable, £2,500/$4,250

Victorian walnut two-tier occasional table. 1850–60, size unavailable, £400/$680

Regency mahogany four-division canterbury. 1800–20, size unavailable, £3,000/$5,100

Italian rosewood tabletop on a giltwood base, with ebony, ivory, and mother-of-pearl marquetry. 1835–60, size unavailable, £4,500/$7,650

George IV mahogany three-tier *étagère* (for displaying ornaments). 1820–30, size unavailable, £4,200/$7,150

Louis XV tulipwood *table ambulante*, with marquetry. 1750–60, size unavailable, £1,100/$1,870

George IV mahogany washstand (the central hole is for holding a washbasin). 1820–30, size unavailable, £350/$595

Anglo-Indian rosewood work table, with ivory and pewter inlay. 1840–60, size unavailable, £1,000/$1,700

Mirrors

The marquetry and oyster walnut veneers are typical decoration often found in large-scale furniture of this period.

William and Mary wall mirror

In the 16th century, the Venetians developed glass-making techniques that were suitable for mirrors. By the 18th century the French and British introduced methods to produce large plate glass. These early mirrors were expensive and remained a symbol of a family's status into the 19th century.
c.1690, size unavailable, £9,000/$15,300

The inlaid crest adds an architectural element – it takes the shape found of a Dutch gable.

The "cushion" frame uses a curved moulding applied with contoured marquetry.

The piece retains its original mirror, which despite being heavily degraded, is highly important to the desirability and value of the mirror – it should never be replaced.

George I giltwood pier mirror, with carved details. 1715–25, size unavailable, £2,800/$4,750

Charles II giltwood mirror, with carved details. 1660–80, size unavailable, £8,000/$13,600

Régence giltwood mirror, with carved details. 1715–23, size unavailable, £3,800/$6,450

George I giltwood mirror, with carved details and Neoclassical motifs. 1715–25, size unavailable, £3,500/$5,950

Louis XV giltwood mirror, with carved details. 1740–50, size unavailable, £1,700/$2,900

Italian cartouche-shaped giltwood mirror, with carved details. c.1750, size unavailable, £500/$850

Irish George III giltwood mirror, with carved details. 1760–80, size unavailable, £3,200/$5,450

George II giltwood mirror, with carved details. 1750–60, size unavailable, £4,000/$6,800

George III giltwood mirror. 1770–1800, size unavailable, £2,800/$4,750

Regency ebonized and parcel-gilt convex girandole (ornate sconce with a mirror backing). 1800–20, size unavailable, £2,400/$4,100

Victorian giltwood console table and pier mirror, in the Chippendale style, with carved details (one of a pair). 1880–1900, size unavailable, £38,000/$64,600

American Furniture

The tradition of American furniture began with the arrival of the Pilgrims during the early 17th century to those parts of the eastern coast later to be known as Massachusetts, Rhode Island, and Connecticut. Their furniture reflected the pieces that they had left behind in their homeland. They were sturdy and constructed from oak, pine, and local indigenous woods, and they often incorporated elaborate carving and turning. Colonial taste continued to follow the trends set in England throughout the 17th and early 18th century, but at the same time the colonists gradually incorporated their own ideas of form and decoration, which eventually developed into a distinctly American style.

The styles that found favour throughout the 18th century are grouped in specific headings that often have little chronological connection to the relative monarch. William and Mary furniture was produced from 1700 to 1730, and Queen Anne designs were produced between 1725 and 1755. These were followed by the Chippendale style, which gave way to the Federal in 1790.

The finest pieces were produced in large cities such as Boston, Philadelphia, and New York. There was also an important regional network of top class cabinet-makers working in Newport, Rhode Island, Chester County, Pennsylvania, and Newburyport, Massachusetts.

Early American Furniture

Queen Anne maple flat-top high chest, New England. 1775–1800, 178cm (70in) high, £3,200/$5,450

Queen Anne maple flat-top high chest of drawers, New England. 1775–1800, 178cm (70in) high, £7,000/$11,900

Queen Anne tiger maple flat-top high chest of drawers, New Hampshire. 1775–1800, 191cm (75in), £6,200/10,550

Queen Anne cherry flat-top high chest of drawers, Connecticut. 1775–1800, 180cm (71in) high, £1,800/$3,050

Chippendale mahogany drop-leaf table, Pennsylvania. 1775–1800, 72cm (28in) high, £700/$1,190

Chippendale tilt-top tea table, on tripod legs, attributed to Joseph Short (1771–1819) of Newburyport, Massachusetts (Short is recorded as a maker of fine mahogany furniture with a workshop in Merrimack Street). 1780–1800, 72cm (28in) high, £4,500/$7,650

The urn-and-flame finials appear to be favoured by American cabinet-makers of high chests, especially in Philadelphia, Boston, and Providence, Rhode Island.

Chippendale chest of drawers

In the United States furniture of this type is known as a highboy, but in England it is recognized as a tallboy. Although few tallboys appear in England after 1730, the American highboy remained popular throughout the 18th century. Its overall form and decorative features make it quite distinct from its English counterpart. *c.1775, 237cm (94in) high, £3,400/$5,800*

The broken scroll pediment terminating with large carved rosettes are features associated with 18th-century American furniture. Flat-top high chests were also made.

The highboy is often constructed in two sections, with the upper part fitted with five rows of drawers and the lower stand raised on cabriole legs with ball-and-claw feet

This Pennsylvanian example is constructed from walnut, although cherry is the usual preference of the Connecticut cabinet-maker.

The elaborate apron, or skirt, below the stand indicates American manufacture.

Federal mahogany Pembroke table, with inlay decoration, New York. 1790–1800, 72cm (28in) high, £6,700/$11,400

Federal marble-top mahogany mixing table, with inlay decoration, New York or Pennsylvania. 1790–1810, 77cm (30in) high, £10,000/$17,000

Federal mahogany card table, with inlay decoration, Mid-Atlantic states. 1790–1810, 72cm (28in) high, £3,000/$5,100

Chippendale walnut slant-front bureau, Pennsylvania. 1775–1800, 104cm (41in) high, £1,000/$1,700

Chippendale walnut tall chest of drawers, Chester County, Pennsylvania. 1775–1800, 161cm (63in) high, £6,000/$10,200

Early American Furniture

Federal mahogany bow-front chest of drawers, Massachusetts. 1790–1810, 81cm (32in) high, £1,000/$1,700

Federal mahogany serpentine-front sideboard, New York. 1790–1810, 97cm (38in) high, £2,100/$3,600

Federal mahogany card table, with inlay decoration, Baltimore or Philadelphia. 1800–10, 74cm (29in) high, £1,500/$2,550

Federal mahogany tilt-top tea table, New England. 1800–25, 74cm (29in) high, £1,400/$2,400

Mixed-wood comb-back Windsor armchair, New England. 1800–25, 114cm (45in) high, £600/$1,020

Federal mahogany sideboard, with inlay decoration, New York. 1800–25, 101cm (40in) high, £8,000/$13,600

Late American Furniture

Federal mahogany butler's secretary or bureau, with inlay decoration, New York. 1810–15, 112cm (44in) high, £1,800/$3,050

Neoclassical mahogany card table, with carved details, New York or Philadelphia. 1800–25, size unavailable, £1,500/$2,550

Federal dressing table, with painted and stencilled decoration, New England. 1800–25, 88cm (35in) high, £1,400/$2,400

Federal mahogany bureau, New York. 1800–25, 152cm (60in) high, £1,500/$2,550

Federal cherry and tiger maple bow-front chest of drawers, Pennsylvania. 1800–25, 98cm (39in) high, £1,200/$2,050

Federal mahogany work table, New York or Philadelphia. 1815–20, 74cm (29in) high, £2,000/$3,400

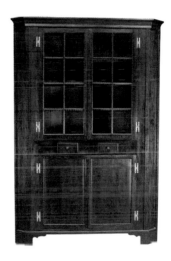

Federal cherry corner cupboard, Pennsylvania or Ohio Valley. 1800–25, 228cm (90in) high, £2,000/$3,400

Neoclassical gilt mahogany bookcase, with gilt-bronze mounts. *c.*1825, 180cm (71in) high, £1,100/$1,870

Neoclassical mahogany parcel-gilt pier table, with a marble top. 1825–50, 94cm (37in) high, £1,100/$1,870

Neoclassical parcel-gilt and ebonized mahogany chest of drawers, New York. 1825–50, 87cm (34in) high, £1,700/$2,900

Late Federal tiger maple and cherry work table, New England, 1850–70, 73cm (29in) high, £550/$935

Chippendale-style mahogany block-front bookcase, in the Boston style. (This bookcase demonstrates the continued demand for "American" antique furniture – a genuine 18th-century example would be worth £4,000/$6,800.) Late 19th century, 208cm (82 in) high, £700/$1,190

Oriental Ceramics and Works of Art

1

2

3

4

1 Chinese coral red stem cup,
18th century
2 Japanese carved-ivory okimono
of a grape vendor, *c.*1900
3 Chinese *famille verte* "Dutch
Province" dish, *c.*1730
4 Chinese gilt-bronze equestrian
figure of Guanyin, Ming Dynasty
(1368–1644)

The earliest Chinese porcelain was produced in the north of the country during the Tang Dynasty (618–906). The Chinese began to export their wares as early as the 9th century to Southeast Asia, India, and the Middle East. It was not until Portuguese explorers found their way to China in the early 16th century that Chinese porcelain was introduced to Europe, where it was highly prized.

The finest porcelains produced during the Ming Dynasty were made at the Jingdezhen potteries during the "middle" period (the 14th to the 15th century), but the demand for the wares was so great that unskilled labour was taken on to meet orders and standards inevitably declined, with hurried decoration painted onto a body prone to chipping. However, there was a revival in quality after the rebuilding of the Jingdezhen kilns, which had been destroyed by fire in 1675. Under the Qing

emperor Kangxi (1662–1722), the body became denser and whiter and the decoration more delicate and refined. The wares were usually blue and white but occasionally three or more colours were used.

By this time, trade with Europe had begun to expand and several nations had established trading posts in Canton, which – apart from being a port – was a centre of porcelain production and enamelling. Kraak porcelain (named for the Portuguese "carrack", a type of ship), often decorated in panels of repeating designs, was among the first Chinese porcelain to be shipped to Europe in quantity. Along with blue and white, the palettes that found favour in the West were green (known as *famille verte*) and pink (known as *famille rose*). The often eggshell-thin wares made during the reign of the emperor Yongzheng (1723–35) were decorated with fine enamelling and are among the most desirable of all 18th-century Chinese porcelain.

5

6

7

8

5 Chinese *qingbai* lotus bowl, Song Dynasty (960–1279)
6 Japanese Ko-Imari figure of a reclining Bijin, *c*.1680
7 Chinese *guri* red lacquer circular box and cover, Ming Dynasty (1368–1644)
8 Japanese iron and bronze *futamono* (a lidded receptacle), *c*.1890

During the reign of the following emperor, Qianlong (1736–95), massive consignments of porcelain were shipped to the West with elaborate table services, which were often especially commissioned and occasionally decorated with European subjects copied faithfully by Chinese decorators from European engravings. They were sometimes painted in black and gilt (referred to as *en grisaille*). Some decoration incorporated elaborate armorial crests or initials in script, often referred to as armorial ware.

Prices were competitive and demand remained keen until the beginning of the 19th century, when the huge technological advances made in the production of European pottery and porcelain began to have an adverse effect on trade with China. By *c*.1830, the quantity of Chinese porcelain exported to Europe had dwindled to a trickle.

Where to begin

Pottery and porcelain are the two principal forms of ceramics – a hard, brittle material formed by firing clay and similar substances in a kiln or oven – and both groups can be subdivided into numerous others, including bone china, stoneware, and earthenware (see page 54).

Your first task is to familiarize yourself with the differences between the types of ceramics, so that you can distinguish between, for example, an earthenware item and a porcelain item. The most difficult challenge will be determining hard- from soft-paste porcelain. It may seem an insurmountable obstacle at first, but every porcelain collector in the world has faced it. Pieces of damaged Chelsea and Meissen, studied together, will help you learn the difference between soft- and hard-paste porcelain.

A good reference book on marks is invaluable, but bear in mind that not all marks are to be trusted – many were faked.

Condition is also important. A chip, a crack, or an area of restoration will detract from the value of a piece.

Types of ceramics

It is essential to be able to recognize the various bodies that come under the generic term "ceramics". Listed below are the primary types that you are likely to encounter.

Earthenware First made when man discovered that raw clay could be dug out from the ground, shaped into a vessel, and hardened by baking in a fire.

Japanese carved-ivory okimono of a farmer, *c.*1900

Stoneware The clay is mixed with fusible rock and fired to a higher temperature than earthenware to produce a dense, hard body.

Salt-glazed stoneware Produced from the early 18th century in Staffordshire, the result of salt being introduced into the kiln and vaporizing to form a covering glaze.

Creamware An opaque white body with a creamy translucent glaze. During the 18th century, pottery bodies became more refined with the discovery of china clay or kaolin (a fine, white clay).

Hard-paste, or true, porcelain First made in China in the Tang Dynasty (618–906), it consists of china clay and a feldspathic rock ("petuntse"). The clay fuses at about 1,700°C (3,100°F), the petuntse at about 1,450°C (2,650°F). The powdered rock is mixed with the clay and fired at the lower temperature until the rock fuses to the consistency of glass. True porcelain is translucent and is often used for figure modelling because of its suitability for casting in moulds.

Soft-paste, or artificial, procelain First made in Italy about 1575 in an attempt to copy true porcelain. Because European potters didn't know the ingredients, they experimented by mixing china clay with powdered glass and soapstone or bone ash.

To tell the difference between hard- and soft-paste porcelain, examine chipped areas. The soft-paste body is slightly porous and granular with a glassy skin of glaze. Hard-paste looks more like opaque glass with a thin, glittering glaze that is fused with the body. Glazes on soft-paste tend to run and absorb enamel colours. Enamel colours on hard-paste rest on top. Dirt sinks into the unglazed soft-paste body but washes off hard-paste porcelain.

Bone china A cross between hard- and soft-paste porcelain, with 25 percent china stone, 25 percent china clay, and 50 percent calcined bones. It is more stable at high firing temperatures than soft-paste porcelain and has lower firing costs than hard-paste.

Decorative techniques

The way a piece is decorated can often help date it or suggest a possible country of origin – and even a specific artist.

Incising Cutting a pattern into wet clay ("sgraffito") was the earliest method of decorating earthenware. In the 17th and 18th centuries, sgraffito was enhanced by painting glaze into the incised areas.

Moulded decoration Involves forming pots in a mould before firing or applying pieces to them to create a moulded effect.

Slip trailing Applied decoration similar to the method used to ice a cake. Liquid slip (clay and water) is trailed onto the body to create a raised outline and provide a barrier for the different colours.

Pair of Chinese export models
of seated hounds, *c.*1770

Pâte-sur-pâte Meaning "paste on paste", creating raised decoration by building up layers of slip.

Underglaze hand painting Decoration applied to the biscuit (once-fired) body using brushes dipped in pigments. The paint is absorbed immediately into the piece and mistakes can never be rectified. The piece is dipped in glaze and fired again.

Overglaze hand painting Used on stoneware, porcelain, and earthenware. Enamel paints are applied to the glazed surface and are fused once the piece is returned to the kiln.

Transfer printing Mainly used for underglaze decoration. A design engraved onto a copper plate is filled with ink; then a sheet of tissue paper absorbs the ink and is laid onto the piece. This paper template burns off in the kiln, leaving the inked design. Perfected in the 18th century, this technique was developed for mass production in the 19th century.

Gilding Gold leaf applied in the final decorative process and fired at a lower kiln temperature. For a raised effect, gold leaf is applied over enamels. Elaborate patterns were made in matt gilding, using an agate stone to burnish them and achieve contrast – this is known as tooled gilding.

The Chinese Dynasties

Shang (*c.*1500–1028 BC)
Zhou (1028–256 BC)
Warring States (480–221 BC)
Qin (221–206 BC)
Han (206 BC–AD 220)
The Six Dynasties (221–581)
Sui (581–618)
Tang (618–906)
The Five Dynasties (907–960)
Song (960–1279)
  Northern Song (960–1127), **Southern Song** (1128–1279)
Jin (1115–1234)
Yuan (1260–1368)
Ming (1368–1644)
  Hongwu (1368–98), **Jianwen** (1399–1402), **Yongle** (1403–24), **Hongxi** (1425), **Xuande** (1426–35), **Zhengtong** (1436–49), **Jingtai** (1450–57), **Tianshun** (1457–64), **Chenghua** (1465–87), **Hongzhi** (1488–1505), **Zhengde** (1506–21), **Jiajing** (1522–66), **Longqing** (1567–72), **Wanli** (1573–1619), **Taichang** (1620), **Tianqi** (1621–27), **Chongzhen** (1628–44)
Qing (1644–1911)
  Shunzi (1644–61), **Kangxi** (1662–1722), **Yongzheng** (1723–35), **Qianlong** (1736–95), **Jiaqing** (1796–1820), **Daoguang** (1821–50), **Xianfeng** (1851–61), **Tongzhi** (1862–74), **Guangxu** (1875–1908), **Xuantong** (1909–11)
Republic (1911–)

Chinese Pottery

The earliest pottery found in China dates from the Neolithic period (about 7000 BC), followed by that produced during the period of the Warring States (480–221 BC), which preceded the unification of China under the first Qin emperor. These early wares were similar in form to contemporary bronzes and were used in burials when pottery was used to make replicas of objects the dead would need in the afterlife. This tradition continued into the Han Dynasty (206 BC–AD 220) and through to the Tang (618–906), by which time the Chinese potters had perfected a sophisticated low fired, white-bodied ware. Glazes at this time were limited to a simple straw colour or to the wider palette found on *sancai* (three-colour) ware, which included ochre, blue, and green.

By the Song Dynasty (960–1279), wares were mostly made for ritualistic and domestic use. Sophisticated olive-green glazed celadon ware was made in the Northern Song Dynasty (960–1127) at the *Yaozhou* kilns of Shaanxi in the northwest of the country, near the capital Xian. *Cizhou* stoneware, often decorated with painted, incised, or punched designs, was made in the northern provinces of Henan, Hebei, and Shaanxi.

Political influence shifted south, and during the period known as the Southern Song (1128–1279), production of celadon ware was centred on Longquan in Zhejiang province. These later wares were more thickly potted and covered in thicker glazes of a bluish green hue, which were neatly applied and sometimes coloured to imitate jade.

Unglazed figure of a prancing horse (with restoration). Tang Dynasty (618–906), 42.5cm (16¾in) high, £1,500/$2,550

Chestnut-glazed horse. Tang Dynasty (618–906), 49cm (19¼in) high, £7,000/$11,900

***Cizhou* bowl** painted in iron-brown with the character Qian, and with chip to rim. Song/Yuan Dynasty (960–1368), 22.5cm (8⅞in) diameter, £1,000/$1,700

Longquan celadon vase, in *meiping* form, with narrow neck/tapering body. Northern Song Dynasty (960–1126), 34.25cm (13½in) high, £3,000/$5,100

***Yaozhou* pale celadon-glazed archaistic tripod censer.** Jin Dynasty (1115–1234), 15cm (6⅛in) high, £20,000/$34,000

Henan olive-glazed jar, with hand-painted decoration. Jin/Yuan Dynasties (1279–1368), 18cm (7in) high, £2,000/$3,400

Chinese Porcelain

Although a type of porcelain was first produced in China during the Tang Dynasty, it was not until the kilns at Jingdezhen came under imperial patronage at the beginning of the 14th century that fine porcelain was made with underglaze decoration, which replaced the glazed stoneware of the Song Dynasty (960–1279) as the most desirable form of ceramics. Most scholars recognize the finest porcelain as having been produced in the Ming Dynasty (1368–1644) during the reigns of the emperors Yongle (1403–24) and Xuande (1426–35). Many of the decorators at that time showed a preference for certain themes such as fish among aquatic plants, grapes and tendrils, windswept figures in landscapes,

and trailing lotus or peony flowers. Fahua ware was a type of decoration using slip trailing to separate the colours.

During the civil war in which the Ming Dynasty was toppled by the following Qing (Ch'ing) Dynasty (1644–1911), the kilns at Jingdezhen were destroyed. They were eventually rebuilt and reorganized by the emperor Kangxi in 1683. The new ware was an improvement on the later and inferior Ming porcelain, and trade with the West resumed. During the 18th and the early 19th century, literally millions of pieces of Chinese "Export" porcelain found their way into the living and dining rooms of Europe and North America's well to do, modelled in both Chinese and European forms.

Ming Porcelain

Underglaze copper-red vase, in *yuhuchun* pear-shaped form. Hongwu (1368–98), 33cm (13in) high, £65,000/$110,500

Rare Ming blue-and-white arrow vase, for the Islamic market. Wanli (1573–1619), 26cm (10¼in) high, £20,000/$34,000

Blue-and-white rectangular plaque. Chenghua (1465–87), 20.5cm x 25.5cm (8in x 10in), £34,000/$57,800

Blue-and-white cat night-light. Late Ming Dynasty (1368–1644), 23cm (9in) high, £8,500/$14,450

Large early Ming blue-and-white dish (restored). Yongle (1403–24), 32cm (12⅝in) diameter, £2,800/$4,750 (a perfect one would be £10,000+/$17,000+)

Large blue-and-white *kraak porselein* dish. Late 16th century, 51cm (20in) diameter, £9,500/$16,150

Ming Porcelain

Blue-and-white "Three Friends" stem bowl. Jingtai (1450–57), 11.5cm (4½in) high, £6,000/$10,200

Large Ming *fahua* jar. *c.*1500, 32.5cm (12¾in) high, £5,000/$8,500

Blue-and-yellow dish. Zhengde (1506–21), 25.5cm (10in) diameter, £5,500/$9,350

Transitional Porcelain

Blue-and-white transitional vase

This vase is typical of Chinese porcelain made *c.*1620–80, during the transition between the Ming and Qing Dynasties. The "transitional" style, often decorated with everyday scenes and naturalistic elements, was one of the most important influences on European pottery in the latter 17th century. *c.1640, 44cm (17⅜in) high, £600/$1,020*

The porcelain body has a grey-white colour. The vase is thickly potted, which often frits (blisters) on the rim. The thickness allows it to be incised with decoration.

The decoration is applied in purplish blue cobalt. Scholars within naturalistic settings are featured on all types of porcelain of this period.

The edge of the base and the underside have been wiped free of glaze.

Large *wucai* (five-coloured) jar and cover. *c.*1640, 45cm (17¾in) high, £6,500/$11,000

Later Porcelain

***Famille rose* soup plate,** depicting a European gentleman in a garden with attendant. Qianlong (1736–95), 22.5cm (8¾in) diameter, £1,000/$1,700

Peachbloom-glazed water pot, in *taibo zun* (bee-hive) form. Kangxi (1662–1722), 9cm (3½in) high, £4,500/$7,650

Pair of *famille rose* jars and covers. Yongzheng (1723–35), 47cm (18½in) high, £12,000/$20,400

***Famille rose* candlestick group.** Qianlong (1736–95), 26cm (10¼in) high, £8,500/$14,450

Large blue-and-white beaker vase. Kangxi (1662–1722), 47cm (18½in) high, £6,000/$10,400

European figure group in *blanc-de-chine* (Chinese white-glazed porcelain). Kangxi (1662–1722), 16cm (6¼in) high, £2,600/$4,400

Famille Verte panel-form vase. Kangxi (1662–1722), 58cm (23in) high, £4,000/$6,800

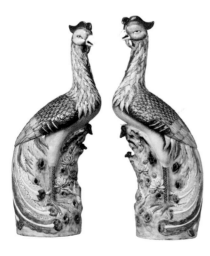

Pair of large *famille rose* phoenix figures. Daoguang (1821–50), 61cm (24in) high, £5,000/$8,500

Pair of *famille rose* elephant candle holders. Qianlong (1736–1795), 16cm (6¼in) long, £4,000/$6,800

Chinese Works of Art

Household items were made in various materials. The Chinese reverence for jade has been known for centuries, and the most desirable colour is the vivid green that is invariably used in modern-day jewellery. Jade is the term applied to two distinct minerals: nephrite, used in China, and jadeite. Other favoured minerals include rock crystal and rose quartz.

Ivory carving is also held in esteem in China. An item's age can usually be determined by the colour and patination of the surface. Older ivory often displays a yellow-brown appearance resulting from centuries of being handled. In the mid- to late 19th century, Canton became the centre of the ivory carving industry and exported finely detailed wares.

Lacquerware has been made in China for two thousand years but the vast majority seen on the market today is from the late 19th or 20th centuries, especially the deep red variety known as "cinnabar". Earlier examples are rare.

Cloisonné enamels were first produced in China in the 14th century and were used initially for religious and ceremonial purposes. These early pieces tend to be heavy because the body is cast from bronze. The decoration mirrors the scrolling floral designs found on contemporary porcelain. Most cloisonné presently in the West was exported from the late 19th century onward and made for western taste with floral and bird decoration.

Large rock-crystal figure of Guanyin (Chinese Buddhist goddess of mercy). Qing Dynasty (1644–1911), 33.5cm (13¼in) high, £8,000/$13,600

Ming-style carved red-and-black lacquer square tray. 18th century, 34.5cm (13⅝in) square, £3,000/$5,100

Ming red lacquer rectangular tray, with carved details. 16th–17th century, 43.5cm (17in) long, £2,000/$3,400

Rhinoceros-horn libation cup. 17th–18th century, 17.5cm (7in) high, £13,000/$22,100

Large, carved and lacquered wooden figure of Guanyin. Qing Dynasty (1644–1911), 48.5cm (19in) high, £1,000/$1,700

Pair of cloisonné elephant candlesticks. Qianlong (1736–1795), 32.5cm (12⅝in) high, £10,000/$17,000

Large mirror painting, depicting an imperial hunting scene. 18th century, 77cm x 46.5cm (30¼in x 18¼in), £10,000/$17,000

Large carved red-lacquer circular box and cover. 18th–19th century, 31.5cm (12⅜in) diameter, £2,100/$3,600

Large rose quartz vase and cover. 19th century, 51cm (20in) high, £2,500/$4,250

Large late-Ming cloisonné enamel charger. 17th century, 47.5cm (18¾in) diameter, £1,500/$2,700

Pair of cloisonné enamel stag figures. Qianlong (1736–95), 16cm (6¼in) high, £3,000/$5,100

Carved celadon jade landscape panel. 18th century, 22.5cm (8⅞in) wide, £13,000/$19,500

Spinach-green jade vase and cover. 19th century, 23.5cm (9¼in) high, £2,000/$3,400

Ivory carving of Shou Lao (god of longevity). Qing Dynasty (1644–1911), 51cm (20in) high, £1,000/$1,700

Japanese Pottery

Although early Japanese wares show a distinct Chinese or Korean influence, original Japanese forms and shapes were also produced. These often had simple decoration such as a leaf, flower, or calligraph applied off-centre. Much Japanese pottery was for ornamental purposes, because utilitiarian pieces were usually made of lacquered wood. The exceptions – and probably the most sought-after wares – are those intended for the tea ceremony, especially the Raku tea bowls, or *chawan,* which invariably have a rustic appearance that belies their importance and age. The rarest bowls date from the 17th century and are valued as national treasures. Other items made for the tea cermony include jars, trays, incense burners (*koros*), tea caddies (*chaires*), and scent boxes.

The main early pottery centre was at Seto. However, the majority of Japanese pottery found in the West tends to be from the Meiji period (1868-1912), when vast quantities were pouring out of kilns in Satsuma, a port in southern Japan, and Kutani, located in Kaga province. The quality of the cream-coloured, finely crackle-glazed ware varied. Those made in artists' studios were of fine quality, while those destined for the European and American export markets were often of poor quality.

In the Seikozan studio in Satsuma and in Kyoto, such potters as Kinkozan IV, Yabu Meizan, Kozan, and Rokuzan all produced finely detailed wares of breathtaking quality. Thickly potted and strong enamelled examples were produced in large sizes and were decorated in more formal designs. Most of the Kutani ware that found its way to the West is decorated in a predominantly iron-red colour, which is applied to porcelain as well as pottery.

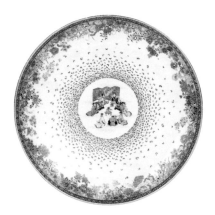

Satsuma dish, by Yabu Meizan. Meiji period (1868–1912), 21.5cm (8½in) diameter, £2,500/$4,250

Pair of large Satsuma vases, with gilt-metal mounts. Meiji period (1868–1912)/European mounts *c.*1900, 87cm (34in) high, £4,000/$6,800

Fine Satsuma bowl, by Yabu Meizan. Meiji period (1868–1912), 9.5cm (3¾in) high, £2,000/$3,400

Satsuma oviform vase. Meiji period (1868–1912), 20.5cm (8in) high, £3,000/$5,100

Satsuma square dish, with river landscape, by Hankinzan. Meiji period (1868–1912), 16cm (6¼in) square, £2,000/$3,400

Satsuma square dish, by Kozan. Meiji period (1868–1912), 16cm (6¼in) square, £850/$1,445

Large *ao* (green) Kutani *koro* and cover.
Meiji period (1868–1912), 59cm (23in) high,
£1,500/$2,550

Small Satsuma vase, by Yabu Meizan.
Meiji period (1868–1912), 12cm (4¾in)
high, £1,500/$2,550

Satsuma vase by Rokuzan

The details of the decoration, applied in
rich enamels and gilt, demonstrate the
high-quality work of this important
Japanese potter.
c.1890, 30cm (12in) high, £4,000/$6,800

*When exposed the cream
coloured pottery exhibits
a fine surface crazing*

*The collar neck is decorated
with a formalized band of
ho-ho birds (phoenixes). These
contrast with the dragon
design applied to the body.*

*The gilt decoration is incised,
finely detailed, and has a matt
surface, all signs of quality.*

*An asymmetrical design of
two three-clawed dragons is
set among celestial clouds
and above turbulent waves.*

*The glazed underside of the
base is fully signed by the
decorator and the cross
within circle mon (arms)
of the Prince of Satsuma.*

Satsuma vase and domed cover. *c.*1890,
35.5cm (14in) high, £4,000/$6,800

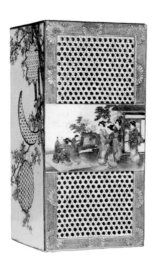

Satsuma vase or *chaire,* by Seikozan. Meiji period
(1868–1912), 13.5cm (5¼in) high, £3,000/$5,100

Satsuma vase, by Ryuzan. Meiji period
(1868–1912), 19.5cm (7⅝in) high, £2,500/$4,250

Japanese Porcelain

The civil war in China, fought during the middle decades of the 17th century, resulted in many of the imperial kilns being destroyed. Consequently, the Dutch, who were the main traders in Chinese wares, turned to Japan to replace the vast quantities of porcelain that arrived in Europe by the shipload. However, from the late 17th century Japan retreated into self-isolation and only small quantities of wares were exported before trade resumed after 1860.

The Japanese porcelain industry was centred in the Arita province. Other factories included Hirado, which produced soft white porcelain painted in blue from the early 17th century, and Nabeshima, whose output was exclusively for the ruling Shogun and feudal lords.

After the reopening of trade, the West was flooded with porcelain from Arita, especially Imari ware, which is easily identifiable by its distinct underglaze blue and overglaze iron-red palette. However, Kakiemon ware is considered by collectors as the most delicate of all the Arita porcelain.

The name "Kakiemon" is derived from the family of potters who are credited with introducing overglaze enamelling in the mid-17th century onto their fine milky-white porcelain, which is known in Japan as *nigoshide*. Their wares were decorated in distinctive red, blue, green, and yellow overglaze enamels applied in asymmetrical designs. They are sometimes heightened with gilding, and their dishes may be edged in chocolate brown.

Arita reticulated dish. *c.*1700, 26.5cm (10½in) diameter, £2,500/$4,250

Arita Kakiemon-style baluster jar and cover (with restoration on the cover). *c.*1700, 39.5cm (15⅝in) high, £1,500/$2,550

Large Imari baluster jar and cover. 18th century, 79cm (31in) high, £2,500/$4,250

Arita five-piece garniture (matching vases or figures). Edo period (late 17th century), 66cm (26in) high, £35,000/$59,500

Large Arita blue-and-white deep bowl and cover. *c.*1700, 28cm (11in) diameter, £2,500/$4,250

Large Arita blue-and-white baluster jar. *c.*1700, 48cm (19in) high, £3,000/$5,100

Pair of Arita blue-and-white bottle vases (with slight damage). Edo period (late 17th century), 28cm (11in) high, £800/$1,360

Arita blue-and-white *kaiseki* dish, used for serving food. Probably 19th century, 29cm (11½in) wide, £700/$1,190

Large pair of Imari circular dishes (only one shown). *c.*1700, 55cm (21¾in) diameter, £8,000/$13,600

Pair of Arita figures of Bijin or Tayu (beautfiul women or high-ranking courtesans). Late 17th century, 37cm (14⅝in) high, £6,000/$10,200

Pair of Nabeshima blue-and-white flaring cups. Early 18th century, 11cm (4¼in) diameter, £4,000/$6,800

Arita blue-and-white baluster jar and cover. 18th century, 86cm (34in) high, £4,000/$6,800

Kakiemon fluted dish,18th century, 24cm (9½in) diameter, £4,000/$6,800

Japanese Works of Art

The single common element found in each type of Japanese work of art produced during the golden age, which extended from the mid-19th to the early 20th century, is the inherent quality of the materials matched to the excellence of design. This is readily apparent in the vast range of decorative lacquerware. Producing this ware involves many hours of preparation to carefully build up layer upon layer of lacquer prior to applying the gilt and blackened surface.

Skilled craftsmen produced netsuke, small, often figurative carvings of ivory, bone, or wood. Netsuke were used as a toggle to secure the cord on an obi, or waist sash, on a kimono, a type of robe. (Inro, small lacquered boxes used for storage, were hung from the obi.) The finest ivories are those

from the Tokyo School, which are carved with incredible facial and anatomical detail. A top-quality ivory carving will carry a signature incised into a mother-of-pearl or red-lacquer rectangular panel inset into the underside of the base.

The art of the cloisonné enameller reached new heights of excellence with the top craftsmen using silver wire in their naturalistic compositions. Many less-skilled craftsmen offered simpler designs outlined with copper wire.

For generations Japanese metalworkers provided swords and decorative armour and fittings to the Samurai classes until an imperial edict in the 1870s prohibited the wearing of swords. Those craftsmen involved turned their attention to a whole range of decorative metalwork, silver, and bronzes.

Ivory okimono of a farmer

This okimono, carved as a chicken farmer standing with a chicken basket beside a hen and four chicks, was designed to stand in a *tokonoma*, or alcove. These were first made in the 19th century and depicted figure or animal forms, often based on smaller netsuke. This one is signed Soko.
c.1900, 13cm (5in) high, £2,600 /$4,400

This okimono is constructed from several pieces of ivory, which have been skilfully assembled.

This example retains most of the original staining, which adds to the value and desirability of the piece.

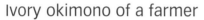

The overall subject matter is of an endearing nature that most collectors find attractive. The fine detail and realistic carving identify this example as by a top craftsman.

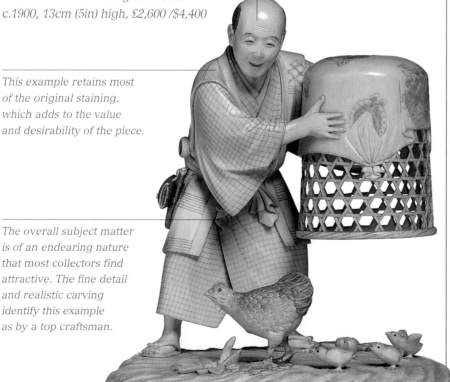

Bronze okimono of a mother and child, by Teidagawa. Meiji period (1868–1912), 52cm (20½in) high, £10,000/$17,000

Large cloisonné enamel circular dish. Meiji period (1868–1912), 87cm (34in) diameter, £4,000/$6,800

Miyao-style gilt-bronze figure of a sennin (a sagelike figure). Meiji period (1868–1912), 54.5cm (21½in) high, £8,000/$13,600

Large midnight blue-ground cloisonné enamel vase. Meiji period (1868–1912), 46.25cm (18¼in) high, £3,000/$5,100

Silver-plated bronze okimono of a cockerel, by Masatsune. 19th century, 65cm (25½in) high, £13,000/$22,100

Nunome zogan (inlaid metal) on iron *kodansu* (chest), by Okunu of Kyoto. Meiji period (1868–1912), 14cm (5½in) high, £9,000/$16,150

Gold-lacquered mixed-metal vase. 1893, 45cm (17¾in) high, £30,000/$51,000

Ivory okimono of a standing elephant. Meiji period (1868–1912), 26cm (10¼in) high, £3,000/$5,100

Two gold, silver, and red/black inros, by Kansai. Late 19th century, size unavailable, £4,000/$6,800 (left) and £5,000/$8,500

Wooden netsuke of Watanabe no tsuna and the demon (Watanabe no tsuna is a warrior in Japanese folklore). *c.*1800, size unavailable, £1,800/$3,050

Wooden netsuke of a seated tiger, with a two-toned striped tail wrapped toward the front. 19th century, size unavailable, £1,800/$3,050

Ceramics from the West

1　**2**　**3**　**4**

1 Staffordshire flatback of Heenan and Sayers, *c*.1855
2 Prattware "Postillion" toby jug, *c*.1800
3 Swansea porcelain "Gosford Castle" plate, *c*.1815
4 Minton majolica garden seat, *c*.1880

Stoneware was favoured by German potters during the later Middle Ages. Elsewhere in Europe the Renaissance (*c*.1500–1650) revived interest in Greek and Roman architecture and works of art, and Italian potters began to decorate their pots using colourful "maiolica" tin glazes (inspired by imported Hispano-Moresque ware). They depicted finely painted mythological beasts and episodes from classical literature. By the 16th century, Dutch potters were influenced by Italian craftsmen who settled in Antwerp, and they produced tin-glazed ware with blue-painted decoration. These techniques and style of decoration were adopted by other potters, but the town of Delft was the premier centre of "Delftware" production. In the late 16th century, Dutch potters who settled in London, England, instigated the beginnings of the British delftware industry, which continued to the late

18th century, before conceding to the printed creamware championed by Josiah Wedgwood.

In the 16th and 17th centuries, potters in the West endeavoured to produce wares emulating the fine Chinese porcelains imported initially by Portuguese traders. A significant amount of tin-glazed ware was produced in Holland, Britain, and Germany, where it was known as "fayence" (but *"faïence"* in France). These were decorated with Chinese motifs and figures. Yet despite the high standards of potting and decoration, they were a pale imitation of Chinese perfection.

Discovering hard-paste porcelain

By 1700 the race was on in Europe to discover the closely guarded secret Chinese formula for making true "hard-paste" porcelain. It was the German alchemist Johann Friedrich Böttger,

5

6

7

8

5 Barr, Flight and Barr "George III Service" teapot, c.1805
6 Höchst porcelain figure of Columbine, c.1750
7 Pilkington's Royal Lancastrian Pottery lustre-decorated vase, c.1925
8 Deruta maiolica tazza, c.1650

incarcerated in Albrechtsburg castle near Meissen by Augustus the Strong, who made the discovery in 1708. The Meissen factory soon achieved universal acclaim for its fine teaware and decorative porcelain and figures. Within a few years its monopoly was lost when workers defected to Vienna and the formula found its way into the hands of potters at Berlin, Nymphenburg, Fürstenburg, Ludwigsburg, Frankenthal, and other German factories.

The French potters' experiments failed to produce true-hard porcelain, but the factories at Chantilly, Mennecy, and St Cloud all managed to achieve an artificial, or soft-paste, porcelain with a warm ivory colour. It was the Vincennes factory, which moved to Sèvres in 1756, that saw the greatest success, having attracted royal and aristocratic patronage. It remains to this present day the national factory of France.

British porcelain

In the mid-1740s, British porcelain production began in London at Chelsea and Bow, followed by the short-lived firms of St James, Limehouse, and Vauxhall. Production at the Bristol factory began in 1749, but it moved to Worcester in 1752. Derby and Worcester were important porcelain centres during the ensuing 250 years, which witnessed great makers such as Swansea and Rockingham rise and fall. The 19th century established Britain as the premier potting nation, exporting wares worldwide and dominated by such giants as Doulton and Minton.

At the end of the century, the reaction against mass production resulted in numerous art potteries in both Britain and the United States dedicated to reviving the art of the potter. Despite their imaginative output, only a handful survived beyond the war clouds of 1945.

Continental Pottery

The earliest advance in European pottery design took place in Spain in the 14th and 15th centuries, with the production of Hispano-Moresque lustreware (pottery with a lustre glaze) in Malaga and Manises (Valencia). The merit of the Spanish ware was recognized by Italian potters, who developed their own tin glazes, which they christened "Maiolica" after the island of Maiorca (Majorca), from where they imported the lustreware. In the 15th and 16th centuries, Italian centres of production ranged from Venice in the north to Palermo in the south.

French tin-glazed ware, referred to as "faience" – after the Italian city of Faenza – commenced in 1512 with the arrival of Italian potters in Lyons. In the 17th century, the pottery made in the city of Nevers used a more native style, and in the 18th century, Rouen and Strasbourg gained importance with their distinct shapes and designs. Italian potters also influenced developments in Holland in the 16th and 17th centuries, which led to the town of Delft becoming pre-eminent. As well as the blue-and-white colours linked with Delft, a polychrome palette was used, including Delft *doré*, a Japanese-inspired decoration in red, blue (or green), and gold. German potters preferred robust stoneware, but at Frankfurt and Hanau they produced tin-glazed ware, known as "fayence", from about 1660.

Stoneware

German stove tile. Dated 1561, 27.5cm x 18.5cm (10⅞in x 7¼in), £570/$970

German stoneware "bellarmine" (bulbous jug with a bearded head), possibly Cologne or Frechen. 1607, 35cm (13¾in) high, £24,000/$40,800

Annaberg fayence apostle tankard, with pewter hinged cover. Inscribed 1673, 17cm (6¾in) high, £2,100/$3,600

Creussen fayence apostle flask. *c.*1660, 25cm (10 in) high, £2,400/$4,100

Westerwald stoneware stein, with hinged pewter cover. Dated 1781, 18cm (7in) high, £200/$340

Westerwald stoneware tankard, with hinged pewter cover. Dated 1706, 23.5cm (9¼in) high, £260/$440

Westerwald stoneware ewer, with hinged pewter cover and footrim mount. 1650–1700, 36cm (14⅛in) high, £250/$425

Dutch Delft Pottery

Dutch Delft *doré* **lobe-shaped plaque** (with restoration). *c.*1770, 38cm (15in) high, £1,000/$1,700

One of a pair of polychrome Dutch Delft plaques. 1725–50, 24cm (9½in) high, £3,600/$6,100

Dutch Delft blue-and-white plate. *c.*1700, 21cm (8¼in) diameter, £250/$425

Dutch Delft multiple tulip vase, by De Metalen Pot factory. 1720, 20.5cm (8in) high, £4,300/$7,300

Dutch maiolica silver tray-shaped porringer. 1610–30, 23cm (9in) high, £1,800/$3,050

Dutch Delft tobacco jars, with brass covers, by the De Porceleyne Bijl factory. 1770–1800, 30cm (11⅞in) high, £500/$850 each

Dutch Delft polychrome plaque, with relief moulded surround. 1750–75, 30.5cm (12in) high, £1,000/$1,700

Garniture of three Dutch Delft vases, with similar dog and bird decoration. *c.*1770, vase with cover 38cm (15in) high, £600/$1,020

Dutch Delft vase, by De Paeuw factory. 1700–10, 27cm (10⅜in) high, £380/$645

Faience Pottery

Hispano-Moresque dish, Manises. 1525–75, 25.5cm (10in) diameter, £1,000/$1,700

Moustier faience fountain and cover. 1700–50, 64.5cm (25in) high, £1,600/$2,700

Frankfurt fayence vase and cover. c.1720, 55cm (21¾in) high, £4,500/$7,650

Erfurt fayence tankard, with hinged pewter cover. c.1740, 23.5cm (9¼in) high, £300/$510

German fayence tankard, with hinged pewter cover, possibly Ansbach. 1730–50, 14cm (5½in) high, £280/$475

German fayence bottle, attributed to Bayreuth. 1720, 23.5cm (9¼in) high, £450/$765

Pair of Strasbourg faience sauceboats. 1760–70, 21cm (8¼in) high, £3,000/$5,100

Three French faience Revolutionary plates. 1790–1810, 23cm (9in) diameter, £400/$680

Maiolica Pottery

Pair of faenza maiolica armorial flasks.
1575–1600, 31.5cm (12⅜in) high, £6,000/$10,200

Urbino maiolica armorial dish

This dish belongs to a suite of maiolica all bearing the arms of the Duke of Ferrara. It is thought to have been made for the Duke on the occasion of his marriage to Margarita Gonzaga in 1579. The scene of the boar hunt indicates that the suite was probably made by the Patanazzi workshop.
c.1579, 37cm (14⅝in) diameter, £16,000/$27,200

The flaming brazier with the ribboned words "Ardet Aeternum" at the top of the dish is the Duke's motto.

The rim has been decorated with trompe l'oeil (trick of the eye) gadrooning, which is found on silver and metalwork in the 16th century and later.

The border was decorated with grotesque beasts and hybrid-humans, which is typical of Renaissance maiolica but was copied in the 19th and 20th centuries.

Although the dish is unsigned, the style and use of specific colours suggest that it was made at the Patanazzi workshop.

Castel Durante maiolica pill jar and cover.
*c.1580, 14cm (5½in) high, £1,350/$2,300

Pair of Venetian syrup jars. *c.1600,* 20cm (7⅞in) high, £2,500/$4,250

Savona octagonal plate. *c.1700,* 17cm (6¾in) diameter, £500/$850

Castelli maiolica plaque. *c.1740,* 30.5cm (12in) high, £1,100/$1,870

British Pottery: 17thC and 18thC

The arrival of Dutch potters in London in the early 17th century led to the introduction of a hand-decorated tin-glazed ware known today as delftware. British decoration included the monarch's portrait applied to a mug or a charger with a blue-dash rim, which was applied in broad strokes.

Slip-glazed ware, which has characteristic naive decoration in white slip (liquid clay) against a brown earthenware body, was made in the 17th and early 18th centuries, as was the green-glazed ware referred to as Whieldon and Wedgwood types. In the 1740s, the Elers brothers, who set up their operation in Stoke-on-Trent, began to make a dense red stoneware emulating the Yixing ware that was exported from China.

In the late 18th century, the industry was revolutionized by Josiah Wedgwood, who was behind the development of black basaltes (a dense, hardened stoneware), creamware and pearlware (see page 54), and jasperware, an unglazed stoneware with fine decoration. He worked in Staffordshire, which increased in importance as a centre for pottery production. However, Nottingham, London, Liverpool, Bristol, Leeds, and various other centres in Yorkshire also produced stoneware, creamware, and delftware, and are all highly collected today.

British Delftware

Charles I delftware bottle, with royal monogram and crown. 1643–45, 19.5cm (7⅝in) high, £44,000/$74,800

London delftware bottle (with restoration). Dated 1647, 17cm (6¾in) high, £1,200/$2,050

London delftware fuddling cup (a type of linked cup). 1675–1700, 8.5cm (3¼in) high, £2,200/$3,750

British delftware "Oakleaf" dish. c.1690, 29cm (11½in) diameter, £720/$1,225

British delftware William and Mary double-portrait bowl. c.1690, 26cm (10¼in) diameter, £5,800/$9,850

London blue-dash charger

This delftware charger is painted with a full-length portrait of Queen Anne holding an orb and sceptre. Royal portrait chargers were made during the reign of Charles I, but their popularity increased significantly with the restoration of the monarchy in 1660 and the return to the throne of Charles II. *1702–4, 34.1cms (12 ins) diameter, £12,000/$20,400*

Although the upper surface is covered with tin glaze, the potter used a clear, untinted, lead glaze on the reverse for economical reasons.

The broad strokes of blue around the rim shows this to be a "blue-dash" charger

The naive painting is a standard type and attributable to the Norfolk House pottery in Lambeth.

Any small chips to the rim and even the odd fine crack are considered to be acceptable to collectors and have a limited effect on the value.

The value of this charger (and any other British delftware) would be greatly enhanced if a date had been present.

British delftware "Popish Plot" tile. *c.*1700, 13cm x 13.5cm (5in x 5¼in), £2,100/$3,600

British delftware Adam and Eve charger. *c.*1720–30, 33.5cm (13¼in) diameter, £1,200/$2,050

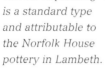

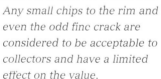

British delftware apothecary's pill jar, inscribed "P Macri" (with restoration to top rim). *c.*1730, 10cm (3⅞in) high, £700/$1,190

"Battle of Portobello" delftware plate. *c.*1741, 21.5cm (8½in) diameter, £3,000/$5,100

British delftware tea canister, probably Bristol (the cover is missing). *c.*1750, 11cm (4¼in) high, £2,900/$4,900

British Delftware

London delftware sweetmeat tray. *c.*1750, 21cm (8¼in) diameter, £1,150/$1,950

London delftware "Cockfighting" plate. *c.*1750, 22.5cm (8⅞in) diameter, £5,800/$9,850

British delftware Adam and Eve dish. *c.*1750, 33.5cm (13¼in) diameter, £3,000/$5,100

Bristol or Wincanton delftware "Woolsack" dish. *c.*1760, 33.5cm (13¼in) diameter, £820/$1,395

Lambeth delftware "Lunardi" ballooning plate, by Thomas Morgan and Abigail Griffiths. *c.*1785, 23cm (9in) diameter, £800/$1,360

Lead-glazed and Salt-glazed Pottery

Staffordshire glazed redware chocolate pot and cover. 1730–44, 21.5cm (8½in) high, £15,000/$25,500

Staffordshire Astbury-type lead-glazed figure of a bagpiper. *c.*1750, 12cm (4¾in) high, £3,000/$5,100

Pair of Astbury-type lead-glazed figures of Mounted Dragoons. *c.*1750, 20cm (7⅞in) high, £10,000/$17,000

Staffordshire solid agateware cream jug.
1745–55, 10cm (3⅞in) high, £400/$680

**Staffordshire salt-glazed enamelled guglet
or decanter.** *c.*1750, 23.5cm (9¼in) high,
£2,000/$3,400

Derbyshlre salt-glazed jug, attributed to
Cockpit Hill. 1764, 16cm (6¼in) high, £800/$1,360

Staffordshire salt-glazed sifter. *c.*1765,
14cm (6.75in) high, £2,000/$3,400

Staffordshire "melonware" teapot and cover.
*c.*1765, 14.5cm (5⅝in) high, £3,500/$5,950

**Staffordshire Whieldon-type food warmer or
*veilleuse*** (night-light). *c.*1765, 24.5cm (11.75ln)
high, £2,000/$3,400

Creamware and Other Pottery

Barnstaple slipware jug, by Thomas Fields.
Dated 1757, 31.5cm (12⅜in) high, £8,000/$13,600

Liverpool-printed creamware mug, featuring
"The Tythe Pig" (with a crack in the rim). *c.*1765,
13cm (5in) high, £400/$680

British lobed silver-shaped creamware plate.
*c.*1770, 21.5cm (8½in) diameter, £850/$1,445

Creamware and Other Pottery

Wedgwood black basaltes teapot and cover, with blue enamelled decoration and widow finial. 1770–90, 24cm (9½in) long, £2,500/$4,250

British creamware melon tureen and cover, with an integral stand. *c.*1775, 19.5cm (7⅝in) long, £1,300/$2,200

Yorkshire creamware jug. Dated 1776, 22.5cm (8⅞in) high, £800/$1,360

Wedgwood blue jasper portrait medallion of Edward Bourne, modelled by William Hackwood. *c.*1778, 15.5cm (6in) high, £1,500/$2,550

Wedgwood creamware teapot and cover, printed with "The Death of Wolfe". *c.*1780, 24cm (9½in) high, £3,400/$5,800

Wedgwood black basaltes inkstand. *c.*1780–82, 14cm (5½in) wide, £550/$935

Liverpool-printed creamware jug. *c.*1790, 18.5cm (7¼in) high, £550/$935

Wedgwood "First Edition" copy of the Portland Vase, in solid black jasper with white reliefs (not numbered). *c.*1793, 26.5cm (10½in) high, £20,000/£34,000

British Pottery: 19thC

In the 19th century, the potteries based in Staffordshire, known collectively as The Potteries, became an important production centre of pottery and porcelain. Mason's and Spode, two of the potteries, pioneered the development of colourfully enamelled, durable stoneware as a less-expensive alternative to bone china. The Pratt family developed pearlware pottery decorated in a distinctive palette of blue, green, yellow, orange, brown, and purple, which is now known as Prattware, regardless of the maker.

Perhaps the most enduring of all 19th-century pottery has to be the Staffordshire portrait figure, which was modestly priced to enable the working classes to own effigies of Queen Victoria or other celebrities of the age, along with a variety of spill

vases (for holding "spills" to light candles), pastille burners (for burning herbs as an air freshener), and the ubiquitous Staffordshire spaniels. The earliest figures had idyllic themes: shepherds and shepherdesses, musicians, and courting couples, with modelling in the round. Most later figures were less well modelled and the backs were not detailed.

Several successful potteries operated in Yorkshire, in the Rotherham and Leeds area, and on Clydeside and in Portobello near Edinburgh. In South Wales the Swansea pottery made earthenware into the 19th century; in the northeast on Tyneside the Maling pottery claimed to be the largest factory in the world; and in nearby Wearside several makers in Sunderland produced a distinctive pink lustreware pottery.

Birch caneware teapot, milk jug and cover, and sugar bowl and cover. c.1800, jug 13cm (5in) high, £750/$1,275

Prattware equestrian model of a Napoleonic officer. c.1810, 24cm (9½in) high, £9,000/$15,300

North Country/Scottish portrait figure of the Duke of Wellington. 1810–15, 28.5cm (11¼in) high, £700/$1,190

Bristol pearlware jug, printed in mauve with "The World in Planisphere". c.1800, 17cm (6¾in) high, £700/$1,190

Creamware jug, inscribed "William Fowler 1826". 23.5cm (9¼in) high, £850/$1,445

British Pottery: 19thC

Mason's ironstone hexagonal dark blue-ground vase and cover. *c.*1815, size unavailable, £1,600/$2,700

Large Mason's "Fenton Stone Works" vase and cover. 1835–40, 146cm (57½in) high, £5,800/$9,850

Spode brown printed "Greek" dinner service, with 67 pieces. 1806–20, size unavailable, £3,200/$5,450

Pearlware group of a performing bear and trainer. *c.*1820, 21cm (8¼in) high, £220/$375

Oldfield and Co. salt-glazed stoneware flask of William IV. *c.*1835, 29.5cm (11⅝in) high, £280/$475

Walton Lion and Unicorn spill vase. *c.*1830, 15.5cm (6in) high, £3,700/$6,300

Pearlware figure of the pugilist Tom Molyneux. 1812–15, 22.5cm (8⅞in) high, £750/$1,275

Staffordshire creamware model of a leopard. *c.*1830, 21cm (8¼in) high, £2,500/$4,250

Staffordshire group

By the end of the Victorian era Staffordshire figures such as this portrait group of King Henry VIII and Anne Boleyn were in many homes. These figures reflected the times in which they were made, often highlighting the latest news, including portraits of both heroes and rogues.
c.1860, 25cm (10in) high, £350/$595

This group has typical early facial details, including feathered eyebrows and rouged cheeks.

Early figures usually display the use of more colour and detail in the costume than later examples.

The "flatback" of this figure has been left undecorated because it was designed to be placed against a wall.

This group would have been more valuable if inscribed with a title in gilt or black.

Wedgwood "Water Lily" footbath (repaired).
1815–20, 50cm (19¾in) high, £380/$645

Wedgwood "Absalom Pillar" dinner service, with
180 pieces. 1825–30, size unavailable, £5,000/$8,500

British Pottery: 19thC

Staffordshire feeder. 1825–30, 19cm (7½in) long, £320/$545

Spode "Caramanian" series platter, printed with "The Triumphal arch of Tripoli in Barbary". 1810, 53cm (20¾in) wide, £550/$935

Minton garden seat. Dated 1872, 48cm (18¾in) high, £850/$1,445

Sunderland lustreware, including a Masonic jug, Moore's Wear frog mug, milk jug, Wear Bridge frog mug, and Masonic creamware frog mug. 1810–60, Masonic jug 18.5cm (7¼in) high, £320/$545, £380/$645, £100/$170, £360/$610, and £260/$440

Pair of Staffordshire portrait figures of Admiral Dean Dundas and Admiral Sir Charles Napier, flanking General Sir William Codrington. All c.1854, 33cm (13in) high, the pair £320/$545 and the General £2,200/$3,750

Staffordshire group titled "The Death of the Lion Queen", modelled as Nellie Chapman. c.1850, 37.5cm (14¾in) high, £750/$1,275

Staffordshire portrait group of the Prince and Princess of Wales. c.1863, 25.5cm (10in) high, £130/$220

Thomas Parr equestrian figure of Guiseppe Garibaldi. c.1861, 38.5cm (15⅛in) high, £900/$1,530

Minton majolica heron stick stand

Inspired by Italian maiolica, Minton developed majolica – a richly enamelled stoneware with high-relief decoration. Controlling the glaze during firing was critical to prevent colours bleeding together. The best majolica is by Minton, George Jones, and Wedgwood.
1873, 98cm (38½in) high, £3,500/$5,950

The heron's beak has suffered damage, which affects the value. Fortunately, a good restorer can convincingly replicate majolica glazes.

The naturalistic modelling is of an exceptional standard and is complemented with authentically coloured plumage.

The bulrushes have been modelled to form a stick stand.

The underside is impress-marked Minton with the year symbol for 1873 and the shape number 1917, which should never be confused with the date of manufacture.

John Ridgway and Co. "Real Stone China" part dinner service, with 57 pieces. *c.*1840, size unavailable, £800/$1,360

Minton majolica figure of a man with wheelbarrow. Dated 1864, 33cm (13in) high, £3,000/$5,100

Minton majolica monkey and cockerel teapot and cover, with a snail finial. *c.*1870, 23.5cm (9¼in) high, £3,000/$5,100

British Art Pottery

The reaction against the mass-produced pottery and porcelain of the early Victorian age led to the rise of the art potter, who made hand-crafted wares. By 1880, probably the largest commercial enterprise making hand-decorated stoneware and pottery was the Lambeth studios of Doulton. Sir Henry Doulton promoted the emancipation of women by employing recent graduates from the Lambeth School of Art to decorate his extensive range of ornamental and utilitarian wares. The popularity of Lambeth stoneware was further enhanced by the work of the Martin brothers in nearby Fulham and later Southall in London.

In the north of Britain, Pilkington's, later Royal Lancastrian Pottery, made some of the finest hand-decorated lustreware near Manchester and the short-lived Della Robbia pottery in Birkenhead exemplified the best in Art Nouveau-inspired design, often using sgraffito, or scratched decoration. In Leeds, the Burmantoft factory produced Turkish-inspired, hand-decorated wares in the manner of William de Morgan, the celebrated London-based Victorian art potter. The most prominent of the Staffordshire art potters was William Moorcroft, who worked for James Macintyre & Co. before setting up his own pottery in 1913 in Cobridge.

Burmantoft Pottery

Three Burmantoft pottery double-gourd vases, encircled by grotesque reptiles. *c.*1890, 63cm (24¾in) high, £900/$1,530 each

Burmantoft pottery faience vase, incised with a daisy chain design and another with a stylized tulip design. Both *c.*1900, 26.5cm (10½in) high, £250/$425

Seven Burmantoft pottery "grotesque" vases. *c.*1885, 12cm–18cm (4¾in–7in) high, £300–£500/$510–$850 each

Della Robbia Pottery

Della Robbia two-handled bottle vase and stopper, with a water lily-pad design and sgraffito decoration, by Ruth Bare. *c.*1900, 52cm (20½in) high, £1,900/$3,250

Della Robbia charger, with a central portrait of a maiden and sgraffito decoration, by William Warwick. *c.*1890, 35cm (13¾in) diameter, £700/$1,190

Della Robbia pottery vase, with flowering plants and sgraffito decoration. *c.*1900, 26.5cm (10½in) high, £260/$440

Della Robbia trumpet-shaped vase

The maiden's head emerging through stylized celandine flowers and honesty plants, painted by Cassandia Ann Walker, is typical of the Art Nouveau style seen on pottery made by Della Robbia (1894–1906), which was sold by Liberty and Co., the London-based retailer. Della Robbia also made plaques and tiles, and its wares were decorated with coloured translucent lead glaze.

Dated 1903, 40cm (16in) high, £4,000/$6,800

Della Robbia two-handled vase, with owls among leafy branches and sgraffito decoration. *c.*1900, 25cm (9⅞in) high, £550/$935

This vase is a large size and is decorated with a highly desirable subject – it shows a close association with the Glasgow School.

The use of the strawberry-pink with turquoise, green, and ochre is an attractive and desirable choice of palette.

The design is incised into the clay using the sgraffito technique and accentuated with ochre and black.

The underside is incised with the Della Robbia boat trademark, the date mark for 1903, and the artist's initials.

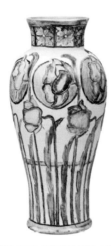

Della Robbia vase, painted with a poppy design (cracked). *c.*1900, 34.5cm (13⅝in) high, £300/$510

Della Robbia two-handled bottle vase and stopper, with a maiden, sinuous flowers, and sgraffito decoration, by Cassandia Ann Walker. Dated 1903, 52cm (20½in) high, £1,500/$2,550

Pilkington's Pottery

Pilkington's lustre-glazed pottery vase, with floral shields and scrolls, decorated by William Salter Mycock. Dated 1916, 20cm (7⅞in) high, £600/$1,020

Pilkington's lustre-glazed pottery vase, with a deer and oak tree design, decorated by Richard Joyce. Dated 1911, 15.5cm (6in) high, £900/$1,530

Pilkington's lustre-glazed pottery tile, with a stag and tree design, modelled in low relief by Albert Hall. Dated 1908, 43cm x 21cm (17in x 8¼in), £2,600/$4,400

Pilkington's Royal Lancastrian lustre pottery vase, with a galleon design, decorated by William Salter Mycock. c.1930, 32.5cm (12¾in) high, £1,800/$3,050

Pilkington's Royal Lancastrian pottery vase, with three fish, modelled in low relief by Richard Joyce. c.1920, 19cm (7½in) high, £150/$255

Pilkington's Royal Lancastrian "Lapis Ware" pottery vase, decorated by Gladys Rogers. c.1930, 22.5cm (8⅞in) high, £100/$170

Lustre-glazed vase

Richard Joyce decorated this Pilkington's Royal Lancastrian vase with fish among aquatic plants in silver and scarlet lustre against a speckled blue-green ground. The firm experimented with several glaze techniques, but its lustreware won it international acclaim.
1915, 25.5cm (10in) high, £2,600/$4,400

The lustre decoration, although complex, is well controlled and in full harmony with the chosen shape.

The value of this vase is dictated by size, subject, the degree of uniform lustre, and the artist involved.

The artist Richard Joyce, as well as William Salter Mycock, was a member of the Pilkington art pottery department for many years and his work is keenly sought after.

The underside of the base is impressed with the company trademark, which is composed of two small bees around a large letter P. It is also painted with the artist's RJ monogram and his specific year symbol for 1915.

Moorcroft Pottery

Macintyre three-handled loving cup, with the "Claremont" pattern and applied silver mounts, designed by William Moorcroft and made for the Shreve Co. of San Francisco. 1904–11, 18.5cm (7¼in) high, £3,000/$5,100

Macintyre Florian Ware vase, designed by William Moorcroft. c.1899, 26.5cm (10½in) high, £700/$1,190

Pair of Macintyre Florian Ware vases, with a "Poppy" pattern, designed by William Moorcroft (with damage to one vase). c.1905, 29.5cm (11⅝in) high, £1,800/$3,050

Moorcroft pottery trumpet vase, decorated with the "Brown Chrysanthemum" pattern. c.1913, 30.5cm (12in) high, £2,200/$3,750

Moorcroft pottery footed jardinière, decorated with the "Claremont" pattern, for Liberty and Co. c.1915, 20cm (7⅞in) high, £2,200/$3,750

Moorcroft pottery two-handled vase, decorated with the "Pomegranate pattern". c.1925, 32cm (12⅝in) high, £800/$1,360

Moorcroft pottery vase, decorated with the "Big Poppy" pattern. c.1925, 26.5cm (10½in) high, £1,500/$2,550

Moorcroft pottery vase, decorated with the "Fish" pattern. c.1930, 20.5cm (8in) high, £2,000/$3,400

Martin Brothers Pottery

Clement Martin stoneware double bird jar and cover. *c.*1923, 17cm (6¾in) high, £10,500/$17,850

Martin Brothers stoneware grotesque bird jar. Dated 1903, 28cm (11in) high, £25,000/$42,500

Martin Brothers stoneware double-sided grimacing face jug. Dated 1913, 28cm (11in) high, £2,500/$4,250

Martin Brothers stoneware flagon, incised with grotesque fish and aquatic creatures. Dated 1888, 34cm (13⅜in) high, £6,200/$10,550

Doulton Lambeth and Other Factories

Minton "Aesthetic" wall plate, painted with a maiden in a garden. Dated 1887, 39cm (15⅜in) diameter, £600/$1,020

William de Morgan "Cavendish" tile, with a flower and leaf design. *c.*1898, 15.5cm (6in) square, £380/$645

Three William de Morgan ruby lustre tiles, painted with partridge, comical ostrich, and bird and snake subjects. *c.*1880, 15.5cm (6in) square, £1,500/$2,550

Doulton Lambeth stoneware jug, with two oval panels enclosing "shaggy dogs", decorated by Hannah Barlow, Florence Barlow, and Frank Butler. *c*.1885, 27cm (10⅝in) high, £1,500/$2,550

Doulton Lambeth stoneware jug, with eight various cats, decorated by Hannah Barlow. *c*.1885, 14cm (5½in) high, £2,000/$3,400

Doulton Lambeth stoneware figural group, as four mice musicians and titled "Waits and Water", modelled by George Tinworth. *c*.1885, 13.5cm (5¼in) high, £5,200/$8,850

Doulton terracotta rectangular plaque, with a biblical tableau, modelled by George Tinworth. *c*.1885, 29cm x 46cm (11½in x 18in), £1,500/$2,550

Ruskin high-fired stoneware vase, covered in an uneven *sang de bouef* glaze (a rich red colour). Dated 1926, 38cm (15in) high, £800/$1,360

C.H. Brannum "Barum Ware" two-handled vase, with fish decoration. *c*.1900, 37cm (14⅝in) high, £470/$800

Morris ware vase, designed by George Cartlidge. *c*.1910, 17.5cm (6⅞in) high, £400/$680

Charles Vyse pottery group of "Punch and Judy", with a musician and dog. *c*.1929, 34cm (13⅜in) high, £5,200/$8,850

American Art Pottery

In the years that followed the Centennial Exhibition, held in Philadelphia in 1876, American art pottery became popular among the affluent in American society. The early pioneers followed either a canvas or sculptural approach: the first is typified by the Ohio Valley School, the second is relevant to wares produced in New England, the South, and California.

Perhaps the most celebrated of all the Ohio Valley enterprises is the Rookwood pottery of Cincinnati, founded by Maria Longworth Nichols in 1880. Prior to 1900, its most accomplished wares included subjects such as flowering plants and the portraits of native Americans, covered in a high-gloss, yellow-brown "standard" glaze. Its main competitor was the Roseville pottery of Zanesville, whose output mirrored that at Rookwood, but at competitive prices.

William Grueby typified the approach of New England potters by embracing organic forms complemented with matt green glazes. In the South, the women-only Newcomb College in New Orleans produced inventive wares, and George Ohr, a truly eccentric potter based in Biloxi, Mississippi, created contorted sculptural extremes. The Arequipa pottery was established in California in 1910 with the aim to provide therapy for women with tuberculosis.

Louis Comfort Tiffany pottery vase, embossed with an arrowroot design and decorated with a random chartreuse crystalline glaze. *c.*1910, 53.5cm (21in) high, £9,700/$16,490

Pewabic pottery vase, covered in a lustred and textured flambé-type glaze. *c.*1920, 48cm (19in) high, £8,000/$13,600

Fulper pottery vase, in Chinese blue flambé laid over a copper dust crystalline glaze. *c.*1910, 28cm (11in) high, £4,000/$6,800

Artus Van Briggle pottery vase, embossed with a leaves and blossom design and covered with a matt raspberry glaze. *c.*1903, 25.5cm (10in) high, £1,800/$3,050

Grueby pottery vase, of organic form, decorated by Ruth Erickson. *c.*1907, 11.5cm (4½in) high, £12,500/$21,250

Newcomb College pottery vase, with yellow and green blossoms against a cobalt and dark green ground, decorated by Leona Nicholson. *c.*1908, 32.5cm (12¾in) high, £12,500/$21,250

Rookwood "standard glaze" loving cup

Native American subjects, such as the one featured on this loving cup, were mostly produced during the latter years of the 1890s. One known source was a series of contemporary photographs taken of members of both the Cree tribe from Montana and the Sicangu Sioux from South Dakota who set up camp, by invitation, in the grounds of the Cincinnati Zoological Gardens in 1895 and 1896 respectively. This cup is more valuable because it has an applied silver band from a popular silver firm.
Dated 1898, 17cm (6¾in) high, £3,400/$5,800

The silver band and shield-shaped medallion on the reverse side were applied by the Gorham Silver Manufacturing Company using an electrolytic technique.

The decoration is the work of Grace Young who, like Matthew Andrew Daly, was considered one of the company's most accomplished portrait artists.

This loving cup is covered in the early "standard" brown glaze, which is applied over slip-painted decoration, giving the pottery its distinctive appearance.

The underside of the base is impressed with the company trademark composed of an R reversed against a P, surrounded by a specific number of flame motifs that determine the date, beginning with a single flame in 1887.

Marblehead pottery vase, with a leaf design covered in mustard over red-green matt glaze, decorated by Arthur Baggs. *c.*1910, 13cm (5in) high, £1,200/$2,050

Teco pottery vase, of organic form, covered in a green-black glaze, designed by Harold Hals. *c.*1910, 34cm (13⅜in) high, £17,500/$29,750

George Ohr pottery vase, of eccentric form, with compressed and twisted body, covered in a raspberry glaze. *c.*1900, 8.5cm (3¼in) high, £4,800/$8,150

Continental Porcelain: 18thC

European potters began trying to imitate Chinese porcelain in the late 16th century, and the first artificial porcelain was made in Italy c.1575, before the French developed a more successful formula at the end of the 17th century. Recognized today as soft-paste porcelain, these variations were adopted by numerous French factories that sprang up in the early years of the 18th century, including those at Chantilly, Mennecy, and later at St Cloud. They used wares from the Orient as their source of inspiration for the decoration.

In Germany, the Elector of Saxony's passion for Oriental porcelain made him determined to find the formula for true porcelain and control its manufacture. His dream was finally realized when Johann Friedrich Böttger, an alchemist imprisoned by the Elector, developed the first successful hard-paste bodies in 1709. His discoveries led to the establishment of the Meissen factory, where J.J. Kändler was one of its most important modellers. The secret was stolen, and toward the end of the 18th century, hard-paste porcelain was manufactured all over Europe. Under the protection of King Louis XV of France, Sèvres (formerly Vincennes) took over as the leader in fashionable porcelain by about 1757.

Successful factories also operated in Holland, Italy, and Denmark during the 18th century. Many of the smaller factories were fairly short-lived – they were unable to compete with the less-expensive creamware pottery popularized by Josiah Wedgwood in Britain.

Meissen Porcelain

Meissen beaker, decorated with a harbour scene. c.1735, 8cm (3in) high, £3,000/$5,100

Pair of Meissen figures of the Prince de Rohan and the Marquise de Pompadour. 1750–52, 24cm (9½in) and 21cm (8in) high, £29,000/$49,300

Meissen teapot and cover, gilded at Ausburg in the Seuter workshop. c.1730, 12.5cm (5in) high, £2,100/$3,600

Meissen teapot and cover, with Kakiemon-style enamelled decoration. 1725–30, 12cm (4¾in) high, £6,000/$10,200

Meissen figure emblematic of Sight, modelled by J.F. Eberlein. c.1750, 15cm (6in) high, £1,000/$1,700

Böttger tea bowl and saucer, with "Hausmaler" (independently home-painted) decoration. c.1720, saucer 14cm (5½in) diameter, £800/$1,360

Pair of Meissen figures of Malabars, modelled by J.F. Eberlein. 1755–70, 35cm (13¾in) high, £10,000/$17,000

Meissen group of two lovers in an ormolu arbour, mounted with French porcelain flowers, modelled by J.J. Kändler. c.1750, 41cm (16in) high, £6,000/$10,200

Meissen teapot and cover. c.1745, 11.5cm (4½in) high, £600/$1,020

Meissen model of a pug and her puppy. c.1750, 17cm (6¾in) high, £800/$1,360

Meissen mother hen and chicks teapot and cover, modelled by J.J. Kändler. 1735–40, 17cm (6¾in) high, £1,400/$2,550

Meissen figure of Harlequin with a Jug, modelled by J.J. Kändler. c.1740, 16cm (6¼in) high, £31,000/$52,700

Pair of Meissen orioles, modelled by J.J. Kändler and J.G. Ehder (with later ormolu bases and some damage and restoration). c.1750, 26.5cm (10½in) high, £3,000/$5,100

Meissen figure of a Japanese woman and child, modelled by J.J. Kändler. c.1745, 11cm (4¼in) high, £1,500/$2,550

Meissen samovar and cover, with six matching tea bowls and saucers. 1740–45, samovar 35.5cm (14in) high, £12,000/$20,400

Sèvres Porcelain

Sèvres green-ground cup and saucer, painted by Jean-Baptiste Noualhier. 1757–60, saucer 15.5cm (6in) diameter, £800/$1,360

Vincennes sucrier, Sèvres plate (painted by Jean-Nicolas le Bel), and Sèvres sucrier with cover. 1750–70, 8.5cm (3¼in) high, 24cm (9½in) diameter, and 10.5cm (4in) high, £300/$510, £300/$510, £500/$850

Sèvres wine-bottle cooler, painted by Rosset. Dated 1767, 19.5cm (7⅝in) high, £500/$850

Sèvres *gobelet* Herbet-shaped cup and saucer. Dated 1757–58, saucer 12cm (4¾in) diameter, £1,000/$1,700

Sèvres chestnut basket and cover, with integral stand. *c.*1758-60, stand 27cm (10⅝in) wide, £2,500/$4,250

Vincennes soup plate. Dated 1755–56, 25.5cm (10in) diameter, £800/$1,360

Sèvres hard-paste porcelain *écuelle* (for serving soup) with cover and stand. Dated 1774, stand 23.5cm (9¼in) wide, £1,400/$2,400

Other Manufacturers

Ludwigsburg figure group of a Chinese mandarin and boy, modelled by Joseph Anton Muller. *c.*1766, 27cm (10⅝in) high, £4,000/$6,800

Vezzi Venetian small bowl or tea bowl. 1720–27, 9cm (3½in) high, £9,500/$16,150

Buen Retiro plate, made to match the Sèvres *Service des Asturies*. *c.*1780, 23.5cm (9¼in) diameter, £1,250/$2,125

Höchst figures of a woodcutter and a boy. *c.*1770, 16cm (6in) high, £500–£600/$850–$1,020

Ludwigsburg white figural group of three dancers. 1760–65, 16.5cm (6½in) high, £2,000/$3,400

Vienna figure of a cobbler. *c.*1770, 13cm (5in) high, £500/$850

Du Paquier Vienna beaker, decorated by Ignaz Preissler of Breslau. *c.*1725, 8cm (3in) high, £1,000/$1,700

Höchst "Slumber Disturbed" group, modelled by J.P. Melchior. *c.*1770, 19cm (7½in) high, £2,500/$4,250

British Porcelain: 18thC

From the mid-1740s, factories at Bow, Chelsea, Worcester, and Derby, among many others in Britain, were producing artificial, or soft-paste, porcelain. The granular consistency was difficult to fire and expensive in comparison with pottery, so pieces were often small. Many of the shapes followed those produced in silver. In fact, Nicholas Sprimont, one of the founders of the Chelsea factory, started out as a silversmith.

William Cookworthy, an eminent citizen of Plymouth, perfected the formula for hard-paste porcelain in Britain. He patented it in 1768 and production began soon afterward. Cookworthy moved his business to Bristol, where his friend

and business partner Richard Champion played an active role. In 1774, Cookworthy retired and Champion took over.

The year 1784 is highly significant in the history of British ceramics. Parliament passed the Communication Act, which reduced the duty paid on tea from 119 percent to 12.5 percent, ending the profitability of smuggling it. Tea became available to a wider range of people, and the demand for pots and cups in which to serve the drink exploded. In addition, Greek- and Roman-inspired decoration eclipsed the fashion for Oriental decoration. By 1798, the East India Company had reduced its imports of Chinese porcelain to almost nothing.

Derby Porcelain

Derby "dry-edge" group of a flautist and a lady companion. c.1754, 16cm (6¼in) high, £18,000/$30,600

Derby cream boat, with Oriental-inspired decoration. c.1755, 11cm (4¼in) high, £500/$850

Derby teapot, with Oriental-inspired decoration. 1758–60, 13cm (5in) high, £8,400/$14,300

Derby two-handled vase. c.1765, 32cm (12⅝in) high, £620/$1,055

Derby model of a squirrel. c.1800, 7cm (2¾in) high, £780/$1,325

Derby sucrier (sugar bowl) and cover. c.1800, 15.5cm (6in) high, £380/$645

Bow Porcelain

Bow vase and cover. *c.*1750, 20cm (7⅞in) high, £1,400/$2,400

Bow model of a lion. 1750–55, 8cm (3in) high, £3,500/$5,950

Bow model of a seated pug dog. *c.*1755, 6cm (2⅜in) wide, £900/$1,530

Bow Kakiemon-style butter tub and cover. *c.*1755, 13cm (5in) wide, £5,750/$9,775

Bow figure of a seated lady. *c.*1758, 12cm (4¾in) high, £400/$680

Bow model of a goat and kid. *c.*1760, 10.5cm (4in) high, £1,000/$1,700

Bow figure of Columbine, a character from the Italian *Commedia dell'arte. c.*1765, 17cm (6¾in) high, £650/$1,105

Bow figure of a huntsman. *c.*1760, 17.5cm (6⅞in) high, £650/$1,105

Two Bow figural groups, modelled as a boy seated before a tree and porcelain flowers. *c.*1765, 27cm (11⅜in) high, £3,850/$6,550

Matching pair of Bow candlesticks, modelled as two buntings among flowering shrubs and a nest with three chicks. *c.*1770, 23cm (9in) high, £750/$1,275

Chelsea Porcelain

Early Chelsea beaker, from the late Triangle/ early Raised Anchor period. 1748–50, 7cm (2¾in) high, £2,000/$3,400

Chelsea saucer, painted in the Vincennes style, from the Raised Anchor period (with chipped rim). *c.*1750–52, 12cm (4¾in) diameter, £2,500/$4,250

Chelsea saucer, painted by Jefferyes Hamett O'Neale, from the Red Anchor period (restored). *c.*1752–53, 10.5cm (4in) diameter, £1,600/$2,700

Chelsea teapot, from the Red Anchor period. *c.*1755–57, 14.5cm (5⅝in) high, £2,750/$4,675

Chelsea figure of Spring, from the Red Anchor period. *c.*1755, 13.5cm (5¼in) high, £4,000/$6,800

Pair of Chelsea vases, from the Gold Anchor period. *c.*1765, 21cm (8¼in) high, £820/$1,395

Chelsea bodkin case, from the Gold Anchor period. *c.*1765, 11.5cm (4½in) high, £2,000/$3,400

Chelsea plate, part of the Duke of Cambridge service, from the Gold Anchor period. *c.*1765, 23cm (9in) diameter, £9,200/$15,650

Chelsea figural watch stand

This watch stand, modelled in the chinoiserie style as a lady in a Rococo-style pavilion, represents a mastery of early British porcelain figural modelling at Chelsea during the Red Anchor period (1752–58). Many collectors prefer objects from this period rather than the more colourful and heavily gilded wares of the Gold Anchor period (1759–69). Earlier periods are referred to as the Triangle period (1744–49) and Raised Anchor period (1749–52). These periods reflect the marks used by the factory, which was bought by Derby in 1769.
c.1757, 26cm (10¼in) high, £4,400/$7,500

The upper section is fitted with a cavity to receive a watch, which was usually placed there in the evening prior to retiring.

The fanciful modelling follows the manner popularized at the Meissen factory in Germany during the previous decade.

The glaze is thick and glassy and had a tendency to pool in recessed areas.

The reverse of the base is signed with an overglaze red anchor mark that places the date of the piece to 1756–58.

Worcester Porcelain

Worcester "Scratch Cross" coffeepot and cover. 1753–54, 22.5cm (8⅞in) high, £11,350/$19,295

Worcester lobe-shaped and fluted teapot. 1754–56, 14.5cm (5⅝in) high, £2,300/$3,900

Worcester baluster-shaped, squared section vase, painted in blue with the "Fancy Bird in a Tree" pattern. *c.*1758–60, 44.5cm (17½in) high, £5,250/$8,925

Worcester Porcelain

Worcester sauce boat

The swollen form of this sauce boat was produced at Worcester for about two years and is always found with the finest decoration. A few later blue and white examples are known. When placed against a strong light most 18th century Worcester porcelain transluces a pale green colour.
c.1753–54, 11.5cm (4½in) high, £7,500/$12,750

The overall shape is inspired by the Rococo style and based upon silver examples of the same period.

The scroll finial is moulded with a dog's head thumb rest, which is peculiar to early Worcester pieces.

The carefully executed decoration fits effortlessly within the Rococo-style moulded panels.

Although unsigned, the perfect harmony of form and delicate enamel work are ample evidence to suggest this sauce boat is of early Worcester origin.

Worcester vase, decorated by J.H. O'Neale (restored). *c.*1770, 34.5cm (13⅝in) high, £5,250/$8,925

Worcester Rococo-style shell centrepiece. *c.*1770, 25cm (9⅞in) high, £5,000/$8,500

Worcester milk jug, with the "Earl Manvers" pattern. *c.*1775, 13cm (5in) high, £1,100/$1,870

Worcester pounce pot, painted in blue. *c.*1772–75, 6.5cm (2½in) high, £6,950/$11,900

Worcester lobe-edged plate, with a "Japan" pattern featuring a central chrysanthemum spray. *c.*1772, 24cm (9½in) diameter, £1,000/$1,700

Other Manufacturers

Limehouse teapot and cover. 1746–48, 9.5cm (3¾in) high, £22,000/$37,400

Bristol Benjamin Lunds factory coffee cup. *c.*1750, 5.5cm (2⅛in) high, £8,800/$14,950

Liverpool Samuel Gilbody's factory mug. 1755–61, 6.5cm (2½in) high, £1,100/$1,870

Vauxhall vase and cover. 1756–58, 14.5cm (4⅝in) high, £2,000/$3,400

Longton Hall figure emblematic of Winter (missing a brazier). *c.*1758, 18cm (7in) high, £320/$545

Lowestoft mug. *c.*1762, 15.5cm (6in) high, £2,000/$3,400

Plymouth teapot and cover, decorated with a Kakiemon-style design. *c.*1770, 14.5cm (4⅝in) high, £1,500/$2,550

Newhall "Robin" jug. 1782–87, 6.5cm (2½in) high, £1,350/$2,300

Continental Porcelain: 19thC

During the early 19th century, the Napoleonic Wars adversely affected the trade in Continental porcelain, and the political instability did little to promote the growth of commerce between the nations. Until about 1830 most porcelain was manufactured for the home markets, but eventually relations with the French improved and much Sèvres porcelain was exported to Britain and the United States. The ornate style was popular in both countries and no wealthy household was complete without its enviable collection of French porcelain. By the end of the 19th century, the most important centre of French porcelain manufacture was Limoges.

In Germany, the Meissen factory held the premier position in porcelain production, relying on the reissuing, remodelling, and adapting of 18th-century and Neoclassical-inspired wares. Nymphenburg and Berlin continued in the same tradition, and the neighbouring Austrian factory at Vienna also went on making richly decorated pieces that demonstrated the skill of their artists, especially the figure painters who worked in the Neoclassical style of the Swiss painter Angelica Kauffmann. The Italian factories in Naples found a market for vases and tableware finely modelled in relief, with classical figure subjects in the manner of the 18th-century Doccia factory.

Meissen Porcelain

Meissen nodding pagoda figure. *c.*1845, 31cm (12¼in) high, £2,500/$4,250

Meissen figure of a tailor riding a goat, originally modelled by J.J. Kandler (restored). *c.*1850, 23cm (9in) high, £860/$1,460

Meissen group emblematic of Liberty. c.1870, 22cm (8⅝in) high, £1,200/$2,050

Meissen musical group. *c.*1850, 26.5cm (10½in) high, £1,400/$2,400

Meissen Rococo-style clockcase. *c.*1850, 38cm (15in) high, £3,200/$5,450

Meissen model of a parrot. *c.*1860, 15cm (5⅞in) high, £400/$680

Meissen group of Love Among the Ruins. *c.*1870, 24cm (9½in) high, £900/$1,530

Two Meissen models of begging Papillon dogs. *c.*1860, 25cm (9⅞in) high, £900/$1,530

Meissen scroll-moulded plaque. *c.*1860, 46cm (18in) wide, £9,000/$15,300

Pair of Meissen groups of The Broken Bridge and The Broken Eggs, modelled by A.V. Acier. *c.*1870, 24cm (9½in) high, £3,000/$5,100

Meissen cabinet plate, with pierced borders and a painting of a lady. *c.*1870, 25cm (9⅞in) diameter, £1,200/$2,050

Meissen group of a lady and her gallant

The modelling of this pair in French Revolutionary dress is distinctly 19th century. Most other contemporary groups were a reworking of 18th-century themes. An 18th-century figure was often marked on the edge of the base at the rear with a small crossed swords – on this group the crossed swords mark is precise and large. *c.1870, 20.5cm (8in) high, £600/$1,020*

This subject matter is slightly unusual because few Meissen figures depict gentlemen wearing bicorn hats.

The choice of subtle pastel shades and lack of any strong colour are unusual on late 19th-century figures.

The raised circular base with moulded frieze heightened with soft gilding is a 19th-century Meissen feature.

The underside of the base is painted in underglaze blue with the Meissen crossed swords mark, but beware that such a mark is not a guarantee of authenticity.

Sèvres and Other Factories

Sèvres topographical coffeepot and cover. Dated 1805, 27.5cm (10⅞in) high, £1,500/$2,550

Pair of Sèvres tureens and covers, with integral stands, from the Château de Randan service. Dated 1841, stands 27cm (10⅝in) wide, £4,200/$7,150

Sèvres cabinet plate. Dated 1846, 24.5cm (9⅝in) diameter, £1,900/$3,250

Sèvres-style coffee can and saucer. c.1860, 16cm (6¼in) high, £720/$1,225

Sèvres-style vase and cover, with gilt metal handles, plinth, and rim. c.1880, 61cm (24in) high, £3,400/$5,950

Pair of Sèvres-style jewelled cabinet plates. c.1880, 23cm (9in) diameter, £500/$850

Sèvres *pâte-sur-pâte* charger, decorated by Jules Archelais. Painted in 1882, 37cm (14⅝in) diameter, £5,750/$9,775

Paris coffee service, including coffeepot and cover, milk jug, sucrier and cover, and five cups and saucers. c.1820, coffeepot 18.5cm (7¼in) high, £800/$1,360

Pair of Paris-based Darte's factory perfume bottles and stoppers. c.1845, 16cm (6¼in) high, £680/$1,155

Jacob Petit jardinière and stand.
c.1860, 28cm (11in) wide, £550/$935

Berlin topographical snake-handled vase. c.1880, 47.5cm (18¾in) high, £2,200/$3,750

Berlin simulated *pietra dura* (inlaid hardstone decoration) coffeepot and cover. c.1820, 18cm (7in) high, £550/$935

Pair of Berlin soup plates, made as replacements for the Meissen Empress Elizabeth of Russia service (only one shown). c.1850, 24cm (9½in) diameter, £600/$1,020

Berlin Russian presentation Easter egg, titled "La Forteresse à St Petersburg". c.1850, 8cm (3in) high, £400/$680

Berlin vase with goat's mask handles and cover. c.1880, 64cm (25in) high, £1,500/$2,550

Three Russian Gardner's factory porcelain figures, of a cobbler, an accordian player, and a wheelwright. c.1890, accordian player 17cm (6¾in) high, £300/$510, £400/$680, and £450/$765

Pair of Vienna-style cabinet plates, titled "*Reflexion*" and "*Erbluht*", painted in the Wagner workshops after Asti. c.1895, 25cm (9⅞in) diameter, £1,400/$2,400

British Porcelain: 19thC to Early 20thC

In the early 19th century, the porcelain factories of Worcester and Derby dominated the market for fine china, although they faced strong competition from Coalport and the Stoke factory founded by Josiah Spode. Meanwhile, at the Nantgarw and Swansea factories in South Wales, William Billingsley pursued the quest to make beautiful soft-paste porcelain equal to that produced at Sèvres during the 18th century. In Yorkshire, the Rockingham factory near Rotherham developed an individual style that embraced the Rococo style, employing lavish decoration on bone china.

By the middle of the 19th century, the Stoke factory of Minton and Co. was rapidly becoming the premier maker of all manner of ceramics – however, the magnificent *pâte-sur-pâte* pieces produced by Marc-Louis Solon are unquestionably the ultimate in craftsmanship. In later decades, the demand for fine bone china continued with makers such as Copeland, Brown, Westhead and Moore, and Coalport providing high-quality wares.

In the early 20th century, both Royal Worcester and Royal Crown Derby retained the importance they had achieved one hundred years earlier. Worcester called upon the talents of great artists such the Stinton family and Harry Davies, while at Derby artists such as Desire Leroy and Albert Gregory produced magnificent floral decoration.

Early Porcelain

Pinxton vase and cover. c.1800, 26.6cm (10¼in) high, £4,000/$6,800

Barr, Flight, and Barr Worcester teacup and saucer, decorated with landscapes within canted panels. c.1804, saucer 14cm (5½in) diameter, £1,140/$1,950

Chamberlain jug, printed with a view of Worcester. Dated 1807, 16.5cm (6½in) high, £550/$935

Rockingham presentation jug. 1830–37, 20.5cm (8in) high, £3,600/$6,100

Garniture of three Bloor Derby vases. c.1830, 30cm (11⅞in) high, £480/$815

Swansea "Marquis of Anglesey" teacup and saucer, with floral decoration. 1815–17, 11cm (4¼in) high, £1,100/$1,870

Pair of Chamberlain's Worcester vases

These vases were painted with square panels enclosing colourful feathers. The value of vases is a reflection of their condition: the feet have been restored, the gilding shows wear, and originally the vases had covers. If they were perfect and complete, the value would be £6,000/$10,200.

c.1815, 13cm (5in) high, £600/$1,020

The handles mirror the lion mask-and-ring design found on furniture of the same period.

The feather decoration is inferior to similar feather decoration on Flight and Barr Worcester porcelain of the same period. It is never signed.

The worn gilding and restored feet are the main factors for the low value. Collectors might accept missing covers.

The underside of the base is painted in script "Chamberlain's Worcester".

Rockingham plate, decorated in the manner of Thomas Steele. *c.*1826–30, 23cm (9in) high, £600/$1,020

Derby campana-shaped vase, decorated by Richard Dodson. *c.*1815, 46cm (18in) high, £3,000/$5,100

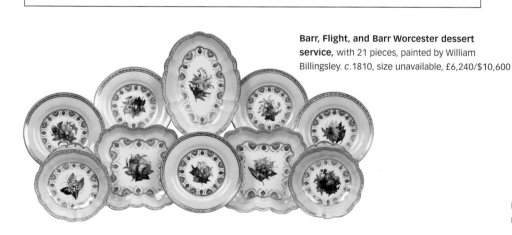

Barr, Flight, and Barr Worcester dessert service, with 21 pieces, painted by William Billingsley. *c.*1810, size unavailable, £6,240/$10,600

Rockingham plate, with scale and shell moulded rim. *c.*1835, 22.5cm (8⅞in) diameter, £400/$680

Early Porcelain

Derby beaded cabinet cup and saucer. *c.*1820, saucer 14.5cm (5⅝in) diameter, £850/$1,445

Minton "New Vase" and cover. 1838–40, 45cm (18in) high, £700/$1,190

Flight, Barr, and Barr Worcester inkstand and covers. *c.*1820, 14.5cm (5⅝in) high, £2,600/$4,400

Coalport garniture of vase and pair of side jardinières, with Italian views, painted in the workshop of Thomas Baxter. *c.*1805, vase 30cm (11⅞in) high, £2,400/$4,100

Nantgarw dish, decorated by Thomas Pardoe. 1818–20, 27.5cm (10⅞in) wide, £5,800/$9,850

Flight, Barr, and Barr Worcester campana-shaped vase. *c.*1825, 30cm (11⅞in) high, £1,500/$2,500

Coalport tea and coffee service, for six settings. 1820–25, size unavailable, £940/$1,600

Pair of Chamberlain and Co. Worcester "Warwick Vases", decorated with London Thames-side views (with restored handles). *c.*1840, 19cm (7½in) high, £1,200/$2,050

Late Porcelain

Pair of Parian figural comports. c.1865, 40.5cm (16in) high, £1,500/$2,550

Brown-Westhead, Moore and Co. vase and cover, decorated in Limoges enamel style, by Thomas John Bott. c.1888, 50cm (19¾in) high, £1,100/$1,870

Copeland cabinet plate, decorated by Charles Ferdinand Hurten. c.1880, 23cm (9in) high, £3,300/$5,600

Copeland vase and cover, decorated by Charles Ferdinand Hurten. c.1875, 48cm (18¾in) high, £2,000/$3,400

Pair of Minton "Elephant vases", styled after the Sèvres originals. Dated 1876, 30cm (11⅞in) high, £6,000/$10,200

Minton Parian figure group of Perseus and Andromeda, modelled by Victor Simyan. Dated 1868, 51cm (20in) high, £1,500/$2,550

Minton "Cloisonné" floor vase. c.1870, 60cm (23½in) high, £17,000/$28,900

Minton "Ship vase and cover", styled after a Sèvres original. c.1895, 43.5cm (17⅛in) high, £8,000/$13,600

Doulton vase, decorated by Edward Raby for the 1893 World Columbian Exhibition. 123cm (48½in) high, £15,000/$25,500

Late Porcelain

Minton *pâte-sur-pâte* **"Cupids Bathing" vase,** decorated by Marc-Louis Solon. Dated 1895, 22cm (8⅝in) high, £37,000/$62,900

Coalport scent bottle and stopper. *c.*1898, 12.5cm (4⅞in) high, £580/$985

Royal Worcester vase, decorated by John Stinton. 1903, 41.5cm (16⅜in) high, £6,800/$11,700

Coalport vase and cover. *c.*1895, 45cm (17¾in) high, £800/$1,360

Pair of Royal Worcester ewers, with swans in flight, decorated by Charles Baldwyn. Dated 1900, 41cm (16⅛in) high, £31,200/$53,000

Pair of Royal Worcester "The Japanese Potters Story" vases, modelled by James Hadley. Dated 1872, 28cm (11in) high, £2,000/$3,400

Garniture of three Coalport vases and covers. *c.*1905, 42cm (17½in) high, £2,000/$3,400

Royal Worcester vase, with sheep in a misty glen, decorated by Harry Davis. Dated 1925, 21.5cm (8½in) high, £4,800/$8,150

Royal Worcester reticulated and double-walled teapot, pierced by George Owen. Dated 1877, size unavailable, £5,500/$9,350

Royal Worcester goblet, bowl, and pair of vases, painted respectively by Harry Martin, Millie Hunt, and Kitty Blake. 1908, 1928, and 1925, 30cm (12in), 24cm (9½in), 18cm (7in) high, goblet and bowl £1,200/$2050, vases £1,300/$2,200

Pair of Derby vases, (only one shown). c.1800, 11.5cm (4½in) high, £2,500/$4,250

Royal Crown Derby two-handled vase, decorated by Desire Leroy. Dated 1904, 13cm (5in) high, £6,200/$10,200

Royal Crown Derby vase

Albert Gregory decorated this vase with a continuous floral band composed of roses, primulas, tulips, and daisies. The firm is noted for richly gilded and painted wares. *Dated 1901, 30cm (11¾in) high. £4,800/$8,150*

The artist's signature is hidden among the decoration. Albert Gregory specialized as a flower painter.

The choice of an exuberant form is typical of the wares made of high-quality Royal Crown Derby bone china.

The fine-quality gilding incorporates flat, beaded, and raised techniques.

The underside of the base is printed in iron-red, with the year symbol below the company cypher mark.

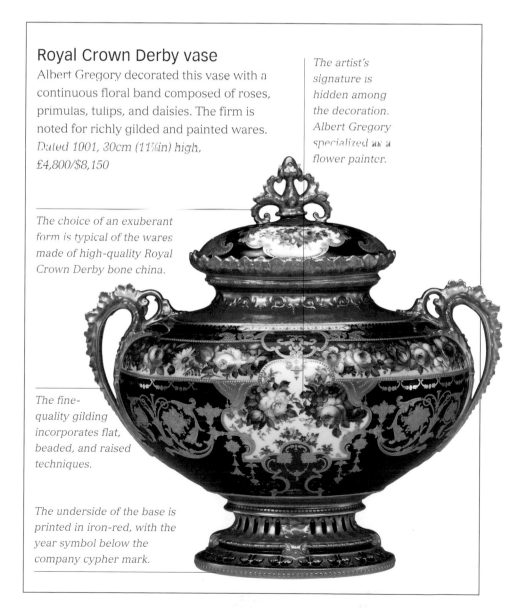

Royal Crown Derby vase and cover, decorated by Albert Gregory. Dated 1905, 25cm (9¾in) high, £720/$1,225

Glass

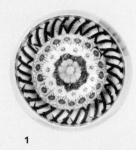

1

2

3

4

1 St Louis mushroom paperweight, *c*.1848
2 American carnival glass footed bowl, *c*.1920
3 Irish decanter and stopper, *c*.1815
4 Dutch engraved armorial wine glass, *c*.1745

Early glass, made from around 3000 BC, contained silicon dioxide (sand); soda made from the ash of the barilla plant gathered in salt marshes and used as the alkaline to help the batch melt; and lime to stabilize it and make it less vulnerable to the adverse effects of water. When heated, this powdery mix became a molten liquid, which could be moulded, cast, or rolled into an endless variety of forms.

After *c*.1000, the composition of glass in Europe changed. Northern glass-makers had relied on supplies of soda from Mediterranean countries, but they found that the ash from burning local supplies of bracken, beech trees, and other plants worked just as well as a flux to lower the melting temperature of the silica. This type of glass, known as *Waldglas* in Germany and Bohemia and *verre de fougère* in France, was made until the 17th century. Unfortunately, it is prone to weathering

so little of it survives today. High-quality, fragile, soda glass continued to be made in Venice.

The term "metal" is applied to glass whether it is molten or cooled and formed into a shape. The metal varies depending on the ingredients. Glass can be shaped using different techniques during the various stages of its malleability. It can be treated as a liquid or as a stone that can be cut, etched, or engraved, making it a highly versatile material. Spun like silk or densely walled, brightly coloured or clear, its properties have been exploited by artists and artisans throughout history for both useful and decorative wares.

A new glass formula

The most significant changes occurred in the glass-making industry until 1676, when experiments in Britain by George Ravenscroft revealed that lead

5

6

7

8

5 British mixed colour-twist wine glass, *c*.1770

6 South Netherlands *Facon de Venise* "leg" drinking vessel, *c*.1600

7 Stourbridge cameo glass vase, attributed to Thomas Webb, *c*.1890

8 Victorian cased, engraved, and cut ewer, by Stevens and Williams, *c*.1890

oxide could provide the fluxing element. This was a turning point in the industry. With this added ingredient Ravenscroft was able to produce a durable and exceptionally clear glass. The Glass Sellers' Company, a City of London guild, had employed Ravenscroft in 1674 to research new techniques in glass production. Success did not come immediately, and his first attempts produced glass that "crisselled", or became covered in minute crackling after a short time.

Once a way had been found to stabilize the mixture, the British glass industry took off (alongside that in Bohemia), and by the end of the 17th century, there were more than a hundred glasshouses operating thoroughout Britain. This laid the foundations for an expansion in glass-making all over Europe and, during the 18th century, British and Irish glass-makers were lured to the Continent and the United States.

Where to begin

One of the most practical ways to learn about glass is to handle it whenever you can at fairs, markets, and auction previews – but ask first, if you think a piece might be a fragile. Examine pieces carefully to become familiar with weight, textures, colours, and styles, and also to look for defects and repairs. You'll begin to recognize a decorator's or manufacturer's style, which is important because most early pieces were not marked.

Main techniques

Core-forming Used from earliest times in Mesopotamia, ancient Greece, western Asia, and the Mediterranean, a technique in which small glass vessels were built up around a central, removable core made of animal dung and clay, modelled to the shape required for the interior and then dipped in molten glass in a furnace. A rod was turned to ensure an even coating while the glass built up, and then it was removed and allowed to cool. The rod was snapped from the core, which was then scraped out. The small vessels produced were sometimes applied with coloured trailed-glass decoration (see *applied*) and used as oil or perfume bottles.

Casting with moulds A method employed from the Bronze Age until Roman times. Jewellery, tableware, inlays, and plaques were made by forcing hot glass into an open mould, or by using two interlocking moulds.

Free blowing Used from *c*.75–50 BC in the Roman world and later worldwide; it is still used today. A blow pipe inserted into the furnace is rotated to pick up an even coating of molten metal. Once removed from the furnace, the glass is rolled back and forth across a metal or stone surface known as a marver to make it cylindrical before the bubble is blown to form the body of the vessel. Once blown and worked to the required shape and size, a rod known as the pontil rod is attached to the base and the blow pipe is removed. Further working while rotating the pontil rod creates the opening. Once complete, the pontil rod is broken from the base with a tap, leaving the characteristic "pontil mark". The mark can be ground and polished away. From *c*.1830, the spring clip replaced the pontil rod and this left no mark.

Blow moulding In ancient times and in the 18th and 19th centuries vessels were made by blowing molten glass into a mould. The metal took the shape and pattern of the mould inside and out. The cooled pieces were removed from the mould and hand finished.

Press moulding Pioneered in the USA in the 1820s and taken up in Europe in the 1830s, an innovative mechanical technique that involved pouring molten glass into a brass or iron mould and pressing it against the sides with a metal plunger. The mould formed the outer surface of the glass, the plunger the inside.

Internal decoration

Many techniques can be applied to glass vessels to form different types of decoration. The principal types of internal decoration, in which elements are added into the metal, are listed below.

Cased Also known as overlay glass, when one layer of glass is applied over another, or three or more layers are fused together and then the outer layer or layers are cut away (see also *cameo*).

Simple coloured tinted The glass is mixed with a metallic oxide while still in powder form.

Three British cordial glasses (centre right with a tear, or elongated air bubble) and a colour-twist wine glass, *c*.1760

Latticino Clear glass embedded with white glass threads to create the appearance of spiral fluting. The threads are woven into the semi-molten metal.

Lithyalin Opaque glass that shows visible striations of various colours and, when polished, has the appearance of agate.

Marqueterie de verre Shaped and coloured lumps of glass pressed into the molten body of a vessel and carved after the glass has cooled. It is found mostly on Art Nouveau glass by Émile Gallé.

Millefiori Meaning "a thousand flowers". Slices of coloured glass canes are embedded in clear glass to form flower heads or other patterns. It is found on paperweights, jugs, and other tableware.

Opaline A translucent, milky white glass that, by adding various metallic oxides, can be coloured pink, mauve, turquoise, green, and several other shades.

Zwischengoldglas The German term used to describe gilt and coloured enamel decoration that is literally sandwiched between two layers of glass.

External decoration

The principal types of external decoration, in which glass is removed or added to the exterior of a vessel, are listed below.

Acid etching The surface of the vessel is covered with an acid-resistant medium such as varnish or gum and a design is then scratched through the resist, using a sharp tool. The piece is then exposed to hydrofluoric acid, which results in a shiny, matt, or frosted decoration of the exposed area.

Applied Clear or coloured molten glass that is applied to the sides of vessels. When strands of glass are applied across the surface, it is referred to as trailing. When applied in the form of small, circular blobs, they are known as prunts.

Cameo Cased glass in two or more layers, with the outer layer carved on a wheel to create a design in relief.

Cut Facets and grooves made by cutting into the surface of glass with an iron or stone wheel. It was used in ancient times and by Irish and British glass-makers in the late 18th and 19th centuries.

Enamelling Fine glass powder is mixed with metallic oxides to create colours that are painted onto the surface of a glass vessel and then fired to fix them.

Engraving Cutting a design into glass with a sharp tool such as a needle or wheel. Wheel engraving involves working the piece on a rotating wheel, which acts as a form of grindstone to remove areas of the surface and create a pattern or inscription. Stipple engraving is achieved by tapping the surface of the glass in varying densities with a sharp needle to create a series of dots, which build up into the desired pattern.

Intaglio The technique of cutting or engraving a design below the surface of the glass to produce an image.

Flashing Applying a thin layer of contrasting colour to the body of a piece by dipping it into thin, transparent, coloured glass enamel in liquid form. The flashed glass can be carved to create an inexpensive version of cased glass.

Two English green-coloured glass spirit decanters and a rinser, *c.*1800, and a Victorian serving bottle, *c.*1850

Drinking Glasses

At the end of the 16th century, Venice still led the world in the field of glass-making, as it had done for 400 years, producing fragile, elegant drinking glasses. Further north, German glass production expanded rapidly after the end of the Thirty Years War in 1648, and, by the middle of the 18th century, the Venetians were beginning to lose their prominent position.

The discovery of the formula for making lead glass, which was pioneered by British glass-maker George Ravenscroft in 1676, transformed the glass-manufacturing industry in Britain. Until this time wine glasses had been imported into Britain from Italy, the Low Countries, and France. Adding lead oxide to a batch produced stronger, clearer bodies, which could also be worked on for longer than previous

types of glass. Lead glass was also especially suited to cutting and engraving techniques so it encouraged the design of many new styles of drinking glasses, which were made available to a wider range of people.

Early 18th-century British drinking glasses tend to be heavy, solid, and plain. However, as the century progressed, glass-makers experimented with a variety of bowl shapes, and, more interestingly, with decorative stems involving air twists, where air bubbles in the molten glass are stretched out, and opaque white and coloured enamel twists, which use rods of white or coloured glass to form the twists. These are still widely available and, although the finest examples command serious money, the vast majority are affordable.

Early Glasses

Engraved cordial glass, inscribed "Trade and Navigation". 1730–40, 17cm (6¾in) high, £1,900/$3,250

Wine glass, with an unusual annulated stem. c.1720, 20cm (7⅞in) high, £3,800/$6,450

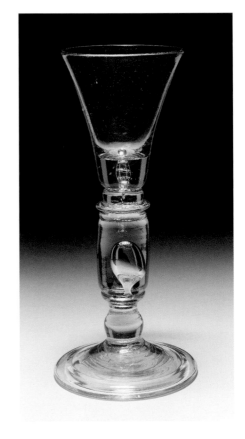

Heavy baluster wine glass, with a funnel-shaped bowl and tears (elongated air bubbles) in the stem. c.1710, 17cm (6¾in) high, £7,200/$12,250

Dutch pedestal-stemmed wine glass, with a funnel-shaped bowl and late 18th-century engraving. c.1720, 22cm (8¾in) high, £1,100/$1,870

Baluster wine goblet, with a rounded funnel-shaped bowl, double-knop stem, and domed foot. c.1745, 21.5cm (8½in) high, £850/$1,445

Jacobite Glasses

Engraved wine glass. *c.*1750, 16.5cm (6½in) high, £1,900/$3,250

Anti-Jacobite wine glass, with Duke of Cumberland. *c.*1730 (engraved 1746), 16.5cm (6½in) high, £5,000/$8,500

Jacobite air-twist wine glass, engraved with roses. *c.*1750, 17cm (7in) high, £1,300/$2,200

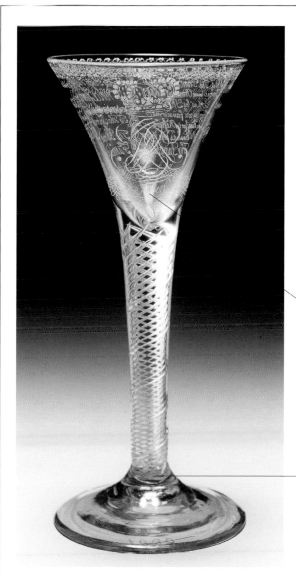

Russell "Amen" glass

A verse and sentiments typical of Jacobite glasses form part of the decoration. This glass is rare and is known as the "Russell Amen" because it belonged to the Russell family of Edinburgh. The other 34 known examples are also named after original or subsequent owners. *c.*1750, 17cm (7in) high, £40,000/$68,000

This Amen glass has a drawn trumpet-shaped bowl and its stem encloses a multiple spiral, air-twist stem. Other examples have a plain stem, which often encloses a single tear.

The circular foot is of conical form. Although this one is plain, other Amen glasses sometimes feature additional engraving on the foot.

The ornate design and script were created with a diamond stylus, which is identified by the irregular edging of the script and the hatched reserves of the crown.

This glass is known as an Amen glass because of the engraved loyal Jacobite verse ending in the word "Amen", enclosed within a cartouche.

Later Glasses

Dutch engraved "Royal Armorial" wine glass.
c.1745, 20.5cm (8in) high, £2,500/$4,250

Light baluster "Kit-Kat" style wine glass.
c.1750, 16cm (6¼in) high, £380/$645

Dutch engraved ceremonial goblet. c.1755,
29.5cm (11⅝in) high, £2,500/$4,250

Bristol "Privateer" opaque-twist wine glass.
1757–60, 15.5cm (6in) high, £7,800/$13,250

"Cyder" engraved cider glass. c.1760,
19.5cm (7⅝in) high, £3,200/$5,450

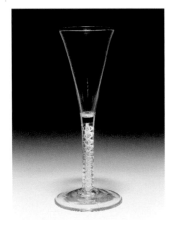

Double series mixed-twist stem wine glass.
c.1760, 19cm (7½in) high, £750/$1,275

Dutch stipple-engraved wine glass, with a
facet-cut stem, by David Wolff. c.1795, 15.5cm
(6in) high, £6,000/$10,200

**Perrin Geddes Prince of Wales service wine
glass,** engraved with the three feathers.
c.1806–10, 14cm (5½in) high, £950/$1,615

"Williamite" rummer, engraved with a
rider on a horse. c.1820, 12.5cm (4⅞in)
high, £1,800/$3,250

Colour-Twist Stems

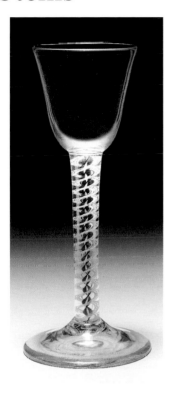

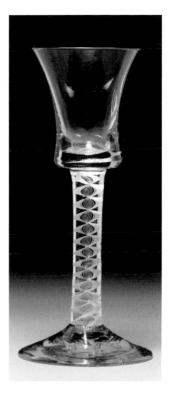

Colour-twist wine glass, with ogee-shaped bowl and white opaque spiral edged in red. *c.*1770, 15.5cm (6in) high, £2,000/$3,400

Mixed-colour-twist wine glass, with a rounded funnel-shaped bowl. *c.*1770, 15.5cm (6in) high, £3,800/$6,600

Canary yellow colour-twist wine glass, with a conical foot. *c.*1765, 14cm (5½in) high, £3,700/$6,300

Tartan colour-twist wine glass, with a knopped stem and flanged foot. *c.*1770, 17cm (6¾in) high, £4,600/$7,800

Enamelled and Gilded Glasses

Opaque-twist wine glass, with enamelling by the Beilby workshop in Newcastle. *c.*1765, 15.5cm (6in) high, £1,700/$2,900

Opaque-twist wine glass, gilded in the Giles workshop in London. 1765–70, 14cm (5½in) high, £520/$885

Decanters and Wine Rinsers

The glass decanter came into its own during the 18th century. Early shapes usually have long necks, wide shoulders tapering slightly toward the base, and spire-shaped facet-cut stoppers. As the century progressed, the straight-sided bottle shape became more prevalent, often engraved with a label to identify the contents it was made to hold, which might have included hop and apple-based drinks, as well as wines, spirits, and liqueurs. When cut-glass decanters became fashionable in Britain in about 1800, the engraving of labels became impractical (engraved silver labels were used instead).

In Ireland, decanters were mould blown with standard-sized bases and vertical flutes. The necks were often decorated with multiple rings, which ensured a firm grip in an age when table etiquette resulted in greasy fingers. The stoppers were produced in bull's-eye and lozenge shapes, although by the end of the 18th century, the mushroom stopper was the most prevalent. Irish decanters enjoyed enormous commercial success and were exported to North America, the West Indies, and Portugal.

The British exported cut-glass decanters to the Continent, and these were rivalled only by the Bohemian glass-makers. By the 19th century, travelling sets were made comprising four bottles with ball stoppers, all in a fitted mahogany box.

The glass rinser became popular during the 18th century. Its single or double lip was designed to allow a wine glass stem to rest at an angle in clear water before removal for the next wine course. Although coloured examples tend to be expensive, clear single rinsers are still inexpensive.

Rodney, or ship's, decanter. 1770–1800, 19cm (7½in) high, £360/$610

Two cruciform serving bottles. 1715–20, 26.5cm (10½in) high, £1,150/$1,955

Irish decanter, moulded on the base Penrose, Waterford (not the original stopper). c.1800, 20.5cm (8in) high, £750/$1,275

"Non-such" Bristol blue-tinted wine glass rinser, with double lips, gilded Greek key motif by Isaac Jacobs. c.1805, 9.5cm (3¾in) high, £1,600/$2,700

Port "sugarloaf"-shaped decanter and stopper, enamelled in the Beilby workshops in Newcastle. c.1765, 24cm (9½in) high, £5,800/$9,850

Set of four blue club-shaped glass decanters and lozenge-shaped stoppers, with gilded labelling and decoration. 1800–10, 23.5cm (9¼in) high, £1,100/$1,870

Paperweights

The French glasshouses of Baccarat, Clichy, and St Louis were responsible for some of the finest and the most inventive paperweights produced between 1845 and 1860. The two main types of decoration are *millefiorie* (meaning "thousand flowers") and lampworking. The former requires glass rods, or canes, arranged concentrically or in a formal or sometimes random arrangement before being cut and imbedded within clear glass. Those that include silhouette canes featuring animals, birds, and occasionally the devil, are always at a premium, as are dated examples.

Lampworking involves individually sculpted flowers, butterflies, fruit, and reptiles, including snakes, made in coloured glass and formed using a direct heat source before being captured within clear glass.

A limited number of English paperweights were made in 1848 at George Bacchus and Sons in Birmingham. However, the American paperweight industry gained impetus with the arrival of two French glassworkers. François Pierre and Nicholas Lutz joined the New England Glass Company and the Boston and Sandwich Glass Company respectively.

Some of the most desirable weights are overlaid with white and coloured glass that has been cut with facets to show the design inside. The condition of a paperweight is important. Bruises and chips will make a paperweight undesirable to collectors and, therefore, they will limit its value. Size also matters. In particular magnums, which are over 10cm (4in) in diameter, and miniatures, which are less than 5cm (2in) in diameter, are popular among collectors.

St Louis garlanded flat bouquet paperweight, facet cut with three bands of circular windows and a starcut base. *c.*1850, 6.5cm (2½in) diameter, £430/$730

St Louis fruit paperweight. *c.*1850, 7cm (2¾in) diameter, £290/$495

Clichy patterned *millefiorie* turquoise-ground paperweight. *c.*1850, 8cm (3in) diameter, £720/$1,225

Baccarat garlanded pom-pom paperweight. *c.*1850, 8cm (3in) diameter, £800/$1,360

Baccarat *millefiorie*/silhouette paperweight. Dated 1848, 7cm (2¾in) diameter, £780/$1,325

British paperweight, by George Bacchus and Sons. *c.*1848, 8cm (3in) diameter, £1,150/$1,950

Cut Glass

British lead crystal glass, the glass developed by George Ravenscroft in 1676, provided the ideal material for cutting and polishing because the lead oxide made it heavier and easier to work than the Continental equivalent. The lead in the glass also refracts, or bends, light, which made it more brilliant than non-lead types. English and Irish cut glass of the 18th century led the world market, so much so that Irish patterns were copied on a grand scale in France, and factories in Norway and North America lured workers from Britain to help them develop the techniques.

A variety of patterns were used to make cut glass. The diamond-shaped pattern was an English innovation and by the end of the 18th century, cut glass tableware was made in large matching services. Other patterns include swags, flutes, slices (or splits), blazes, hobnails, and combs. The English and Irish also monopolized the manufacture of cut glass lustres and chandeliers during this period, but they were challenged in the mid-19th century by the French factory of Baccarat.

By the early 19th century, the art of cutting glass was well-established in the United States, with several factories in Pittsburgh. This industry was so successful that it adversely affected the export of Irish glass. The Irish industry's decline was exacerbated after 1825 by the removal of tax advantages in Ireland and the introduction by Britain of excise duties.

German sugarloaf-shaped decanter and stopper, with slice-cut reserves and wheel engraved cartouche. *c.*1750, 29cm (11½in) high, £1,150/$1,950

Jelly glass, with shallow cutting. *c.*1750, 11.5cm (4½in) high, £60/$100

Ale decanter with scallop-cut stopper and facet-cut decanter with stopper. Respectively, *c.*1770 and *c.*1760, ale decanter 28cm (11in) high, £520/$885 and £320/$545

Facet-cut sweetmeat glass, with shallow cutting, knopped stem, and domed foot. *c.*1770, 14cm (5½in) high, £300/$510

Facet-cut and moulded candlestick and sconce. *c.*1780, 21.5cm (8½in) high, £450/$775

Boat-shaped shallow-cut table salt, with an unusually shaped rim. *c.*1790, 8.5cm (3¼in) high, £90/$155

George IV cut-glass rummer

The bucket-shaped bowl is cut with a strawberry diamond pattern. When compared with a modern rummer, this antique represents good value for money. This is true of many antique glass items, which often hold their value while the value of modern pieces depreciates quickly. *c.1820, 13cm (5in) high, £90/$155*

The bowl is thickly walled to allow for dense and basal flute cutting into the outer surface.

The strawberry diamond-cut band helps to create a secure grip – diners sometimes had greasy fingers.

The short stem with a facet-cut knop gives the shape a low centre of gravity, thus reducing the risk of the rummer being knocked over.

The robust circular foot has a rounded rim and is cut with a starburst on the underside.

Two-part pedestal bowl (probably Irish) and Irish pedestal bowl, with Van Dyke rim. *c.1790, bowl with Van Dyke rim 38cm (15in) high, £300/$510 and £1,900/$3,250*

Pair of Irish decanters and stoppers, with shallow cutting. *c.1800, 27.5cm (10⅞in) high, £750/$1,275*

Pair of cut-glass decanters and stoppers, entirely cut with facet diamonds. *c.1805, 29cm (11⅛in) high, £1,000/$1,700*

Pair of bon-bonières and covers, with shallow diamond and hobnail cutting. *c.1810, 18.5cm (7¼in) high, £575/$980*

Celery vase, with strawberry diamond cutting in the central band. *c.1820, 22.5cm (8¾in) high, £180/$305*

Cut Glass

Salt and stand, with diamond arch and pillar cutting. *c.*1820, 7cm (2¾in) high, £125/$210

Decanter and stopper, with step cutting above diamond cutting. *c.*1825, 27cm (10⅝in) high, £180/$305

Decanter and stopper, with slice cutting on the decanter and diamond cutting on the stopper. *c.*1840, 28cm (11in) high, £170/$290

Comport and cover, with heavy scallop cutting. *c.*1850, 23cm (9in) high, £475/$810

Cut and engraved claret jug and stopper. *c.*1870, 32cm (12⅝in) high, £395/$670

Claret jug and stopper, with lens cutting. *c.*1870, 29.5cm (11⅝in) high, £150/$255

Champagne jug, with hobnail flute cutting. *c.*1880, 30.5cm (12in) high, £250/$425

Water jug, with polished intaglio cutting. *c.*1900, 21.5cm (8½in) high, £200/$340

Spirit decanter and stopper, with dense hobnail cutting. *c.*1910, 22cm (8⅝in) high, £75/$130

Pressed and Moulded Glass

The technique for making pressed, or moulded, glass was pioneered and developed in the United States during the 1820s, and in Britain and on the Continent during the 1830s. It requires a particular quantity of molten glass to be poured into a mould, which is then pressed against the sides of the mould with a plunger, thereby forming the pattern in the glass. When removed from the mould after cooling, the two halves of the object are annealed together and the seam lines polished away. The seams are occasionally visible, but pressed glass often has the appearance of cut glass and employs similar patterns, although the definition of pressed glass is not as sharp.

The method was easy to use in mass production and less expensive than producing cut glass. Large quantities of pressed glass could be made and sold at affordable prices, thereby making decorative glass available to the masses. At first only a limited range of solid objects such as door handles was made, but it was not long before the range extended to dishes, tumblers, bowls, and many other items.

In Britain, the principal pressed and moulded glass-makers were established in the northeast, in the Gateshead and Sunderland area, and in Manchester and St Helens in the northwest. In Europe, the French factories of Baccarat and St Louis were making pressed glass by 1830.

Pressed glass salt dish, by the Boston and Sandwich Glass Company. 1830–40, 6.5cm (2½in) high, £80/$135

Frosted glass model of a seated lion, by John Derbyshire of Manchester. 1873–76, 16.5cm (6½in) long, £150/$255

American marigold "Octagon" pattern carnival glass decanter and six wine glasses, by the Imperial Glass Company, Bellaire, Ohio. c.1920, 20cm (7⅞in) high, £200/$340

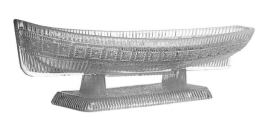

Sea-green opal glass boat, on original stand, by Sowerby of Gateshead. c.1880, 36cm (14⅛in) long, £800/$1,360

"Giallo", or yellow, vitro-porcelain glass swan vase, by Sowerby of Gateshead. c.1880, 9.5cm (3¾in) high, £500/$850

Black glass model of a seated sphinx, by Molineaux, Webb, and Co. of Manchester. c.1875, 20.5cm (8in) long, £1,400/$2,400

Engraved Glass

In the 18th century the Dutch glass engravers produced some of the finest and most inventive engraved glass designs, alongside master engravers working in Bohemia, using diamond-point engraving. However, by the second half of the 19th century, British glassware had also established a reputation for quality engraving. Many skilled craftsmen from Bohemia had emigrated to Britain, which is undoubtedly the reason so many top-quality pieces were made there. They worked in London for various retailers, decorating blanks supplied by the leading manufacturers such as Thomas Webb of Stourbridge.

The practice of engraving a pattern or design on glass is a delicate one, requiring great steadiness and accuracy. In the 19th century, the piece was held in a treadle powered by a machine fitted with wheels that ranged in size from a pinhead to about 10cm (4in). The size of the copper wheel determined the intricacy of the finished pattern or scene. This method is known as wheel engraving and produces finely detailed engraving. The other main types are diamond-point engraving and the more skilful stipple engraving (both use a diamond needle, or "nib", to draw or tap out a pattern), and acid etching, which looks like wheel engraving but has a more even finish.

Dutch ceremonial goblet, engraved by Otto Robart. Dated 1724, 18cm (7in) high, £3,200/$5,450

Dutch engraved armorial wine glass. c.1735, 19.5cm (7⅝in) high, £1,600/$2,700

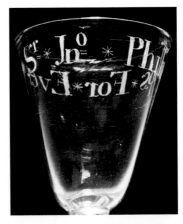

Wine glass of electioneering or Jacobite significance, with plain stem and shoulder knop, engraved "Sr Jno Philipps for ever". 1745–55, 16cm (6¼in) high, £2,600/$4,400

Mercurial-twist cider glass, with a fruiting apple branch engraved on the bowl. *c.*1760, 16.5cm (6½in) high, £3,600/$6,100

Franco–Belgian engraved sugarloaf-shaped magnum decanter and stopper, depicting a dyer beside a steaming vat. *c.*1770, 35cm (13¾in) high, £1,200/$2,050

Engraved "Britannia" goblet, *c.*1775, 19cm (7½in) high, £2,600/$4,400

Dutch-engraved "Seven Provinces" wine glass

The shape of this wine glass is in the "Newcastle" light-baluster style, but the rounded funnel bowl was diamond-point engraved with the provinces of Holland. The glass would have been used to toast the united Dutch provinces.
Engraved c.1760, 19cm (7½in), £1,600/$2,700

The fine crosshatching on the decorative detail is indicative of diamond-point engraving. If shallow wheel engraving was used, it would have a more uniform surface.

The complex design features the Dutch lion rampant surrounded by the arms of the seven provinces of the Netherlands: Gelderland, Zeeland, Friesland, Groningen, Overijssel, Utrecht, and Holland.

The baluster style of the glass suggests it was imported to Holland from Newcastle, but this is now an area of debate, with some experts proposing that these glasses were made in Holland.

The conical foot is raised so that the sharp pontil mark on the underside of the base does not come into contact with and scratch a wooden table surface.

Coloured and Decorative Glass

Glass-makers in ancient times discovered that iron oxides and other impurities added colour to glass that they intended to be clear. It was discovered that by adding copper to a batch you could produce blue and green glass, manganese created purple glass, and cobalt made dark blue glass.

Venice emerged as the dominant European producer of coloured glass in the 16th century. The factories were based on the islands of Murano north of the city. Glass-making techniques in the 18th century included white and coloured enamelling and gilding. *Milchglas*, or milk glass, an opaque white glass that resembled porcelain and was decorated with opaque coloured enamels, was produced in Germany and

Britain during the 18th century. In the 19th century, factories in Bohemia introduced cased glass, which combined colourfully enamelled floral decoration with gilt surrounds. Also in Bohemia, Friedrich Egermann developed yellow and ruby staining to cover clear glass in a technique known as flashing.

In France, Britain, and the United States, mechanization resulted in the mass production of colourful, decorative glass. Vitro-porcelain, sometimes used to produce 19th-century pressed glass, was also made opaque to appear like porcelain. In Britain, the Stourbridge firm of Thomas Webb attracted international praise for the fine-quality cameo glass that was hand-carved by George and Thomas Woodall.

Bohemian *milchglas* tankard, colour enamelled with flower sprays. *c.*1760, 16cm (6¼in) high, £500/$850

Pair of white-on-clear cased decanters and stoppers, attributed to Richardson's glassworks at Stourbridge. 1845–50, 16.5cm (6½in) high, £360/$610

Bohemian ruby-on-clear overlay beaker, relief carved with a racehorse, attributed to Karl Pfohl. 1860–65, 15.5cm (6in) high, £600/$1,020

Cased glass two-handled moon flask, with an intaglio carving of a lively fish, by Thomas Webb and Sons. *c.*1880, 20cm (7⅞in) high, £2,000/$3,400

French opaque glass vase, colour enamelled with butterflies among flora. *c.*1880, 24cm (9½cm) high, £100/$170

"Gem Cameo" Islamic-shaped vase, by Thomas Webb and Sons. *c.*1885, 11.5cm (4½in) high, £900/$1,530

Webb and Sons scent bottle

This cameo scent bottle is attributed to George or Thomas Woodall. The candy-pink glass is cased in white and finely carved with a putto (boy or cherub) among scrolling foliage. George Woodall is recognized as probably the most renowned of all 19th-century glass cameo sculptors, who along with his brother Thomas produced extremely fine cameo wares for the Stourbridge glass-maker Thomas Webb and Sons. *c.1885, 12.5cm (4⅞in) high, £5,500/$9,350*

The embossed hinged cover should lift to reveal a small clear glass internal stopper.

The silver mounts should bear a late 19th- or early 20th-century date mark; usually with the Birmingham assay office anchor mark, lion passant, and maker's initials (see pages 130–31).

The raised white cameo has subtle surface carving, closely akin to the contemporary pâte-sur-pâte bone china decorated by Marc-Louis Solon at Minton and Co.

This scent bottle is not signed, but similar putti are found on other Woodall pieces and the quality on this scent bottle is consistent with the high level of artistry associated with their work.

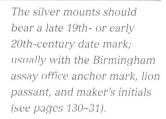

Pair of white-on-scarlet cameo glass vases, made at Stourbridge. *c.*1890, 21.5cm (8½in) high, £1,900/$3,250

Cranberry graduating to pink glass epergne. *c.*1890, 60cm (23½in) high, £680/$1,155

Rectangular cameo glass plaque, with the figure of Sappho, by Thomas Webb and Sons, with engraving by George Woodall. *c.*1890, 32cm x 19.5cm (12⅝in x 7⅝in), £38,000/$64,600

Silver

1

2

3

4

1 Sheffield-plate chamberstick,
*c.*1810
2 George II silver candlestick,
by John Café, *c.*1750
3 Victorian silver sugar basket,
*c.*1880
4 George II silver teapot, *c.*1740

Silver is too soft to be used in its pure state, so it is alloyed with other metals, usually copper, in varying proportions, depending on the country in which it is manufactured. Many countries operate a hallmarking system. A hallmark consists of a series of stamps in the form of punched marks that indicate the quality of the precious metals used to make the piece as well as information on when, where, and by whom the piece was made.

Great Britain operates the most rigorous system of hallmarking anywhere in the world. The first statute governing standards was passed in 1238, but the proper system came into operation with the introduction of the leopard's head mark in 1300, to be struck on both silver and gold throughout the realm. The standard for coinage (92.5 percent) was also used for silver objects. In 1363, a further statute was passed in which every gold and silversmith added his maker's mark to

pieces (at this time in the form of symbols because few people could read or write) to counteract the practice of forging the leopard's head mark on substandard wares. In 1478, the third mark was added in the form of a letter. From this date all work had to be taken to Goldsmiths' Hall for testing and marking by touchwardens.

With this third mark, originally called the Assay Master's mark, the Assay Master or touchwarden could be identified if a marked piece was found to be substandard. Because this letter mark changed each year, usually running in alphabetical order and varying a little between assay offices, it soon came to be regarded as the date letter. In 1544, the fourth symbol, the sterling lion (also known as the lion passant) came into being to symbolize the royal control over the assay office, replacing the leopard's head as the mark of the silver's standard. The leopard's head then became the town mark for

5 Pair of Elizabeth II silver candlesticks, *c.*1955
6 Edwardian silver tea caddy, by Nathan and Hayes, Chester, 1909
7 Victorian silver toast rack, 1847
8 George II silver cow creamer, by John Shuppe, London, 1756

London. When other assay offices began to be established in the 18th century, they used their own town mark, but sometimes they retained the leopard's head. Provincial assay offices were set up in centres all over Britain. Among the earliest were Chester, Bristol, Norwich, and York. Sheffield and Birmingham were established in 1773. Today, all sterling silver is sent to one of four centres – London, Birmingham, Sheffield, or Edinburgh.

In Scotland and Ireland a thistle and a crowned harp were the respective marks used instead of, or sometimes as well as, the sterling lion.

Britannia Standard

A radical change in British hallmarking took place between 1697 and 1720 when the Britannia Standard was introduced. With the passing of the Wrought Plate Act, the standard for silver was

raised from 92.5 percent to 95.84 percent, and the marks were changed. The sterling lion was replaced by the figure of Britannia, the crowned leopard's head by the lion's head in profile, and the first two letters of the maker's surname replaced his initials. In 1720, the original marks were revived, but some Britannia Standard silver continued to be made because certain silversmiths preferred working with the softer, purer metal. The option to use it continues today.

The duty mark

Silver made between 1784 and 1890 had a fifth mark added in the form of the reigning monarch's head, struck to show that the duty had been paid. After 1890, the standard set again comprised four marks: the sterling mark; the town mark; the maker's mark; and the date letter.

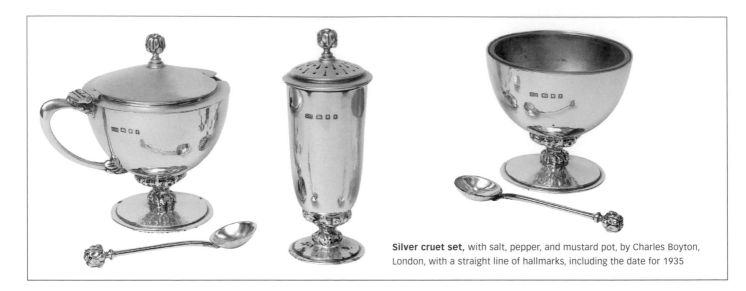

Silver cruet set, with salt, pepper, and mustard pot, by Charles Boyton, London, with a straight line of hallmarks, including the date for 1935

American hallmarks

An attempt was made to imitate English hallmarking in the United States during the late 18th and early 19th centuries and items were stamped with a date letter, a duty mark, and a lion. The strongest efforts were made in Philadelphia and Baltimore, but the practice was abandoned and most examples of American silver are stamped with the maker's signature alone. Many objects were stamped with the silversmith's name in full. By the late 1860s, the sterling standard was often used by Baltimore silversmiths, expressed as 925/1000 below the signature.

Where to begin

You can learn about silver by visiting fairs, markets, and auction previews and handling silver objects. Examine pieces carefully to become familiar with weight, tones, and styles, and also to look for defects and repairs. Avoid purchasing pieces that have been repaired and where armorials or initials have been polished out – the metal will be thinner in these areas.

Decoration

The type of decoration on a silver object can be a good indication of its date, because styles varied in different periods. Pay attention to the condition of the decoration because it has a bearing on value. The main types of decoration are listed below.

Engraving A decorating technique where metal is removed from the surface of the silver by incising lines and patterns by hand with a pointed steel tool held on an engraver's block or by machine.

Bright-cut engraving A form of engraving where the metal is cut in small gouges at an angle and removed by a tool with two cutting points so that the work is accomplished in narrow channels with slanting sides to give a faceted, bright appearance.

Chasing Decorating the surface of the metal by indenting it and raising the design without cutting into or removing the metal. The work is done with tools known as tracers and a chasing hammer. When the same technique is used to create a pattern but without raising the surface of the metal, it is referred to as flat chasing.

Applied Ornament that is not part of the basic form of the object. Cut-card work is a type introduced in the late 17th century, where thin sheets of silver were cut into decorative patterns, often based on leaf shapes, and soldered onto the main body of the piece. It was often used to embellish the bases of bowls or cups, or around the handle sockets of tea- or coffeepots. Other types of applied ornament include beaded wire and sectional casting.

Gilding A method of applying gold to silver to give it the appearance of gold. A parcel-gilt object is partially covered with gold. The earliest technique used is mercurial gilding, where the gold is combined with mercury, brushed onto the silver and heated until the mercury burns off. This was a toxic process and by 1840 had given way to electroplating.

Piercing Also known as openwork. The metal is pierced to make a pattern of small holes for purely decorative effect. Until the late 18th century, it was done with hammers and a selection of small chisels, but, from the 1770s, the fretsaw enabled the silversmith to make a series of tiny, precise vertical cuts. This type of work is most often seen on strainers, covers of casters, mustard pots, fish slices, wine coasters, and baskets.

Embossing Or "repoussé", creating a relief pattern by hammering on the reverse with plain or decorative punches and dies.

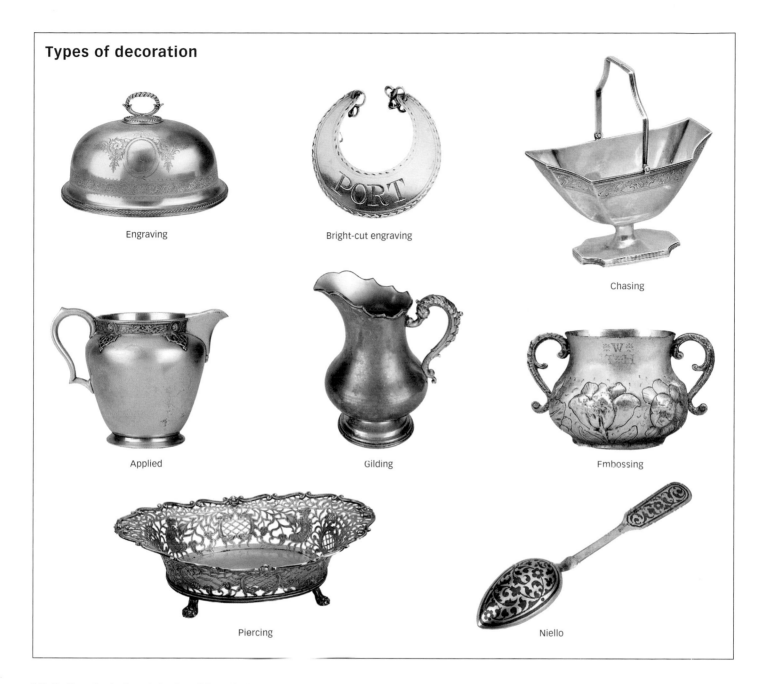

Types of decoration

Engraving

Bright-cut engraving

Chasing

Applied

Gilding

Embossing

Piercing

Niello

Niello Popular in Russia in the 18th and 19th centuries, niello is a compound of silver, lead, copper, and sulphur applied to designs cut into the metal and fired to produce a lustrous black surface.

Types of metals

As well as sterling silver, there are two other types of silver metal in which pieces are fashioned: Sheffield plate and electroplate. Both types of metalware are collected and each has its own distinguishing features and marks.

Sheffield plate The method in which a thin sheet of silver is fused to a much thicker sheet of copper and then passed through a rolling mill to create a sheet from which objects can be made.

Thomas Bolsover of Sheffield made the discovery in 1743, but it was not until 1765 that the new method spread to other cities in Britain. In the late 18th century, some pieces of Sheffield plate were marked with a set of marks that closely resembled those used for sterling.

Electroplate The process of depositing a thin layer of silver onto the surface of a base metal by means of an electric current. The technique was discovered by John Wright of Birmingham in 1840 and patented by the Birmingham company of G.R. and H. Elkington. Electroplate has a whiter colour than Sheffield plate, which has a bluish tone. It is not hallmarked but carries various marks such as "EP" (electroplated), "EPNS" (electroplated nickel silver), or the words "hard soldered".

Tea, Coffee, and Chocolate Wares

The popularity of tea increased in Britain from the 1650s, but coffee remained more popular on the Continent and in North America, where it had become a part of the daily routine. The first coffee house opened in Britain in 1652 and in Boston in North America in 1670. Chocolate was also served in coffee houses, but was in fashion for only a brief period. At first tea, coffee, and chocolate were expensive beverages.

Silversmiths began to make pots for coffee and chocolate, and then for tea, along with kettles, urns, caddies, spoons, jugs, trays, and many other accessories. Early coffeepots had lips like those on wine jugs before adopting spouts. Many coffeepots were probably also used to serve chocolate. However, only those with a removable finial in the centre of the cover, through which a stick, or molinet, can be inserted to stir the contents, can be described as a chocolate pot.

Early teapots imitated the tapering cylinder and straight-spout shape of contemporary coffeepots. Teapots in the early 18th century were pear-shaped and octagonal, but they took on the bullet form in the 1730s. By the mid-18th century, drum-shaped teapots reflected the Neoclassical style and oval teapots were made from the 1770s. Low, boat-shaped teapots were popular by the late 18th century.

George III kettle on stand, by Samuel Eaton, London. Hallmarks for 1773, later embossed in 1825, size unavailable, £700/$1,190

Old Sheffield plate two-handled tea urn. c.1790, 33.5cm (13¼in) high, £250/$425

Belgian silver chocolate pot, with the maker's mark "BC" below a crown, Brussels. 1761, 34.5cm (13⅜in) high, £5,000/$8,500

George III navette-shaped teapot, on pedestal foot, by Henry Chawner. Hallmarks for 1788, 17cm (6¾in) high, £1,000/$1,700

George III silver teapot and stand. c.1815, size unavailable, £400/$680

George III silver coffeepot, with an ivory handle (for insulation), by Royes and Dix. London hallmarks for 1817, 20cm (7⅞in) high, £600/$1,020

George III silver Argyll

Reputed to have been designed by the Duke of Argyll in the mid-18th century, this device is not a coffee- or teapot, but was used to keep gravy warm at the table. Examples with a double wall fitted to hold hot water have a second filling spout with a hinged cover at the rim. They can be found in silver, "old Sheffield plate", and, later in the 19th century, in electroplated nickel silver. *c.1790, 18cm (7in) high, £1,700/$2,900*

Most examples have either a wooden or silver strap handle bound with string and fitted at a right angle to the spout.

Two variations of Argyll exist; both are double-walled. This example has a central tube, which would have had a cover, fitted to receive a hot iron rod, which maintained the gravy at a high enough temperature to prevent it from thickening.

The pouring spout has a much smaller diameter when compared with a contemporary coffeepot or teapot.

Originally, this Argyll would have been marked, but the hallmarks have been rubbed away with wear over the past two centuries, hence the suggested date, c.1790.

Victorian four-piece silver tea set, by Joseph Angell. London hallmarks for 1845, size unavailable, £1,000/$1,700

Victorian silver wine jug, with a wooden handle (for insulation) and Neoclassical decoration. London hallmarks for 1886, 23cm (9in) high, £500/$850

Four-piece Indian silver tea service, by C. Krishniah Chetty of Rangalore. *c.*1910, size unavailable, £470/$800

Flatware

In medieval Europe, most people carried a wooden or pewter spoon with them at home and if they visited others, with the wealthy few having silver examples. Slightly later, a knife was added, but silver spoons, hammered from a single, small ingot, have survived in greater numbers than knives of the period – the blades are often replaced.

Charles II returned from exile in France in 1660, bringing with him the idea of setting a table for eating. Sets of flatware were made in only small numbers before the first decades of the 18th century and it is highly unusual to find complete sets that date from before the late 18th century.

Individual designs each have their own names. In Britain, the Trefid pattern gave way to the Dog Nose pattern in about 1702. By 1710, the Hanoverian, or Rat's-tail, pattern was in use, followed by the Old English pattern by 1760, Fiddle pattern by 1770, and King's pattern by 1810. These patterns, which can be seen below, and their variants have been reproduced ever since, so always check hallmarks instead of using patterns as a way of dating. Antique silver services are expensive so collectors often build a service slowly. It is acceptable to buy single pieces of the same pattern. If you want a challenge, buy pieces by the same maker from the same period.

George III silver and ivory-handled fish slice and pastry/serving slice, the former by Edward Aldridge of London; most or all marks lost in piercing. c.1770 for the latter, sizes unavailable, £700/$1,190 and £320/$545

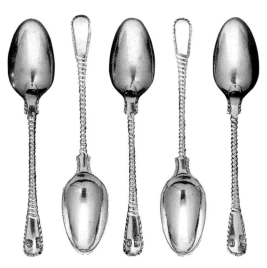

Set of 12 George III silver teaspoons, with spiral twist stems, by Thomas Chawner (only maker's mark and lion passant). c.1775, sizes unavailable, £600/$1,020

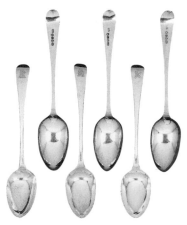

Six George III silver Old English pattern tablespoons, by Hester Bateman, London. Hallmarks for 1790, sizes unavailable, £350/$595

Pair of George III silver hour-glass ice spades, by William Eley and William Fearn, London. Hallmarks for 1806, 27cm (10⅝in) long, £950/$1,615

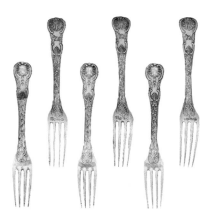

Set of six George III silver desert forks, by Eley and Fearn, London. Hallmarks for 1817, sizes unavailable, £150/$255

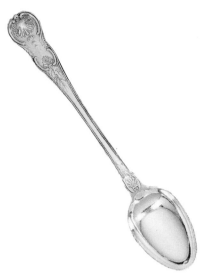

William IV silver King's Honeysuckle-variant pattern basting spoon, by William Eaton, London. Hallmarks for 1832, 31cm (12¼in) long, £140/$240

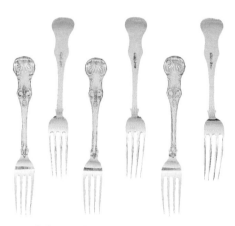

Set of six Scottish silver William IV Queen's pattern table forks, by Peter Aitken, Glasgow. Hallmarks for 1832, sizes unavailable, £140/$240

James II and 17thC silver Trefid pattern spoons

With the exception of the apostle variety (which had cast finials representing the apostles), spoons were not made in sets until the end of the 17th century. Individual silver spoons were often given as presents on special family occasions and handed down through generations, which is the reason that so many have survived. The Trefid pattern spoon was popular in the late 17th century, giving way in about 1702 to the Dog Nose variant, where the end of the stem has a central curve with a smaller one on each side. *Respectively, London hallmarks for 1685 and 17th century (indistinct hallmarks for Robert King and London), sizes unavailable, £360/$610 and £330/$560*

The reverse of each bowl is cast with a "rat's-tail", which helps strengthen the junction of the bowl with the stem.

The reverse of the stems were often personalized by the engraved initials of the owner or recipient, and some were dated.

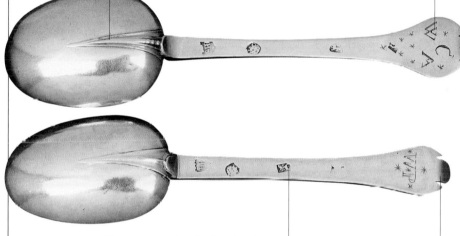

The reverse of each stem has been individually struck with the lion passant sterling standard mark, the maker's mark, the town assay office, and the year mark, which are rubbed on both examples shown here.

The term "trefid" is derived from the broad, flat stem that terminates in a trefoil.

Victorian silver Fiddle pattern fish slice and two William IV Fiddle pattern fish slices, with pierced decoration, respectively by David Phillips, Charles Shipway, and Lias Bros, all of London. Hallmarks for 1839, 1836, and 1836, sizes unavailable, £140/$240, £130/$220, and £180/$305

Victorian silver Albert-pattern table service, with 70 pieces, predominantly by Samuel Hayne and Dudley Cater. London hallmarks for 1845 and 1853, sizes unavailable, £1,200/$2,050

American silver table service, with 188 pieces, by Tiffany and Co. *c.*1900. sizes unavailable, £3,400/$5,800

Candlesticks

Although silver candlesticks have been made in great quantity from the late 17th century, they have always been expensive items, intended for the wealthiest members of the population. The majority lit their way through the dark with far cheaper rush lights or candles burning in brass or pewter candlesticks. This exclusivity is reflected in prices today, and it is possible to pay over £10,000/$17,000 for a fine pair of English silver candlesticks by a well-known silversmith. Single sticks are a lot more affordable, often below half the value of a pair.

Candlesticks fall into two main categories: cast and loaded. The former is cast in moulds and soldered together, the latter is stamped or hammered out from sheet silver, soldered together, and then filled with pitch or plaster of Paris to give it weight and stability. Cast candlesticks have hollow bases, which were often wide to make them more stable. Loaded examples have filled-in bases, covered with green baize to protect the surface on which they sit. Cast candlesticks are made from a much heavier gauge of silver than the loaded variety. Cast candlesticks were made in Britain and the Continent in significant quantities from the early 18th century. In the United States, candlesticks were manufactured in quantity from the mid-19th century.

George II silver candlestick, by William Café, London. *c*.1730, 20cm (7⅞in) high, £700/$1,190

George II silver taperstick. *c*.1730, 10cm (3⅞in) high, £800/$1,360

Pair of George II cast silver candlesticks, by William Café, London. Hallmarks for 1753, 21cm (8¼in) high, £1,800/$3,050

Pair of George III cast candlesticks, by Ebenezer Cocker, London. Hallmarks for 1767, 28cm (11in) high, £2,100/$3,600

George III silver loaded candlestick, by John Carter, London. Hallmarks for 1768, 24cm (9½in) high, £400/$680

George III silver "French-style" candlestick, by Thomas Heming, London. Hallmarks for 1776, 28cm (11in) high, £700/$1,190

George III silver wax jack (or taper stand),
London. Hallmarks for 1778, 10cm (3⅞in) high,
£2,000/$3,400

Victorian silver chamber-style tapersticks,
with extinguishers. 1842 and 1897, sizes
unavailable, £280/$475 and £200/$340

Late Victorian silver three-light candelabrum,
with two sinuous branches and a central socket.
c.1890, 41cm (16in) high, £500/$850

George II candlestick

This is one of a pair of cast
silver candlesticks by John
Carter of London. The shape of
the nozzle can indicate the age
of the candlestick. An early
example follows the design of
the base; if there is a detachable
nozzle, it should be post-1740.
Square-shaped bases with
circular nozzles became popular
later in the 18th century.
*Hallmarks for 1759, 28cm (11in)
high, £2,000/$3,400 for the pair*

*This particular shape of
candlestick was also produced
by other British silversmiths.*

*The stem of this candlestick is
cast and of solid form. Loaded
sheet-metal candlesticks with
an internal weight tend to
rattle when shaken.*

*Pairs should be marked in
different positions. Identical
marks suggest that one
example has been cast
from the other as a later
replacement.*

*The gadrooning
decoration that adorns
both the base and stem
adds to the desirability
of this candlestick.*

Small Silver and *Objets de Vertu*

The novice collector can build up a respectable silver collection by concentrating on small objects. Many of them, particularly when combined with gold, tortoiseshell, porcelain, or enamel, come under the heading of *objets de vertu*, or "objects of vertu". A plain example may sell for less than £100/$170. There is a wealth of material available to any collector, especially when limited display space is something to be considered.

Menu holders can be found in hundreds of differing designs, as can vesta cases, which once enclosed the vesta, or short match, used by Victorian and Edwardian smokers.

Snuff boxes have survived in quantity, so always choose good examples, as have vinaigrettes, which once contained a small sponge loaded with smelling salts and were essential for 19th-century ladies who began to feel faint, often as a result of wearing a tight corset.

Wine labels have always been popular because they are still functional and lend extra gravitas to a plain or cut-glass decanter. If you want an item made by a highly skilled early 19th-century silversmith such as Paul Storr, be prepared to pay in excess of £500/$850, but remember that the majority of Georgian and Victorian wine labels start at about £100/$170.

Charles II silver tankard, with hinged cover and mid-Victorian redecoration. 1683, 16cm (6¼in) high, £1,500/$2,550

Pair of George I tazze, or footed salvers, by David Tanqueray. Hallmarks for 1719, 20.5cm (8in) high, £8,500/$14,450

James I silver-gilt steeple cup and cover, by F. Terry. Hallmarks for 1623, 41cm (16in) high, £10,000/$17,000

George III silver inkstand, by Samuel Meriton, London. Hallmarks for 1787, 10.5cm (4in) long, £420/$715

George III silver five-bottle oval cruet, by Robert (I) and David (II) Hennel, London (one stopper is missing). Hallmarks for 1795, 25cm (9⅞in) high, £300/$510

George III silver soup tureen, by Paul Storr, London. Hallmarks for 1809, size unavailable, £8,000/$3,600

George III silver cake basket

Philip Freeman of London made this late 18th century silver cake basket. Most silver baskets dating from this period used hand piercing only on the finest baskets. This example was probably pierced using the newly developed fly punch, a mechanical process that resulted in smooth, regular edges. Because the gauge of silver used at this time is thinner than on earlier pieces, it is important to ensure that the pierced decoration is intact before making a purchase.

Hallmarks for 1776, 33cm (13in) high, £1,000/$1,700

This basket is unusual because the handle includes a cartouche engraved with the owner's crest – this was usually reserved for the main body of a piece.

The basket is hallmarked and the swing handle stamped with the sterling lion passant and the maker's mark. Look for marks on all components of a piece.

The basket is made from a thinner gauge of sheet silver in comparison with those produced earlier in the 18th century.

Late 18th-century baskets usually have a simple form in comparison with those produced in the earlier years, and they often have strong geometric pierced detail.

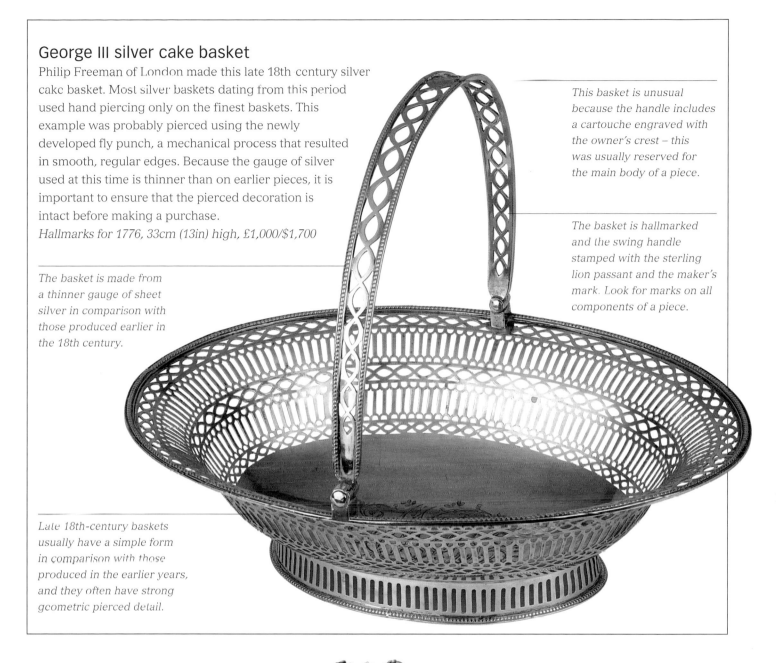

George IV "Old Sheffield plate" entrée dish and cover, engraved with an armorial crest. *c.*1825, size unavailable, £180/$305

Pair of George III silver-gilt "Claret" and "Madeira" wine labels, single "Claret" wine label, and larger "Sherry" label, the pair by Paul Storr, London. Hallmarks for 1815, 1816, and 1812, the pair 7cm (2⅜in) high, £6,000/$10,200 (for the pair), £700/$1,190, and £2,100/$3,600

French silver two-handled tureen and cover, by Jean-Baptiste-Claude Odiot. 1819–38, 25cm (9⅞in) high, £6,000/$10,200

Small Silver and *Objets de Vertu*

George IV silver sauceboat, London. Hallmarks for 1820, 11.5cm (4½in) high, £3,000/$5,100

George IV silver entrée dish and cover, by J. Cradock and William Reid, Birmingham. Hallmarks for 1821, size unavailable, £800/$1,360

George IV "Old Sheffield plate" centrepiece. *c.*1825, 50cm (19½in) high, £2,000/$3,400

George III silver plate, by Philip Rundell, London. Hallmarks for 1815, size unavailable, £500/$850

George IV silver six-division toast rack, by J. and T. Settle, Gunn and Co., Sheffield. Hallmarks for 1826, 16cm (6¼in) high, £270/$460

Pair of George IV silver-gilt double coaster trolleys, for wine bottles, by Benjamin Smith (II), London. Hallmarks for 1828, 48.5cm (19in) long, £72,000/$122,400

George IV silver snuff box, by Thomas Shaw, Birmingham. Hallmarks for 1829, 9.5cm x 5.5cm (3¾in x 2⅛in), £300/$510

One of a pair of silver-plated wine coasters, by Elkington and Co. of Birmingham. *c.*1830, size unavailable, £500/$850 (for the pair)

Victorian silver mug, engraved with various root vegetables, by Barnet and Scott, Birmingham. Hallmarks for 1877, 13cm (5in) high, £300/$510

Victorian silver novelty pepper pot, modelled as a dog. *c.*1890, size unavailable, £800/$1,360

Victorian silver lighthouse spirit lighter, by John Batson, London. Hallmarks for 1883, 12cm (4¾in) high, £650/$1,105

Dutch silver wager cup. Import marks for London 1890, and Edinburgh hallmarks for 1895, 27cm (10⅝in) high, £780/$1,325

Victorian silver tea caddy, decorated with classical figures, Birmingham. Hallmarks for 1895, 13cm (5in) high, £500/$850

Victorian silver wishbone toast rack, on ball feet, Birmingham. Hallmarks for 1896, size unavailable, £100/$170

Austrian silver vesta case, enamelled with a young woman with red parasol. *c.*1890, 3cm (1⅛in) wide, £800/$1,360

German silver vesta case, enamelled with the portrait of a gundog. *c.*1890, 3cm (1⅛in) wide, £500/$850

A silver vesta case, enamelled with the arms of Trinity College, Oxford, by John William Barrett, Chester. Hallmarks for 1919, 4cm (1½in) wide, £260/$440

Edwardian silver two-handled trophy, by H. Woodward and Co., London. Hallmarks for 1904, 60cm (23½in) high, £4,200/$7,150

Clocks and Watches

1   **2**   **3**   **4**

1 French engraved brass cased carriage clock, *c.*1880
2 18ct-gold pocket watch, by James Gibb, *c.*1855
3 British brass skeleton clock, *c.*1870
4 French ormolu mantel clock, *c.*1870

These days, clocks are taken for granted, but until the 19th century the clock was considered to be the most sophisticated machine in the world. Ever since man began to measure time, not only by dividing its passage into years (the time-lapse necessary for the earth to complete its journey round the sun), but by further dividing it into units of months, weeks, days, hours, minutes, and seconds, he has sought to increase the accuracy of the clock.

The first clocks

Salisbury Cathedral in Britain claims to have the earliest example of a clock in working order, made in 1386, and it is still keeping good time. It had neither a face nor hands, but was designed to mark the hours by its strike, calling the monks to prayer. Clocks were being made in the 14th century in Italy, and the earliest portable timepieces were produced in Nuremberg, Germany, by the early 16th century, when the advent of spring-driven mechanisms allowed clocks to come down off the wall and be carried about or placed on a table. The invention of the long pendulum in the mid-17th century was a revolutionary design, leading to the development of the longcase clock. Later came carriage clocks, pocket watches, and, ultimately, wristwatches.

The earliest clocks were made of iron by the local locksmith or blacksmith, until brass began to replace iron for part of the mechanism in *c.*1550. By the 17th century, clockmakers were highly skilled and respected craftsmen, who formed powerful guilds. British clockmakers such as George Graham and Thomas Tompion were so widely respected that, on their death, they were buried inside Westminster Cathedral in London.

5 Walnut longcase brass dial clock, *c.*1690

6 Rolex 9ct-gold tonneau shape gentleman's wristwatch, *c.*1935

7 Scottish mahogany longcase clock, by John Hill of Montrose, *c.*1780

8 GPO wall timepiece, *c.*1930

Where to begin

Clocks and watches are not only attractive decorative objects made in a variety of shapes, sizes, and materials, but they are also complicated precision instruments, making this a fascinating subject for the collector. What is going on inside a handsome walnut or mahogany case is often of more interest to the enthusiast than the outward appearance of the clock.

The movement

If you are new to the subject, it is helpful to try to understand the evolution of clockmaking. The mechanisms are the same in principle. The motive-power of a clock is provided by either a weight or a fusee and spring, which drive a series (or train)

of meshing toothed wheels and pinions (gears), which send the hands around a dial marked with the hours. The train is usually located between two brass plates.

In a clock with a spring, the fusee is a conical-shaped brass drum, with the gut line from the spring wound around it like a spindle filled with thread. It controls, in different ratios, the power output of the spring to enable the clock to keep a regular time. Fusees were used on clocks and watches until the late 19th century, and they were not given up until slimmer Swiss watches became fashionable in the early 20th century.

Types of escapement

The escapement in a clock, watch, or timepiece allows the power driving the mechanism to escape, thereby controlling the speed at which a clock runs down. The various forms of escapement release the escape wheel at regular short intervals (giving the "tick tock" sound), allowing the driving force to operate, lock, and release again in a regulated sequence.

The earliest types of clock mechanism had verge escapements, with a balance wheel on a short pendulum. These were used from the second half of the 17th century in bracket or table clocks, lantern clocks, and, more rarely, longcase clocks. The verge escapement and pendulum continued to be used until 1800, although it was an inaccurate method of timekeeping.

The anchor escapement was developed around 1670. Shaped like an anchor, it allowed either a short or long pendulum to be used, and it provided greater accuracy than was possible with the verge escapement. It was used in longcase clocks and in bracket and wall clocks. The arc of the swing was much smaller than that required by the verge escapement, and so it was seen as an enormous advance. Clocks with a verge escapement generally use a small, pear-shaped bob on the end of the pendulum because a large weight is not needed. Anchor escapements require a larger disc-shaped bob, which is lead-filled to give it weight. The position of the bob on the pendulum's rod can be altered to adjust the speed of the clock.

Among the other varieties of escapements are cylinder, lever, and balance wheel escapements, which were mounted onto platforms on the top of carriage clocks or mantel clocks from c.1840 and continue to be used today. The platform on which these escapements are carried is detachable as a unit, as opposed to being an integral part of the clock.

Striking mechanisms

In auction catalogues, and when you talk to experts, you will read and hear descriptions of both clocks and timepieces. Clocks strike, while timepieces do not. The earliest striking mechanisms determined the hours by using a locking plate incorporated into the mechanism, with notches cut out of it to determine the number of hours a clock needed to strike, the maximum being 12. The locking plate, developed by the 1670s, was used on French clocks up until the late 19th century.

The "rack and snail" is another form of striking mechanism. A snail-shaped disc attached to the hour hand, with steps cut away equalling the number of hours to be struck, controls how many times the chime will sound. This is a more reliable type of mechanism and ensures that the wrong number of hours cannot be struck, as can happen with a locking-plate strike. The "rack and snail" is still used on clocks today.

The majority of clocks strike on the hour only. However, chiming clocks were developed in the early 18th century and they can sound on a number of bells at the hours and quarter hours, playing popular tunes. Wire gongs became popular in the 1840s

French ormolu lyre-shaped timepiece, with Neoclassical decoration, including floral swags, acanthus leaves, and beading, *c.*1780

and developed in the latter half of the 19th century into large gong rods, like pipes. They are found in high-quality longcase clocks made in England and Germany in c.1900. In the 20th century, German clocks often had two wire gongs to provide a "ting tang" strike at the quarters.

The dial

The face of the clock that incorporates the numbers is known as the dial. It is attached to the movement. The earliest examples were brass dials, and they can be found on lantern, bracket, and longcase clocks. Brass dials were probably once silvered, but the silvering has been polished away over the years. The effect is achieved by using silvering salts, which change the colour of the brass. Re-silvering is not expensive, but should only be done by a specialist. Like re-gilding, this kind of restoration is regarded as sympathetic and is acceptable to most collectors.

By 1730, enamel dials were common on British pocket watches, and they were sometimes produced in the 1780s for longcase clocks, but they are otherwise rare. More common are painted metal dials on longcase and bracket clocks, which were fitted to high-quality pieces. The painting became more elaborate in the 19th century.

Enamel sections are most frequently found on French clocks. Often the dials are gilt, with the numerals set against enamel reserves. Enamel dials are extremely prone to cracking and chipping, so examine examples carefully. Hairline cracks are often camouflaged by bleaching, but you should be able to spot the differences in colour. Cracking creates a cobweb effect over the dial and if you come across this, the price should reflect the damage that has occurred.

Wooden painted dials were used for tavern clocks in Britain from the mid-18th century and on Black Forest clocks in the early 19th century. The latter are usually 30cm (12in) square, with an arch above, painted white and then decorated with flowers before being varnished. Wooden dials are susceptible to woodworm and the wood has often split. However, they can be properly restored by a specialist.

The hands

Early clocks had simple, finely sculpted blued-steel hands (whereby the steel was polished and blued with a flame, preventing the metal from rusting and giving a distinctly burnished blue appearance) in straightforward designs. Along with the style of dials, the hands became more elaborate. Blued steel gave way to gilt metal in the latter half of the 18th century on country longcase clocks. Hands get damaged and are often repaired, but it only affects value greatly if the clock is an absolutely top-quality one and the replacements are obvious.

Victorian mahogany travelling clock, with gilt-metal mounts, by Frodsham, London, c.1850

Moving a longcase clock

Major problems can occur when it becomes necessary to move a longcase clock, an operation which should be done carefully in various stages and involves completely disassembling the clock. First of all, slide off the hood, which protects the face and the movement. Finials may be loose so remove them if a long journey is involved and wrap them separately. Mark the weights, left and right, and then unhook the pendulum, possibly attaching it to a wooden rod to keep it straight and to protect the delicate suspension spring. The mechanism may fall out once the weights are removed, so be prepared. Otherwise, lift it down carefully. Protect the dial from getting scratched, and the crutch piece on the back of the movement from being bent. Wrap all the pieces separately and make sure you keep all the keys in a safe place. The case itself can be moved in the same way as a piece of furniture, but take care as you are disassembling the clock that it does not fall over. You may want to secure the case to the wall once it reaches its new destination, something which is considered a sensible safety precaution since longcases can topple over. You won't spoil it if you do it carefully.

Longcase Clocks

The development of the long pendulum in 1657 was probably the most significant invention in the history of timekeeping. Most authorities agree it can be attributed to the Dutch physicist and mathematician Christiaan Huygens van Zulichen. Ahasueras Fromanteel introduced his work to Britain the following year. Shortly afterward, he began to manufacture and sell long-pendulum clocks.

The advantage of the long pedulum is its accuracy. Early clocks are weight-driven with a verge escapement and a short pendulum with a wide swing, which is prone to error. The long pendulum with an anchor escapement has a swing that takes one second exactly and is maintained by its own momentum. Shortly after its development the pendulum was encased to protect it from accidental knocks, keep the dust out of the movement, and conceal the workings.

The earliest British longcase clocks date from the 1660s and had cases of ebony-veneered oak with architectural pediments; these were followed by walnut-veneered ones with flat or crested tops. Marquetry decoration was favoured from 1680 but had waned in popularity by 1710. The type of dial used is often indicative of a clock's age: the arched top or break arch dial appeared in about 1715, silvered dials about 1760, white dials about 1770, and circular dials 1800. Longcase clocks are often signed by their makers on the dial.

Walnut marquetry longcase clock, by Nathaniell Birt (sic), London. *c.*1690, 211cm (83in) high, £6,000/$10,200

Oak longcase clock, with 30-hour movement, by James Whittaker. *c.*1720, 216cm (85in) high £3,200/$5,450

Mahogany musical longcase clock, with Dutch strike, by John Ellicot, London. *c.*1750, 239cm (94in) high, £7,000/$11,900

Oak longcase clock, by Robinson, Staines, Middlesex. *c.*1750, 194cm (76in) high, £800/$1,360

Oak longcase clock, with moon-phase and high-tide indication at both London Bridge and Bristol Quay, unsigned. *c.*1770, 211cm (83in) high, £1,500/$2,550

Mahogany longcase clock

This brass-mounted longcase clock by John Sidaway of London has an alarm and an eight-day movement. It is a desirable piece because it was made by a London maker and the case has retained its strong colour, which helps to emphasize the rich flame figure of the mahogany. *c.1780, 232cm (91in) high, £3,000/$5,100*

The maker's signature is inscribed on the strike/silent subsidiary dial set into the arch.

The dial is fitted with a subsidiary seconds and alarm set disc within the silvered chapter ring, as well as a small calendar aperture.

The snug-fitting brass plate is made in one piece, suggesting that it is original to the cabinet and not an earlier square dial adapted to fit the later fashionable break arch dial.

The height of the case, the arched door panel, and the use of quarter columns on the cabinet are features that indicate a London maker.

Mahogany "London Style" longcase clock, by Benjamin Heeley, Deptford. *c.1775, 241cm (95in) high, £4,000/$6,800*

Oak longcase clock, with a 30-hour movement, by Thomas Strange, Kingston. *c.1780, 183cm (72in) high, £340/$580*

Scottish mahogany longcase clock, by James Wylie, Saltcoats. *c.1830, 229cm (90in) high, £1,000/$1,700*

Mahogany longcase clock with circular hood, unsigned. *c.1830, 192cm (76in) high, £950/$1,615*

Bracket and Mantel Clocks

Weight-driven lantern clocks first appeared in British homes in about 1620. Spring-driven bracket clocks, which sat on a wall bracket in the mid-17th century, were later put on a shelf or table. These clocks were designed to be portable. Clocks were luxury items and a single household often contained only one or two, which were moved from room to room. Only a few bracket clocks have retained their original bracket.

Bracket clocks are often signed on the backplates, which are also engraved. The earliest examples date from the 1660s and are usually cased in ebony and walnut, with either a pediment-shaped or domed top. They had square brass dials, but by the early 18th century arched dials were more common. In the 18th century the preference was for ebony and walnut until about 1725, when mahogany became popular. At the end of the 18th century and into the Regency period several diverse styles were produced. Bracket clocks had become more of a stationary feature, so the top carrying handle disappeared in preference to decorative side handles. The large round convex dials that typify the period were made from white enamelled copper, painted sheet iron, or silvered brass. With the arrival of the Victorian era, growing importance was given to the case design, and by the 1870s Arabic numerals were fashionable.

"Ting tang" quarter-striking lantern clock, by Henry Spendlove, High Metfield. The dial and pillars early 18th century, the movement late 19th century, 38cm (15in) high, £1,300/$2,200

Mahogany and ebonized six-tune musical bracket clock, with brass inlay, by Willm. Ritson, Cripplegate, London. c.1780, 65cm (25in) high, £7,000/$11,900

Mahogany brass-bound quarter-chiming domestic table regulator, with Berthoud-type detent escapement, by Thomas Reid, Edinburgh. c.1790, 48cm (19in) high, £16,000/$27,200

Black marble mantel clock, with ormolu mounts, by the King's clockmaker, Benjamin Vulliamy of Pall Mall, London. 1809, 18cm (7in) high, £8,000/$13,600

French gilt- and patinated-bronze mantel clock, mounted with the figure of Napoleon, movement by Grange and Betout. c.1850, 57cm (22in) high, £1,450/$2,475

Rosewood bracket clock

The clock chimes on the quarter hour and has a repeating mechanism, which allows it to repeat the previous hour. These are indicators of a quality clockmaker, and this clock was made by John Grant of Fleet Street (the son of John Grant, also of Fleet Street), born in 1796. He was liveryman of the Clockmakers Company in 1817 and Master, 1838–67. *c.1820, 57cm (22in) high, £2,500/$4,250*

The sides are fitted with lion mask and ring handles primarily as a decorative rather than functional feature.

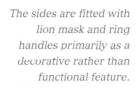

The carrying handle fitted to the top of earlier bracket clocks has been discarded in favour of a gilt-brass pineapple finial.

Regency bracket clocks feature a round convex dial

By 1820 it was fashionable for the hands to have been cut from blued steel or brass.

The mechanism chimes the quarter hours on eight bells and hammers, and the hour on a larger bell.

Gothic-style rosewood mantel clock, retailed by Simson, Southampton, movement by Japy Frères. *c.*1850, 26cm (10¼in) high, £350/$595

French pink marble and ormolu-mounted mantel clock garniture, with candlestick side pieces, movement by Japy Frères. *c.*1870, clock 25cm (10in) high, £1,000/$1,700

French gilt-brass oval four-glass mantel clock, with mercury jar pendulum. *c.*1875, 35cm (13¾in) high, £1,150/$1,950

Oak-case table regulator, with visible chronometer escapement by J. Grant, London. *c.*1880, 45cm (17¾in) high, £1,200/$2,050

French cut brass and tortoiseshell mantel clock, movement by Japy Frères. *c.*1900, 30cm (12in) high, £500/$850

Wall Clocks

A wall clock is literally a clock that can be positioned on a wall, and there is a large variety of shapes and sizes available. These clocks are driven by either weights, which run for 30 hours, or springs, which can keeping going for 8 days. The category ranges from the often imaginative Black Forest clocks – simple types were first made in the 17th century by country craftsmen, sometimes with a dial painted with a rustic scene – to the highly ornamental French cartel clock, and the expensive, high-quality, early 19th-century Vienna regulators, with their severe, architectural lines and ebony or boxwood cases. American wall clocks, made from the 1780s onward, were exported to Britain in great numbers during the mid-19th century.

Lantern clocks and bracket clocks were originally designed to sit on a bracket attached to the wall (see pages 150–51). The largest wall clocks are the weight-driven tavern clocks that graced the walls of 18th-century drinking houses or coaching inns, so the traveller was able to keep track of time before boarding the stage coach.

Drop-dial clocks, popular in Britain in the Victoiran era, have a long movement box below the dial – sometimes as much as 30cm (12in) long. The vast majority of wall clocks produced in the 18th and 19th centuries are simple dial clocks, circular in form with a white dial and plain wooden rim. A thin rim suggests an early date. Many dial clocks were used in offices, train station waiting rooms, and public buildings.

Drop-dial mahogany wall clock, with painted wooden dial, by Recordon, late Emery, London. *c.*1790, 68cm (27in) high, £2,800/$4,750

Cartel giltwood clock, by James Muirhead, Glasgow. *c.*1825, 69cm (27in), £2,000/$3,400

Mahogany wall timepiece, by Ebenezer Sewell, Liverpool. 1820–40, 36cm (14in) diameter, £700/$1,190

Drop-dial walnut wall timepiece, by R. Beck, Bradford. *c.*1850. 75cm (30in) high, £320/$545

Drop-dial mahogany wall timepiece, by J.W. Benson, Ludgate Hill, London. *c.*1890, 47cm (19in) high, £270/$460

Continental Vienna-style walnut wall timepiece. *c.*1880, 102cm (40in) high, £300/$510

Carriage Clocks

The carriage clock is a French innovation, developed from larger portable clocks, and it was made in great numbers there from the 1840s until World War I. The demand was created during the Napoleonic Wars when it became necessary to supply armies on the move with a portable method of telling the time. Abraham-Louis Breguet was the earliest carriage clockmaker and his works are in demand.

This type of clock was made in varying sizes, with a carrying case, and it was fitted with a spring-driven mechanism. Depending on the complexity of the mechanism, the clock could strike quarter to hourly, and some had alarms and calendars set into the dial. In order to remain unaffected by movement, the escapement was placed on a horizontal platform at the top of the clock, which is visible through a glazed aperture and referred to as a platform escapement.

The fully glazed case and carrying handle distinguishes the carriage clock from other types of portable clocks. The finest cases were gilded and engraved with floral designs, but toward the end of the 19th century, some examples were decorated with colourful *champlevé* (inset) enamels or inset with porcelain panels painted in the manner of 18th-century Sèvres porcelain.

British carriage clocks were made in relatively smaller numbers. The clocks themselves are of higher quality than their French counterparts, but they were incorporated into plainer and heavier cases.

French porcelain-mounted repeating carriage clock, with engraving on the case. *c.*1880, 18cm (7in) high, £3,600/$6,100

French gilded brass carriage clock, with Japanese-inspired decoration. *c.*1870, 18cm (7in) high, £900/$1,530

French porcelain-mounted carriage clock, with the movement by Margaine and the dial signed for the retailers Howell, James, and Co., London. 1880, 15cm (6in) high, £2,600/$4,400

French engraved brass one-piece carriage clock, with engraving, retailed by Wurtl, Horologer, Plc Vivienne à Paris. *c.*1860, 16.5cm (6½in), £600/$1,020

Miniature silver carriage timepiece, with French movement. *c.*1900, 9cm (3½in) high, £700/$1,190

French brass carriage timepiece, with enamelled decoration. *c.*1880, 15.5cm (6in) high, £350/$595

American Clocks

Throughout the 18th century the American clockmakers continued to work in tandem with developments in Britain and the Continent, but they adopted a distinctive regional approach to the choice of design elements provided on the cabinetwork. This is evident in the use of carved mahogany, block and shell motifs, and the urn-and-flame finials on the cabinet and hood of tallcase (longcase) clocks attributed to the Goddard-Townsend workshops in Newport, Rhode Island.

By the early 19th century and the advent of the Federal period, "Banjo" wall clocks became popular. This type of clock has a circular dial above an elaborate mahogany cabinet, which was often inset with reverse painted or *verre églomisé* (glass with gilded decoration) panels and sometimes fitted with a thermometer. At this time, the carved wooden finials of the Chippendale-style years had given way to gilt brass ball-and-spire finials and the arch top of the hood was adorned with an elaborate pierced fret crest.

American clocks made for the home market had wooden movements, but with the introduction of inexpensive rolled brass by the mills in Waterbury, Connecticut, the cost of brass clock movements came down to a level where almost everyone could afford a simple mantel clock.

Federal mahogany and *églomisé* (painted glass) banjo clock, New England. 1800–25, 84cm (33in), £1,000/$1,700

Federal mahogany and *églomisé* banjo clock, by Aaron Willard Jr, Boston. 1815–25, 100cm (39in), £3,650/$6,200

Chippendale mahogany tallcase clock, with carved details, attributed to Goddard-Townsend, Rhode Island. 1770–90, 254cm (100in) high, £450,000/$765,000

Federal mahogany tallcase clock, with inlaid details, made in New York or New Jersey. 1800–10, 238cm (94in) high, £3,900/$6,600

Federal mahogany regulator wall clock, by Aaron Willard, Boston. *c.*1820, 76cm (30in) high, £3,650/$6,200

Gilt-bronze "George Washington" shelf clock, with movement by Isidore Genot. 1820–30, 52cm (20in) high, £4,500/$7,650

Novelty Clocks

The earliest surviving working novelty clocks are German automata made in Augsburg in the 1650s. These pieces incorporated mechanical figures – either of human or animal form – which performed each time the hour struck. In the 19th century automaton clocks were made, mainly in France, in forms that reflected the new industrial age, including steam locomotives, water wheels, and steam hammers.

The brass skeleton clock, with its elaborate brass fretwork, found a ready market with the Victorian public. These clocks had an open framework, with the mechanism exposed, and were often enclosed in a glass dome. Elaborate types were modelled after famous buildings and some include chimes.

The 19th century was the great age of the mystery clock. The "mystery" was usually related to how the clock worked, because there was no visible connection between the movement and pendulum or the movement and the hands. If a figural support is used, the value of a clock is often dependent upon whether it is bronze or spelter (a cheaper zinc alloy) and the size of the figure itself. The ultimate mystery clocks were produced in the Art Deco years of the 1920s and 1930s by Cartier of Paris. These are often jewel encrusted or inlaid with semiprecious stones, which probably accounts for present-day price tags well in excess of £100,000/$170,000.

French patinated and lacquered brass novelty industrial clock, modelled as a beam engine. *c.*1880, 17cm (6¾in) high, £950/$1,615

Exhibition-quality, quarter-chiming skeleton clock, attributed to Smiths of London. *c.*1860, 51cm (20in) high, £22,000/$37,400

French enamel and brass "World Time" mantel timepiece. *c.*1880, 24cm (9½in) high, £4,000/$6,800

"Gravity" mantel timepiece. *c.*1910, 26cm (10in) high, £200/$340

Oak mantel clock, with metal mounts, in the form of a longcase clock. *c.*1910, 45cm (18in) high, £380/$645

French spelter figural "mystery" clock. *c.*1900, 25cm (10in) high, £800/$1,360

Pocket Watches

The invention of the spring mechanism triggered the evolution of the pocket watch, but early examples remained inaccurate until *c.*1675. The earliest types were about 5cm (2in) in diameter, and made in France and Germany in about 1550. Pocket watches were initially thick in section, but became slimmer after 1800. Early pocket watches were wound by a key. The first keyless watch was made *c.*1790, wound by turning the knob at the top of the case, but most examples date from the late 19th and early 20th centuries.

Pocket watches have always been collected as much for their cases as for the complexities of their movements, and some cases are works of art, made from silver or gold, often engraved or enamelled. Cases were originally intended to protect the dials – glass faces were not introduced until the 17th century. An open-faced watch has an unprotected glass. A hinged case known as a hunter was first used to protect the glass *c.*1840; if it has an aperature, it is known as a half-hunter.

The first American pocket watch on record, *c.*1809, was made by Luther Goddard of Shrewsbury, Massachusetts. Edward Howard and Aaron Dennison began the Waltham Watch Company in about 1850, and by the late 19th century, American pocket watches were mass-produced and exported. In Europe, precision watches were made in Switzerland by makers such as Patek Philippe and Vacheron Constantin.

Gold-cased fusee verge pocket watch, by A. Bigot, Rouen. *c.*1750, 4.5cm (1¾in) diameter, £300/$510

Silver pair-cased quarter-repeating verge alarm pocket watch, by Eardley Norton, London. *c.*1780, 6.5cm (2½in) diameter, £800/$1,360

Silver pair-cased verge pocket watch, with painted dial, by J. Richards, London. Hallmarked 1820, 5.5cm (2in) diameter, £260/$440

Gold open-face, wind through the dial, pocket watch, with enamel and pearl set bezel. *c.*1820, 4.5cm (1¾in) diameter, £320/$545

Swiss 18ct-gold centre second key wind pocket watch, with stop seconds. *c.*1850, 4.5cm (1¾in) diameter, £240/$410

American 14ct three-colour gold, keyless wind half-hunter pocket watch, by Elgin National Watch Company. *c.*1883, 4.5cm (1¾in) diameter, £1,300/$2,200

18ct-gold open-face lever pocket watch, with dual winding, by Barraud and Lunds, London. Hallmarked 1889, 4.5cm (1¾in) diameter, £480/$815

Swiss 18ct-gold and enamel keyless wind fob watch. *c.*1890, 3.5cm (1⅜in) diameter, £150/$255

The rim of the gold case has been given a coin-edged (milled) band fitted with an inset repeating slide, which when operated sets into motion the quarter-repeating mechanism, that strikes the number of quarters past.

Open-face pocket watch

This 18-carat gold, key wind, quarter-repeating pocket watch was made by E.J. Dent, London. The firm of Dent is recognized for making high-quality watches, as noted in this example, which has many features and is hallmarked. The firm became watchmakers to Queen Victoria. *Hallmarked 1844, 4.5cm (1¾in) diameter, £1,000/$1,700*

All parts of the 18ct gold case are either fully hallmarked or stamped with the London assay and maker's mark.

The white enamel dial has black roman numerals and an outer minute track. The watch is both signed and numbered by the maker.

The dial also features a subsidiary seconds dial.

Swiss 18ct-gold full-hunter quarter-repeating, keyless wind pocket watch. *c.*1890, 5cm (2in) diameter, £440/$750

18ct-gold open-face pocket watch, with stop seconds and up-down indicator, by Thomas Russell and Son. Hallmarked 1894, 5.5cm (2¼in) diameter, £420/$715

18ct-gold full-hunter keyless wind pocket watch, by Edwin Flinn, Allesley Rd, London. Hallmarked 1899, 5cm (2in) diameter, £700/$1,190

Wristwatches

Cartier made the first true wristwatch in 1904 for the aviator Alberto Santos Dumont, but it was during World War I that the wristwatch was first recognized as a more convenient method for soldiers to tell the time than by trying to consult a pocket watch on a chain. Just after the war, small fob watches were converted to wristwatches by having strap fittings attached to them.

During the 1920s the Swiss led the way in being able to produce wristwatches of every quality in numbers large enough to satisfy the public clamouring for this latest method of timekeeping. Many new Swiss firms started up during this period, but older organizations such as Movado and Patek Philippe adapted readily to the new methods. In the 1930s, Rolex led the way by producing one of the first fully automatic and waterproof wristwatches.

The early watches were usually of circular form. During the years between World Wars I and II, following the fashions of the time, different styles were introduced that made use of clean lines and bold numerals, including square, rectangular, oval, and octagonal cases.

Today collectors seek classic designs from the 1930s, 1940s, and 1950s, while also recognizing the merits of more recent years. Value is determined by a combination of factors including maker, model, style, mechanism, and condition.

Movado gent's 14ct-gold rectangular wristwatch. *c.*1935, 2cm (¾in) wide, £900/$1,530

Rolex 9ct-gold cushion-cased wristwatch, Glasgow. Import mark for 1936, 2.5cm (1in) wide, £450/$765

Rolex lady's 9ct-gold bracelet watch, Glasgow. Import mark for 1936, 2cm (¾in) wide, £220/$375

Longines 14ct-gold hour-glass-shaped rectangular wristwatch. 1940s, 2cm (¾in) wide, £1,000/$1,700

Ebel 18ct-gold chronograph wristwatch. 1940s, 3.5cm (1⅜in) wide, £800/$1,360

Breitling gent's steel chronograph wristwatch, on bracelet, Cadette. 1940s, 3.5cm (1⅜in) wide, £400/$680

Gentleman's rectangular wristwatch

The mechanism in this wristwatch is a 15 jewel Swiss movement imported by the famous Old Bond Street company of Asprey, who would have been responsible for commissioning the design of the watch to then sell through its London store. This retailer of gold, silver, and jewellery is known for the quality of its goods and produced many luxury items.
c.1948, 2.5cm (1in) wide, £380/$645

Replacement leather straps are inevitable and acceptable to collectors.

The rectangular 9ct-gold case suggests a 1930s or 1940s year of manufacture.

The dial is silvered and has black Arabic numerals.

The hands are cut in the distinctive Breguet style.

On this example, the 9ct-gold deployment buckle (not visible) is a replacement supplied by Asprey and dated 1971. If the buckle were contemporary with the case, the watch would be more valuable.

Jaeger le Coultre gent's 9ct-gold wristwatch, London. Hallmark for 1965, 3.25cm (1¼in) wide, £300/$510

Jaeger le Coultre lady's 18ct-gold bracelet watch. 1960s, 2cm (¾in) wide, £250/$425

Vacheron Constantin gent's slim 18ct-gold wristwatch, on bracelet with presentation box. *c.1970, 3.25cm (1¼in) wide, £720/$1,230*

Baume and Mercier gent's 18ct-gold wristwatch. 1970s, 2.5cm (1in) wide, £400/$680

Omega stainless-steel automatic chronograph wristwatch, Speedmaster professional mark IV. 1970s, 4cm (1½in) wide, £540/$920

Art Nouveau

1   3   2   4

1 Gilt-bronze bust of a maiden, by A. Gruber, *c.*1900
2 Intarsio Ware twin-handled pottery vase, by Wileman and Co., *c.*1910
3 Green stained and leaded glass screen, attributed to George Walton, *c.*1901
4 Cameo glass vase, by Émile Gallé, *c.*1900

Art Nouveau refers to the "New Art" that permeated the decorative and applied arts in the late 19th and early 20th centuries in Britain, the Continent, and the United States. The style first appeared in Belgium *c.*1892, before spreading to France at the end of the 19th century. The term is traditionally held to be derived from the name given to the Parisian gallery "Maison de l'Art Nouveau" by its owner Siegfried Bing.

Inspired by nature, the style is dominated by sinuous fluid forms such as the shape of flowers, asymmetrical lines, insect motifs, ethereal maidens, and opalescent colours. Bing's gallery promoted the sensually charged style by introducing the talents of international exponents, including Georges de Feure, Louis Comfort Tiffany, Henri Van de Velde, Max Lauger, and Edward Colonna. These were only some of the names that featured at Bing's pavilion at the 1900

Paris Exposition Universal, where the designers and craftsmen received great acclaim as members of the Paris School. A similar approach advocated by the Nancy School in France was also given critical praise, bringing international attention to design luminaries in the guise of Émile Gallé, Louis Majorelle, Eugène Vallin, and the output of the Daum glassworks.

Outside France the style was embraced and adapted at both national and regional levels, and although the curvilinear extravagances evident in the French treatment are recognized as the epitome of the style, it is in stark contrast to the severe geometry incorporated into the designs emanating at the same time in Vienna and Glasgow. Nevertheless, despite the different interpretations, all are perceived as variations of a movement unified beneath the all-encompassing banner of Art Nouveau.

5

8

5 Tudric pewter mantel clock, designed by Archibald Knox, *c.*1905
6 Gilt-bronze figure of a snake charmer, by Borse, *c.*1900
7 Carved walnut chair, by Louis Majorelle, *c.*1900
8 Tiffany Studios Favrile glass and bronze vine-leaf border chandelier, *c.*1910

Early influences

The seeds of the style had been sown in the 1870s after trade with Japan had been resumed and Britain, the Continent, and the United States rediscovered a passion for all things Oriental. It was the Japanese observation and interpretation of the subtle forms and features evident in the natural world, and their eventual translation into works of art, that was so greatly admired by influential artists and designers of the time such as Whistler, Rossetti, and William Morris. The influence became manifest in the Aesthetic Movement, which sought to bring beauty back into the homes of late 19th-century society and what followed over the next 30 years was a natural progression described as "a quest for beauty".

By the 1890s, designers and craftsmen had begun to appreciate that the home itself was worthy of being recognized and treated as a work of art in its own right, and a new emphasis was put upon the harmony between the interior and all that was placed in it. This is probably best explained in the creations of architect-designers such as Charles Rennie Mackintosh in Scotland, Hector Guimard in France, Frank Lloyd Wright in the United States, and Victor Horta in Belgium.

In Britain, the style grew in tandem with the Arts and Crafts Movement, which was happy to borrow from nature but unwilling to sanction the machine, preferring to pursue a hand-crafted idealism, which eventually floundered because it was economically unsustainable.

The graceful sensuality of Art Nouveau lasted a mere 20 years from the 1890s until the outbreak of World World I. After the guns fell silent in 1918, the seeds of modernism, sown before the war, took root and flourished, and found initial expression in the style recognized as Art Deco.

Metalware

At the beginning of the 20th century, the Art Nouveau style managed to find its way into the decorative elements of everyday metalwork, whether it was a candlestick, coal scuttle, or crumb scoop. The style helped to restore the waning fortunes of the German and British pewter industries, with the wares produced by Kayser, Orivit, and WMF managing to incorporate the organic, sensual, and fantasy themes of Art Nouveau. Their works include figural candlesticks, claret jugs, vases, and bowls.

The success of German art pewter at his Regent Street store prompted Arthur Liberty to introduce his own Tudric pewter range, synonymous today with its principal designer

Archibald Knox. Liberty had already launched his Cymric silver range produced by Knox and other designers, but he recognized the potential of the cheaper pewter alternative. Machine-made Tudric pewter often has the hammered appearance of the handmade metalwork that is generally associated with the Arts and Crafts metalwork and silver produced by the Guild of Handicraft, under the guiding hand of Charles Robert Ashbee.

In Austria, the stylized and geometric silver designs of Josef Hoffmann, Koloman Moser, and other members of the Wiener Werkstatte, offered a stark contrast to the asymmetrical and curvilinear excesses of French silver and pewter.

Liberty and Co. Cymric silver bowl on stand, with turquoise and mother-of-pearl, designed by Archibald Knox. Hallmark for 1902, 26cm (10¼in) diameter, £3,000/$5,100

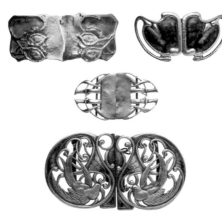

English silver buckles, three with enamel by William Haseler, William Hutton and Sons, and Liberty and Co., one without, by Liberty and Co. 1901–11, 6.5–11cm (2½–4¼in) wide, £300/$510, £300/$510, £500/$850, and £180/$305

William Hutton and Sons silver and enamel photograph frame. Hallmark for 1903, 20cm (8in) high, £1,350/$2,300

Guild of Handicraft silver, enamel, and amethyst cup and cover, by Charles Robert Ashbee. c.1901, 31cm (12¼in) high, £5,000/$8,500

WMF plated-pewter figural table mirror. c.1905, 37cm (14½in) high, £1,000/$1,700

Liberty and Co. Tudric pewter and abalone timepiece, designed by Archibald Knox. c.1905, 17cm (6¾in) high, £5,000/$8,500

WMF plated-pewter and cranberry glass claret jug. *c.*1905, 41cm (16in) high, £500/$850

WMF plated-pewter three-light candelabrum. *c.*1910, 41cm (16in) high, £400/$680

Liberty and Co. Tudric timepiece

This pewter mantel clock is from a range of timepieces attributed to the designer Archibald Knox that feature organic designs, such as stylized foliage, cast in low relief and embellished with enamel or mother-of-pearl detail. Liberty did not allow commissioned designers to sign their work.
c.1905, 20.5cm (8in), £3,000/$5,100

The decoration of stylized heart-shaped leaves supported upon sinuous slender stems is cast in low relief only on the front plate.

This example is enhanced by a circular glazed bezel, but other more sculptural timepieces feature larger hands that cannot function within a bezel.

The German-made mechanism is stamped Lenzkirch. It is of secondary importance in comparison with the decorative pewter case.

The enamel is usually a peacock blue colour or mottled with turquoise and occasionally scarlet.

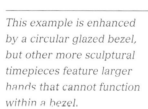

Georg Jensen Blossom tea and coffee service. *c.*1910, size unavailable, £3,500/$5,950

Viennese bronze figural vase, *c.*1900, 20cm (7⅞in) high, £700/$1,190

Liberty and Co. Tudric pewter and enamel tea set, designed by Archibald Knox. *c.*1905, size unavailable, £1,200/$2,050

Glass

The plasticity of glass proved the perfect property for craftsmen to express the concepts of the Art Nouveau style as they moved away from the traditional cut-glass techniques in preference to exploring the medium's sculptural possibilities.

In France Émile Gallé established himself as the country's master glass-maker, working in Nancy. His early creations focused on enamelled themes, while his later work made strong use of organic form inspired by the beauty of nature. The vast majority of Gallé's output both before and after its founder's death in 1904 concentrated on decorative and industrially produced cameo glass, a type of carved glass with two or more layers in different colours. The neighbouring

Daum glassworks are credited with a range of equally inventive wares, including cameo and enamelled wares.

In the United States and Austria, emphasis was placed upon controlled iridescence, with the glassworks of Tiffany and Loetz recognized as the most important exponents of the effect. Although Tiffany's iridescent creations sold well, it was the colourful leaded glass lamps that had become the ultimate status symbol in every middle-class American home by 1915.

The Austrian glassworks of Meyers Neff produced a range of drinking glasses in a severe geometric form with blue flashed decoration designed by Otto Prutscher. These exemplify the modernist doctrine of the Wiener Werkstatte.

Émile Gallé cameo glass table lamp, overlaid with trailing morning glory flowers. 1900–20, 71cm (28in) high, £16,000/$27,200

Set of six Theresienthal enamelled wine glasses, with green stems. *c.*1910, 21cm (8¼in) high, £550/$935

Quezal Jack-in-the-Pulpit iridescent glass vase. *c.*1900, 22cm (8⅝in) high, £1,200/$2,050

Loetz glass bowl, with three bronze dancing maidens mounted on the rim. *c.*1900, 22cm (8⅝in) high, £600/$1,020

Meyers Neff blue-on-clear flashed glass beaker, designed by Otto Prutscher. *c.*1910, 11cm (4¼in) high, £500/$850

Müller Frères cameo glass three-arm chandelier, with iron mounts. *c.*1900, 91cm (36in) diameter, £4,700/$8,000

Tiffany Favrile glass lamp

The "Peony" pattern shade is one of about five hundred different designs matched with a similar number of decorative bronze bases for both table and standard lamps. The early examples were designed as oil lamps, but with the growing availability of electric power, Tiffany found it necessary to provide a conversion service. *1899–1920, 80cm (31in) high, £95,000/$161,500.*

This example has retained its pierced cover with pear-shaped finial.

The leaded framework displays a bronzed, or verdigris, surface, which should never be removed.

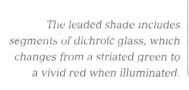

The leaded shade includes segments of dichroic glass, which changes from a striated green to a vivid red when illuminated.

The interior rim of the shade is impressed Tiffany Studios/New York/1505.

The brown patinated bronze base is cast in the "Roman Helmet" design and stamped Tiffany Studios/New York/1529 on the underside.

Lobmeyer engraved glass vase and cover, designed by Michael Powolny. *c.*1913, 35.5cm (14in) high, £1,700/$2,900

Handel interior painted glass and copper lamp. *c.*1910, 25.5cm (10in) high, £2,700/$4,600

Loetz iridescent glass vase, with silver overlay in a sinuous flower and stem design. *c.*1900, 21cm (8¼in) high, £270/$460

Loetz iridescent blue glass vase, with silver water lily overlay. *c.*1900, 18cm (7in) high, £1,600/$2,700

Loetz Creta Glatt glass vase, by Josef Hoffmann. *c.*1900, size unavailable, £3,000/$5,100

Glass

Daum acid-etched overlay glass vase, with lug handles and geranium design. *c.*1900, 21.5cm (8½in) high, £3,500/$5,950

Daum acid–etched and enamelled vase, with rosehip and leaf design. *c.*1905, 11.5cm (4½in) high, £700/$1,190

Daum cameo and applied glass vase, with a berry and leaf design. *c.*1900, 21cm (8¼in) high, £2,800/$4,750

Daum cameo and applied glass vase. *c.*1900, 34.5cm (13½in) high, £6,500/$11,000

Émile Gallé cameo glass landscape vase. *c.*1900, 21cm (8¼in) high, £2,900/$4,900

Émile Gallé cameo glass vase, with shrub rose design. *c.*1900, 25.5cm (10in) high, £2,100/$3,600

Émile Gallé internally decorated and surface carved glass bowl, with an overall leaf design. *c.*1900, 14cm (5½in) diameter, £5,500/$9,350

Gallé mould-blown cameo glass vase, with a "Cala Lily" pattern. *c.*1920, 36cm (14⅛in) high, £30,000/$51,000

Émile Gallé cameo glass vase, acid cut and fire polished with an iris design; it has a chipped base. *c.*1900, 40cm (15¾in) high, £1,200/$2,050

Müller Frères cameo glass table lamp, with
mushroom shade. *c.*1900, 58cm (22¾in) high,
£4,800/$8,150

Louis Comfort Tiffany paperweight glass vase,
with trailed water lily and pad leaf design. *c.*1905,
16cm (6¼in) high, £2,000/$3,400

**Louis Comfort Tiffany carved paperweight
iridescent glass vase,** with trailed leaf design.
*c.*1915, 25.5cm (10in) high, £2,500/$4,250

**Tiffany Studios Favrile glass and bronze "Acorn"
lamp, on a blown-glass gourd base.** 1899–1922,
shade 40.5cm (16in) diameter, £15,300/$26,000

Louis Comfort Tiffany Favrile glass vase, with
a slender onion form. 1892–1928, 51cm (20in)
high, £3,000/$5,100

**Louis Comfort Tiffany Favrile applied glass
vase.** *c.*1908, 23cm (9in) high, £5,600/$9,500

**Tiffany Studios Favrile glass and bronze
"Apple Blossom" table lamp.** 1899–1922,
shade 41cm (16in) diameter, £20,000/$34,000

**Tiffany Studios Favrile glass and patinated
bronze "Dogwood" hanging shade.** 1899–1922,
shade 65cm (25½in) diameter, £37,000/$62,900

Louis Comfort Tiffany gold Favrile glass vase,
*c.*1919, 41cm (16in) high, £2,000/$3,400

Ceramics

The French potters were content to cover their busts and figures of tousled-haired maidens with glazes that emulated bronze. Meanwhile, the Bohemian potters, including Royal Dux, Ernst Wahlis, and the Amphora works, were responsible for a massive output of figures and vases in tones of ivory coloured in green. In Hungary, the Zsolnay pottery produced iridescent-glazed wares of sculptural inspiration covered in a myriad of colours, including vibrant crimson, purple, and green lustre. The Rozenburg pottery located at the Hague in the Netherlands produced eggshell porcelain, the most delicate of all Art Nouveau ceramics. This was hand-painted with complex flower, bird, and fish subjects. In Germany, the robust slip-trailed vases of Max Lauger were decorated with

tall grasses and plants. Villeroy & Boch and Nymphenburg also made Art Nouveau wares.

William Moorcroft, another advocate of slip decoration, introduced his celebrated Florian Ware by 1898, which was recognized by many as the finest British contribution to Art Nouveau ceramic design. Meanwhile, at nearby Minton and Co., a similar technique was applied to the abstract patterns decorated in vivid colours, designed by Leon Solon and John Wadsworth, and sold as Secessionist Ware.

In the United States, Grueby Faience and Teco developed matt and semi-matt glazes, and Rookwood Pottery specialized in painting coloured slip on unfired clay. All three potteries experimented with new decorative forms and patterns.

Austro-German copper-mounted ceramic floor vase. c.1900, 86.5cm (34in) high, £3,000/$5,100

Rozenburg eggshell porcelain vase, decorated by Samuel Schellink. Dated 1908, 11cm (4¼in) high, £850/$1,445

Zsolnay of Pecs lustre vase, decorated with geese. c.1900, 26cm (10¼in) high, £1,800/$3,050

Austrian two-handled organically shaped vase. c.1910, 32.5cm (12¾in) high, £55/$95

Wileman and Co. Intarsio Ware gourd-shaped vase. c.1900, 19cm (7½in) high, £350/$595

Macintyre Florian Ware vase, designed by William Moorcroft. *c.*1900, 26.5cm (10½in) high, £800/$1,360

J. von Schwartz rectangular tile, with a maiden and harp, designed by Carl Sigmund Luber. *c.*1900, 36.5cm x 12cm (14⅜in x 4¾in), £300/$510

Reissner Stellmacher and Kessel vase, decorated with the profile portrait of a maiden. *c.*1900, 28cm (11in) high, £650/$1,105

Minton Secessionist Ware jardinière. *c.*1905, 23cm (9in) high, £500/$850

Minton Secessionist Ware vase, *c.*1905, 37cm (14⅝in) high, £600/$1,020

Minton Secessionist Ware vase, *c.*1905, 31cm (12¼in) high, £150/$255

Royal Doulton Burslem ewer and basin, printed with the "Howard" pattern. *c.*1905, basin 37cm (14⅝in) diameter, £130/$220

Wileman and Co. Intarsio Ware ceramic timepiece, designed by Frederick Rhead, *c.*1900, 29cm (11½in) high, £400/$680

Ceramics

Austrian figural illuminated vanity mirror.
*c.*1905, 63.5cm (25in) high, £1,550/$2,650

Goldscheider terracotta bust of a maiden,
signed Pecheur. *c.*1900, 43cm (17in) high,
£800/$1,360

Reissner Stellmacher and Kessel vase,
decorated with the profile portrait of a maiden.
*c.*1900, 28cm (11in) high, £650/$1,105

Kandern Tonwerke slip-trailed vase,
designed by Max Lauger. *c.*1905, 19.5cm
(7⅝in) high, £300/$510

Zsolnay of Pecs lustre vase, decorated with
fish. *c.*1900, 18.5cm (7¼in) high, £1,500/$2,550

**Royal Dux figural centrepiece and shell-
shaped bowl.** *c.*1900, centrepiece 36cm
(14⅛in) high, £400/$680 and £200/$340

Maurice Dufrene 11-piece porcelain tea and coffee set.
*c.*1905, coffeepot 23.5cm (9¼in) high, £1,500/$2,550 (for the set)

**Zsolnay of Pecs organically
shaped ewer,** with lustre
decoration. *c.*1910, 30.5cm
(12in) high, £1,500/$2,550

Royal Dux figural plant-shaped vase,
embraced by two maidens. *c.*1900,
57.5cm (22¾in) high, £800/$1,360

Rozenburg kettle

This Rozenburg chocolate kettle was produced in fine eggshell porcelain and was delicately painted with a design of exotic fish. Rozenburg eggshell porcelains were slip cast and intended for the display cabinet, and not necessarily the table, although their output also included cups and saucers.
1903, 25cm (9⅞in) high, £3,500/$5,950

The elegant and inventive form appears to evolve organically.

The finely painted decoration often includes reserves (areas left blank for decoration) of complex Javanese Batik inspiration.

The base of vases usually have a square shape, and they are concave underneath with a narrow, flat foot rim that has been wiped free of glaze.

The underside of the base is printed with the "Stork" factory trademark in black, and is painted with the artist's monogram or initials and year symbol.

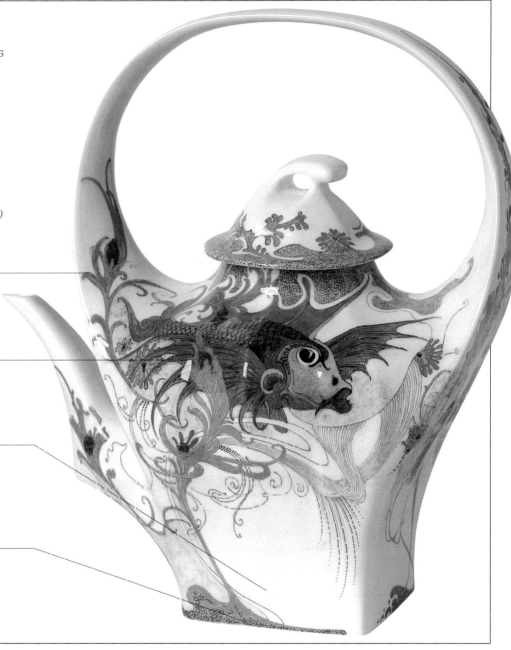

Gouda Zuid-Holland two-handled vase.
c.1910, 20cm (7⅞in) high, £300/$510

Villeroy and Boch Mettlach charger, with a maiden in a forest, designed by R. Chevenin.
c.1890, 40cm (15¾in) high, £800/$1,360

Pierre-Adrien Dalpayrat two-handled high-fired stoneware vase. *c*.1895, 8cm (3in) high, £1,000/$1,700

Sculpture

The female form appears to have monopolized the interest of virtually all the Art Nouveau sculptors. Invariably, she was depicted with long flowing tresses, or with her hair *en chignon* (worn in a knot at the nape of the neck) and adorned with flowers. Sometimes the inhabitant of a fairy-tale realm, where subjects might include wood and sea nymphs or butterfly-winged maidens alongside others of a similar metamorphic nature, sprang from the imagination of the sculptor. Often combined with the ethereal is the symbolist air of mystery, evident in Maurice Bouval's Ophelia and Cadet Julien Causse's La Fée des Glaces, where his ice maiden awaits upon an opalescent glass pedestal. Leopold Savine's Peacock Girl makes play on another metamorphic theme, which revolves around the fascination with this exotic bird and its iridescent plumage.

The work of Agathon Leonard, including his Scarf Dancer from a series of dancers that were produced in porcelain at the Sèvres factory in Paris, is reputed to represent the celebrated American dancer Loie Fuller, whose act was a great attraction when performed at the Paris exhibition of 1900. Ms Fuller's immortality was also ensured by Rauol-François Larche, who modelled two gilt-bronze figural lamps with the light fixtures hidden within her billowing drapery.

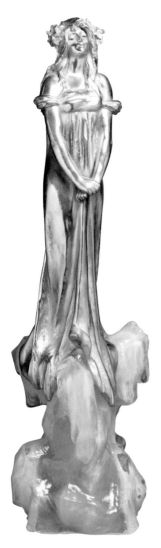

Silvered bronze figure of La Fée des Glaces, cast after a model by Cadet Julien Causse, raised upon an ice-form opalescent glass pedestal by Eugène Rousseau. *c.*1900, 58.5cm (23in) high, £8,200/$13,950

Gilt-bronze figural lamp of The Scarf Dancer, cast after a model by Agathon Leonard. *c.*1900, 60.5cm (23¾in) high, £9,200/$15,650

Patinated bronze figure of a dancing maiden, cast after a model by Ernst Seger. *c.*1905, 32cm (12½in) high, £980/$1,665

Enamelled and patinated-bronze figure of a butterfly dancer, cast after a model by Louis Chalon. *c.*1900, 42cm (16½in) high, £7,000/$11,900

Gilt-bronze figural Peacock Girl vase, cast after a model by Leopold Savine. *c.*1900, 39.5cm (15½in) high, £2,300/$3,900

Although lacking on this example, the presence of a foundry mark is the seal of a quality bronze.

Bronze figural vase

Louis Chalon (born 1866) is considered to be one of the finest exponents of the Art Nouveau style and consequently his work, such as this La Fée des Glaces bronze figural vase with parcel-gilt, is keenly sought after.
c.1900, 47cm (18½in) high, £16,000/$27,200

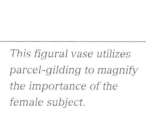

This figural vase utilizes parcel-gilding to magnify the importance of the female subject.

The vase is inscribed on the reverse with the sculptor's signature, L Chalon, Made in France.

The importance of the subject is further enhanced by the ice crown, which signifies the status of the subject, a fairy queen, and makes her more exotic. Ordinary fairies have headdresses but not crowns.

Parcel-gilt bronze figural vase, cast after George Flamand. *c.*1900, 38.5cm (15⅛in) high, £2,500/$4,250

Gilt-bronze bust of Ophelia, cast after a model by Maurice Bouval. *c.*1900, 45cm (17¾in) high, £9,600/$16,320

Gilt-bronze figure of a butterfly nymph, cast after a model by Francis Renaud. *c.*1900, 26cm (10¼in) high, £1,450/$2,475

Gilt-bronze bust of Ophelia, cast after a model by Josef Ofner. *c.*1900, 28cm (11in) high, £1,600/$2,700

Parcel-gilt bronze figure of an orchid nymph, cast after a model by Louis Chalon. *c.*1900, 54.5cm (21½in) high, £10,400/$17,680

Furniture

The French were the foremost exponents of the Art Nouveau style and the two main centres of furniture production were in the French cities of Paris and Nancy. The Nancy School was inspired by natural form and was championed by the designers Émile Gallé and Louis Majorelle, both of whom had achieved great acclaim at the Paris exhibition held in 1900. The furniture they designed incorporated marquetry panels, which were often set into furniture carved with elaborate organic supports. The Paris School was also influenced by nature, but its designers chose a more restrained approach, with emphasis placed on sculptural form rather than decorative inlay. This style is demonstrated in the work of Hector Guimard and Eugène Gaillard.

The Scottish designer Charles Rennie Mackintosh, based in Glasgow, produced furniture using simplified straight lines and gentle curves, which was decorated by his wife, Margaret MacDonald. His work was well received overseas, especially in Vienna, although it drew little attention in Britain at the time. The Mackintosh high-back chair has become a furniture icon in recent years, yet it represents a fraction of his output.

The simplistic Mission furniture designed by the American Gustave Stickley suggests a connection with the architect Frank Lloyd Wright. In Vienna designers such as Moser and Hoffman provided simplistic ideas for bentwood furniture, which were purely functional and pre-empt modernism.

Walnut *buffet a deux corps,* with carved details. *c.*1905, 221cm (87in) high, £1,200/$2,050

Walnut five-piece salon suite, comprising sofa, two armchairs, and two side chairs (not shown), with carved details. *c.*1905, sofa 97cm (38in) high, £2,800/$4,750

L. and G. Stickley oak reclining rocker, model 831. *c.*1912, 140cm (55in) high, £900/$1,530

English mahogany display cabinet, with coloured leaded-glass panels and marquetry. *c.*1905, 158cm (62in) high, £1,300/$2,200

Ernest Archibald Taylor mahogany sideboard, retailed by Wylie and Lochhead, Glasgow, Scotland. *c.*1900, 168cm (66in) high, £2,000/$3,400

Louis Majorelle walnut and rosewood vitrine, with carved details. *c.*1910, 190cm (75in) high, £8,000/$13,600

J. and J. Kohn bent-beechwood cabinet, designed by Kolomon Moser. c.1906, 192cm (76in) high, £4,000/$6,800

Charles Rennie Mackintosh oak dining chairs, designed for the Argyll Street Tearooms, Glasgow. c.1898, 137cm (54in) high, £400,000/$680,000

Émile Gallé mahogany and walnut vitrine, with marquetry and carved details. c.1900, 183cm (72in) high, £80,000/$136,000

Carved vitrine

Louis Majorelle, who was influenced by Émile Gallé, was one of the most important furniture designers working in the tradition of the Nancy School. The Orchid vitrine forms part of a series of gilt-bronze furniture designed by Majorelle after 1903. c.1906, 221cm (87in) high, £80,000/ $136,000

The hinged glazed door mounts are in gilt-bronze (these mounts are sometimes also referred to as "ormolu").

The cabinet is sculpted with the flowing, curvilinear lines typical of the style, which, along with the mounts, illustrate Majorelle's structural approach to furniture.

Majorelle's use of gilt-bronze mounts dates this piece to after 1903.

The gilt-bronze mounts are finely cast as the flowers, stems, and pendant buds of orchid plants, and they are harmoniously integrated with the piece.

The mahogany and rosewood cabinet is inlaid with panels of fruitwood parquetry.

Art Deco

1

2

3

4

1 Clarice Cliff Isis vase, with the "Sliced Circle" pattern, *c.*1930
2 Macassar ebony sideboard, *c.*1925
3 Preiss bronze and ivory figure of a woman and hoop, *c.*1935
4 Gustavsberg Argenta Ware vase, *c.*1930

After the experiences of World War I, the populations of all countries concerned looked for a brighter tomorrow. The arrival of the 1920s heralded a decade that discarded the old in preference of the promise of a new future. This was, after all, the age of "Thoroughly Modern Millie" when it became stylish to raise your skirts and bob your hair, and the bright young things of the moment were able to dance the Charleston.

The "Roaring Twenties"

This was the age of speed. Luxury transatlantic liners were fashioned as floating Art Deco palaces, each determined to win the prestigious Blue Ribbon for the speediest crossing between Le Havre in France and New York. Travel by rail had also become far more elegant and decidedly faster, epitomized by the French Compagnie Des Wagon-Lits, who could speed you to the Côte d'Azur while offering you the best of Gallic cuisine in coaches decorated with Lalique glass panels. Meanwhile, Imperial Airways offered the quickest route to the Middle East and India, while the more sedate zeppelins, or airships, crossed the Atlantic Ocean. For those determined to push the limits of the internal combustion engine, the gladiator of the day came in the form of a goggle-clad racing driver behind the wheel of a Bentley or Bugatti.

This was also the age of Hollywood, with generous helpings of glamour and elegance courtesy of Busby Berkeley and his synchronized *Gold Diggers*. At the same time, Fritz Lang's *Metropolis* offered a chilling projection of things to come, predicting a human race enslaved by the machine – this was also the age of the machine.

Above all else, the silver screen offered the masses a form of escapism where they might

5 Dining chair, by Jacques-Émile Ruhlmann, *c.*1925
6 Schneider internally decorated glass vase, *c.*1925
7 Chiparus bronze and ivory dancer, *c.*1930
8 Lalique Oran opalescent vase, *c.*1930

laugh out loud at the exploits of Laurel and Hardy or, in the case of the ladies, swoon at the sight of Rudolf Valentino dressed as "The Sheik". All these emotions might be vented within the streamlined, modernistic surroundings of the local cinemas, which were literally "Picture Palaces".

A new, modern style

In 1925, Paris provided the venue for the Exposition des Art Decoratifs, from which in post-war years the term "Art Deco" has been derived. Despite being an international event, the exhibition was more of a pretext for France to reaffirm its position as the world leader in the best of luxury furnishings and interiors. Art Deco borrowed elements from the 18th century, the Cubism of Picasso, and the tribal art of Africa. The many diverse characteristics varied from country

to country. The dynamism and spirit of those inter-war years are perfectly captured in the bronze and ivory sportsmen and women of Ferdinand Preiss, while the theatrical creations of Chiparus and Colinet hint at the exoticism and hedonism prevalent in the world of cabaret and speakeasies.

The 1920s continued to roar until the party came to a sudden halt in 1929 with the Wall Street Crash. However, the decorative arts managed to survive and prosper and herald the age of modernism, personified by New York's Rockefeller Center.

This was now the age of all things streamline, where plate glass and tubular steel were accepted as ready alternatives to the more traditional materials of mahogany and cast iron. The new approach survived the trauma of yet another world war, leaving the Art Deco years behind to be remembered in the music of Gershwin and the dancing feet of Fred Astaire and Ginger Rogers.

Metalware

Metalwork in the Art Deco period reflected the same use of geometric and faceted forms promoted by modernist designers and the 18th-century-influenced traditional designs. These elements featured strongly in the French approach to the style and are exemplified by the work of two important designers – the silversmith Jean Puiforcat and the metalworker Edgar Brandt.

Puiforcat launched a range of tea and coffee wares that relied on simple geometric and panel forms and were devoid of applied or engraved decoration. In the United States, a similar streamline approach was embraced in the modernist designs of Norman Bel Geddes, Kem Webber, and Louis Rice.

Brandt's metalwork designs have a more traditional feel, whether applied to bronze, copper, or wrought iron. His revival of decorative wrought iron was well received after being shown in the 1925 Paris Exhibition. He worked in Paris and New York on architectural commissions and domestic wares. The fashion for quality decorative metalwork is also reflected in the work of Paul Kiss, who included cast figural elements in his compositions, and Raymond Subes who used minimal iron supports in his tables, radiator covers, and lamps.

The Bauhaus design school in Germany was an influential source for the modernist cause before being closed by the Nazi party in 1933. The same holds true for the Wiener Werkstatte in Vienna, whose output reached a wider audience.

Wiener Werkstatte hammered white metal bowl, designed by Dagobert Peche. c.1920, 20cm (8in) high, £870/$1,480

Silver-plated Skyscraper range, including pair of candlesticks, two-handled dish, cocktail shaker, brazier, and water jug, designed by Louis W. Rice. c.1928, sizes unavailable, £1,100–£4,400/$1,870–$7,500

Wrought-iron boudoir lamp, with Sabino frosted-glass shade. c.1925, 25cm (10in) high, £580/$985

Georg Jensen "Cactus"-pattern 81-piece set of silver flatware, designed by Gundorph Albertus, with London hallmarks. 1931–38, sizes unavailable, £3,600/$6,100

Silvered bronze and alabaster chandelier, cast from a model by Albert Cheuret. c.1925, 66cm (26in) tall, £5,000/$8,500

Wrought iron chandelier

The visual signature of Edgar Brandt – the leading metalworker of the Art Deco period – is always the harmonious balance of overall form and decoration of a piece. Brandt often preferred to work on a grand scale.
c.1925, 69cm (27in) tall, £5,500/$9,350

These shades are well-turned and polished alabaster. Brandt also used glass shades, usually from the Daum glassworks of Nancy and marked as such, including the cross of Lorraine.

Brandt marked his work with the stamp "E. BRANDT", often on the foot rim of a lamp or table, or on a chandelier hoop support.

The use of well-defined organic motifs such as feathered leaves, scroll-tipped tendrils, and berries is typical of Brandt's designs.

Other design elements used by Brandt include ring-bound uprights, ripple-hammered surfaces, and textured ceiling roses.

Copper-plated desk lamp, designed by Jacques Adnet. *c.*1935, 26cm (10¼in) high, £1,100/$1,870

Silver bowl, designed by Charles Boyton. Hallmarks for 1930, 32cm (12½in) diameter, £300/$510

Vellum and chromed metal standard up-lighter lamp. *c.*1935, 173cm (68in) high, £2,000/$3,400

Glass

The market for decorative glass during the 1920s and 1930s was dominated by the French and, in particular, the Lalique glassworks. Lalique's 12m- (40ft-) high illuminated glass fountain was recognized as the focal exhibit of the 1925 Paris Exhibition and his legacy continues to this day. In contrast, the work of Maurice Marinot is that of a studio glass-maker who explored the sculptural possibilities of the medium and whose output was tiny in comparison with Lalique.

The factory run by the Daum family in Nancy, France, had successfully made the transition from Art Nouveau to Art Deco. Their output included an exciting range of decorative vases, dishes, table lamps, and ceiling lights that were

patterned using acid-cut techniques to achieve a granular textured surface. Cameo glass continued to be made by the firm of Schneider, using formalized floral designs. The popularity of *pâte-de-verre* vases and figures by Argy-Rousseau, which were made by casting ground-glass paste in a mould, and the enamelled work of Marcel Goupy also contributed to the variety available at the marketplace.

In the United States, the Steuben glassworks produced a range of distinctly Art Deco wares designed by Sidney Waugh and Walter Dorwin Teague. Meanwhile, the Consolidated Lamp and Glass Company introduced its stylish multifaceted "Ruba Rhombic" range.

Daum dark turquoise blue-etched glass vase. *c.*1930, 18.5cm (7¼in) high, £500/$850

Almeric Walter *pâte-de-verre* dish, modelled with a chameleon. *c.*1920, 26cm (10¼in) long, £4,500/$7,650

Degue mottled glass and wrought iron three-light chandelier. *c.*1925, 71cm (28in) high, £800/$1,360

Dark green glass lampbase, with a deer hunt in the manner of William Hunt Diederich. *c.*1930, 48cm (19in) high, £1,000/$1,700

Le Verre Français globular-shaped, acid-cut overlay vase. c.1925, 26.5cm (10½in) high, £650/$1,105

Monart ginger jar and cover. c.1930, 20cm (7⅞in) high, £250/$425

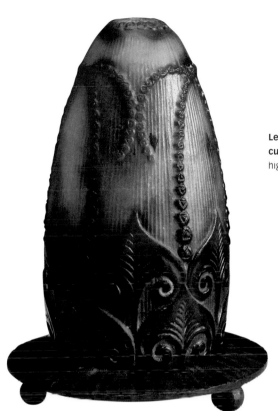

Gabriel Argy-Rousseau *pâte-de-verre* and wrought iron nightlight. c.1925, 15cm (5⅞in) high, £2,900/$4,900

Gabriel Argy-Rousseau *pâte-de-verre* vase, decorated with maidens' heads. c.1925, 18.5cm (7¼in) high, £10,000/$17,000

Le Verre Français acid-cut overlay vase. c.1925, 41.5cm (16⅜in) high, £500/$850

Lalique

Lalique frosted, polished, and stained "Aigrettes" glass vase. Introduced 1926, 25cm (9⅞in) high, £4,300/$7,300

Lalique green glass "Amphitrite" perfume bottle. Introduced 1920, 9.5cm (3¾in) high, £2,300/$3,900

Lalique blue "Phalenes" dish, banded with butterflies. Introduced 1931, 39cm (15⅜in) diameter, £2,000/$3,400

Lalique

Lalique table lamp

This Lalique "Bague Figurines" glass table lamp is moulded, frosted, and charcoal stained. It provided ambient light and was available with a choice of three collars, or *bagues*, modelled with a serpent, leaf, or figural nude females. *Introduced 1922, 46.5 cm (18½in) high, £8,000/$13,600*

The lamp displays an organic influence and a uniform frosted surface.

The low-relief figural detail of nude females is highlighted with a charcoal stain, which wears with excessive handling and cleaning.

The moulded glass form sometimes retains subtle mould lines and the foot rim is ground and polished.

The lamp is engraved on the underside of the base R. Lalique France.

Lalique frosted "Source de la Fontaine – Doris" figure, holding a fish. Introduced 1924, 63cm (24½in) high, £7,000/$11,900

Lalique topaz two-handled "Margaret" vase. Introduced 1929, 23cm (9in) high, £2,000/$3,400

Lalique black "Oeuvres de Lalique" display plaque. Introduced 1931, 16.5cm x 15cm (6½in x 6in), £8,000/$13,600

Lalique clear "Deux Anneaux Scarabees" vase, with frosted and moulded handles. Introduced 1919, 33cm (13in) high, £8,200/$13,950

Lalique amber and white stained "Penthievre" vase, with the Angel Fish pattern. Introduced 1928, 25.5cm (10in) high, £6,800/$11,600

Lalique pale amethyst, frosted, and sepia stained "Bacchantes" vase, with bronze base. Introduced 1927, 28cm (11in) high, £6,000/$10,200

Lalique opalescent "Deux Colombes" clock case. Introduced 1926, 22cm (8⅝in) high, £2,800/$4,750

Lalique clear and black enamelled "Tourbillons" vase, with bronze base. Introduced 1926, 23cm (9in) high, £22,000/$37,400

Lalique amber-toned "Vers le Jour" perfume bottle, for Worth. Introduced 1926, 11cm (4¼in) high, £800/$1,360

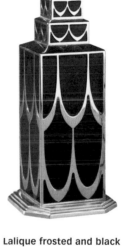

Lalique frosted and black enamelled perfume bottle, with black enamelled and chrome presentation case, for Lucien Lelong. Introduced 1929, 11.5cm (4½in) high, £3,000/$5,100

Lalique clear and frosted "Victoire"/"Spirit of Wind" car mascot. Introduced 1928, 25.5cm (10in) long, £6,000/$10,200

Lalique clear and grey stained "Grande Ovale Tête Penchée" figural plaque. Introduced 1919, 28cm (11in) high, £6,500/$11,000

Lalique deep amber "Serpent" vase. Introduced 1924, 26cm (10¼in) high, £12,500/$21,250

Ceramics

In France, the potters at the national factory at Sèvres were able to call upon the services of eminent designers such as Jacques-Émile Ruhlmann and André Rapin. Competition came from René Buthaud and Primavera, while the Belgian factory of Boch Frères found success with the bright and heavily enamelled designs of Charles Catteau.

In Austria, pottery figurines produced by Goldscheider reflected the glamorous and often theatrical costume of the era. The Italian response came courtesy of the Lenci pottery of Turin, who made finely detailed figural groups that give an insight into the fashions, attitudes, and humour of the 1930s.

In the United States, the Cowan pottery, with their Jazz bowl decorated with silhouettes of the Manhattan skyline, epitomized the vibrancy of the New World potters, many of whom produced equally stylistic wares.

Britain was slow to accept the shock of the new angularity but warmed to the bright "modern" geometry offered by Clarice Cliff, and the more subtle palette and streamline contours of Susie Cooper. The clean colours and inventive patterns used by the Poole pottery and the simple modernity of Keith Murray, designing for Wedgwood, are considered by some to be the "Best of British" ceramic design for the period.

Minton *pâte-sur-pâte* vase, with male athletes, designed by John Wadsworth. *c.*1940, 9.5cm (3¾in) high, £250/$425

Wedgwood "Moonstone" glazed vase, designed by Keith Murray. *c.*1935, 28cm (11in) high, £250/$425

Carlton Ware "Rouge Royale" coffee set. *c.*1930, size unavailable, £260/$440

Carlton Ware vase, enamelled and lustred with the "Carp" pattern. *c.*1930, 21cm (8¼in) high, £950/$1,615

Crown Ducal pottery charger, designed by Charlotte Rhead, *c.*1935, 32.5cm (12¾in) high, £250/$425

Crown Devon Oriental-shaped jar and cover. *c.*1930, 43cm (17in) high, £3,500/$5,950

Poole pottery vase, designed by Truda Carter. *c.*1930, 32cm (12⅝in) high, £8,000/$13,600

Ashstead pottery jar and cover, made for the British Empire Exhibition. *c.*1924, 10cm (4in) high, £800/$1,360

Poole pottery charger, with "The Leipzig Girl", painted by Margaret Holder. *c.*1927, 45cm (17¾in) high, £6,000/$10,200

Beswick pottery wall plaque. 1936–40, 31cm (12¼in) high, £400/$680

Susie Cooper console-shaped pottery vase. *c.*1931, 15cm (5⅞in) high, £8,000/$13,600

Clarice Cliff "Idyll" pattern charger, *c.*1930, 34cm (13⅓in) diameter, £950/$1,615

Clarice Cliff conical-shaped coffee set, decorated in the "Applique, Blue Lugano" pattern. *c.*1930, coffeepot 17cm (6¾in) high, £4,600/$7,800

Clarice Cliff pottery vase, shape No. 37, decorated in the "Sunray/Night and Day" pattern (with hairline crack). *c.*1930, 38.5cm (15in) high, £1,150/$1,950

Ceramics

A.J. Wilkinson figural lamp base, designed by Laura Knight for the Circus series. *c*.1934, 48.5cm (19in) high, £12,000/$20,400

Clarice Cliff Age of Jazz figural plaque, modelled as two pairs of ballroom dancers. *c*.1930, 21cm (8¼in) high, £12,500/$21,250

Lenci pottery figural group, modelled as a pair of student sweethearts sitting upon a bench. *c*.1930, 19.5cm (7⅝in) high, £2,200/$3,750

Two Essevi pottery figures of bathing belles, with respective pale and tanned skin, modelled by Sandro Vacchetti. *c*.1930, 32cm (12⅝in) long, £2,600/$4,400 and £4,500/$7,650

Lenci pottery figure of a female skier. *c*.1930, 43cm (17in) high, £1,600/$2,700

Lenci figural dish, with a naked girl seated upon a fish. *c*.1930, 45cm, (17¾in) high, £3,000/$5,100

Primavera stoneware vase, decorated with deer among stylized foliage. *c*.1925, 15.25cm (10in) high, £500/$850

Gustavsberg Argenta pottery vase and cover, designed by Wilhelm Kage. *c*.1940, 28cm (11in) high, £400/$680

Pair of Boch Frères pottery vases, with grazing deer, designed by Charles Catteau. *c*.1925, 40cm (15¾in) high, £1,200/$2,050

Goldscheider figure

This pottery figure of the Fan Dancer, after a model by Paul Dakon, is part of a huge range, made in varying sizes, of female subjects modelled by freelance sculptors, including Josef Lorenzl. They epitomize the Art Deco style.

c.1925, 45cm (17¾in) high, £1,600/$2,700

The risqué subject matter alludes to fan dancing, usually with a pair of large Ostrich feather fans, which was popular during the 1920s and 1930s.

This example has retained its original silvered paper retail label, which adds to its desirability and value.

The figures are usually supported on a low panel form, or domed bases of elliptical sections, covered in a black glaze.

The sculptor's signature is usually stamped onto the underside of the base beside the pottery trademark.

Stylized pottery cat, with raised paw, modelled by Louis Wain. *c.*1925, 13cm (3in) high, £3,000/$5,100

Goldscheider terracotta wall mask, of a stylish woman with mask. *c.*1930, 28cm (11in) high, £1,200/$2,050

Goldscheider pottery figural lamp, fitted with three lights. *c.*1925, 38.5cm (15⅛in) high, £700/$1,190

Pair of Royal Dux figural book ends. *c.*1925, 23cm (9in) high, £260/$440

Stylized pottery cat, modelled by Louis Wain. *c.*1920, 14cm (5½in) high, £1,800/$3,050

Sculpture

The sculpture of the Art Deco period constantly mirrored the fashions and attitudes of the age. Gone were the simpering fairy maidens emblematic of the Art Nouveau years, supplanted by strong and athletic Amazons that signalled the arrival of the emancipated woman – with the right to vote. This new "modern" woman became the favoured subject of most commercial sculptors, who gravitated to the salons and galleries of Paris, Berlin, and Vienna.

The novelty of incorporating bronze with carved ivory heads and limbs was popularized by many sculptors, including Ferdinand Preiss, C.J.R. Colinet, Dimitri (later Demetre) Chiparus, Josef Lorenzl, and Bruno Zach. Preiss is considered the master of anatomical perfection that touches upon the German pursuit of athletic idealism, while Chiparus provided the most futuristic attired dancers in tight-fitting cat suits or razor-pleated ankle length skirts. Colinet could be relied on to bring a strong theatrical element into her exotic range of dancers of the world, and Josef Lorenzl showed a tendency toward lean and extremely "leggy" dancers, often modelled on single tiptoe. The repertoire of Bruno Zach concentrated on the quasi-erotic, Zach preferring to attire his assertive females in leather suits or scant lingerie.

Bronze Offering figure, cast after a model by Pierre Laurel. *c.*1925, 28cm (11in) high, £1,800/$3,050

Bronze and ivory Dourga figure, cast after a model by Demetre Chiparus. *c.*1925, 63cm (24¾in) high, £14,000/$23,800

Bronze and ivory Invocation figure, cast after a model by Ferdinand Preiss. *c.*1925, 36cm (14⅛in) high, £9,000/$15,300

Bronze and ivory The Leather Suit figure, cast after a model by Bruno Zach. *c.*1925, 73.5cm (29in) high, £13,000/$22,100

Bronze and ivory Bather with Cap figure, cast after a model by Ferdinand Preiss. *c.*1930, 25.5cm (10in) high, £11,000/$18,700

Bronze and ivory Fan Dancer figure, cast after a model by Demetre Chiparus. *c.*1925, 39cm (15¼in) high, £14,000/$23,800

Antinea, a carved ivory bronze figure

This carved ivory, silvered, and cold-painted bronze figure of an exotic young woman is typical of the work of Romanian-born Dimitri Chiparus, especially the choice of costume. The majority of his female subjects are given dramatic postures and are attired in futuristic and exotic clothes. He had a preference for skin-tight bodysuits, pleated skirts, and streamlined headgear. This example is one of his largest and most powerful creations.

c.1930, 67cm (26½in) high, £34,000/$57,800

The quality of the patinated bronze casting should always be crisp and well defined.

The quality of the carving should be the best and should include fine details such as fingernails.

Examination of the ivory should reveal a subtle, slightly irregular grain.

Where it has been difficult to include the sculptor's signature on the bronze figure, it is often inscribed onto the top or back of the marble base.

The composite panelled base features a sunburst design picked out in colourful marble and onyx, a favourite motif among Art Deco designers.

Bronze and ivory Cabaret Girl figure, cast after a model by Ferdinand Preiss. *c.*1925, 39cm (15⅜in) high, £3,900/$6,600

Bronze and ivory The Torch Dancer figure, cast after a model by Ferdinand Preiss. *c.*1930, 41.25cm (16¼in) high, £7,800/$13,250

Bronze and ivory The Stile figure, cast after a model by Ferdinand Preiss. *c.*1930, 25cm (9⅞in) high, £8,000/$13,600

Furniture

The changing lifestyle that followed World War I resulted in a demand for new types of furniture such as cocktail cabinets and coffee tables. Mass-production techniques made possible by technological developments were introduced to cope with these growing demands. At the same time designers began to experiment with new materials, including stainless and tubular steel, plate glass, and laminated plywood.

French designers such as Jacques-Émile Ruhlmann worked in a traditional and opulent style that borrowed from the best of the 18th and 19th centuries to create expensive furnishings for the French elite. Ruhlmann's work exhibits a preference for highly grained exotic timber. Other top French cabinet-makers include Jules Leleu and the Swiss-born Jean Dunand, who revived the painstaking craft

of decorative lacquerwork to great acclaim at the 1925 Paris Exhibition. The partnership of Süe et Mare, which was established by two French designers, resulted in the production of large-scale Art Deco furniture inlaid with colourful marquetry and mother-of-pearl.

In Germany and Finland, the possibilities of laminated plywood furniture were developed into the furniture designs of Marcel Breuer, who was working at the Bauhaus (an influential 20th-century design school), and Alvar Aalto, who established the Finmar Company in 1935 to distribute his streamline laminated furniture in Britain. Their work was generally devoid of decoration. The designer Betty Joel also produced furniture in simple forms, using pale wood, which found a following among British buyers seeking modern design allied to traditional craftsmanship.

Token Works sycamore dressing table and stool, and matching bedside cabinet, designed by Betty Joel. *c*.1932, 110cm (43in) and 100cm (39in) high, £1,600/$2,700 and £150/$255

Isokon long chair, designed by Marcel Breuer. *c*.1935, 148cm (58in) long, £3,600/$6,100

Ebonized side table with glass top. *c*.1930, 58.5cm (23in) high, £600/$1,020

Bird's-eye maple wardrobe, with drawers, by Chanaux and Co. *c*.1925, 169cm (66½in) high, £5,400/$9,200

Carved giltwood three-piece salon suite, attributed to Paul Follot. *c*.1930, settee 152cm (60in) long, £7,200/$12,250

Ivory-mounted mahogany armchair

Furniture designed by Jacques-Émile Ruhlmann such as this chair (one of a pair) displays a fusion of elegant forms, which often echoes the lines in 18th- and early 19th-century French furniture. *c.1922, 80cm (31½in) high, £36,000/$61,200*

This chair has been sympathetically re-covered and the high-gloss polished surface evident on original Art Deco furniture has been restored.

The front seat rail is canted and not bowed.

The shapes of both the front and out-swept back legs are refinements that typify Ruhlmann's lightweight, feminine style.

The small ball finials were optional motifs. However, the ivory feet, or sabot, are recurring features in Ruhlmann's furniture.

Ruhlmann's highly distinctive signature has been branded on the underside of the chair; it is often hidden when a piece is re-upholstered.

Fruitwood upholstered three-piece salon suite, with carved details, designed by Maurice Dufrene. *c.*1920, settee 136cm (53½in) long, £8,000/$13,600

Mirrored-glass and lacquered-wood nest of three tables, designed by Paul Dupré-Lafon. *c.*1935, 44cm (17⅜in) high, £7,000/$11,900

Post-war Design

1

2

3

4

1 Finn Juhl 45 settee, *c*.1945
2 Monart "Paisley Shawl" glass vase, *c*.1935
3 Scandia dining chair, designed by Hans Brattrud, *c*.1958
4 Isokon Penguin Donkey bookcase, designed by Egon Riss and Jack Pritchard, *c*.1938

Once again, after the devastation and deprivation created by war – this time World War II – Britain and the Continent set out on the road to a new, brighter tomorrow. It was this sense of optimism that prompted the emergence of the "New Look", which was encapsulated in the yards of, hitherto scarce, fabric consumed in the gowns and skirts unveiled to the world in 1947 by the celebrated dress designer Christian Dior.

The 1950s was a dynamic time, when architects and designers – their creative output on hold since 1939 – set out to reshape society and carry it into the second half of the 20th century. Cities had to be rebuilt, so in many senses they were blank canvases waiting to be painted. Materials that had previously been associated with industry such as aluminium, plastics, and fibreglass were used to make furniture and many basic domestic items designed for the home. Ornamentation no

longer reflected the historical styles of the past but was deliberately simple.

It was the Scandinavian and Italian designers who offered the greatest influences, using fluid lines, clean forms, and a new appreciation and use of colour. The Scandinavian approach to furniture design was based on the use of simplified organic forms complemented by textured fabrics, with a bias toward a neutral palette.

The designs offered by the Finnish architect-designer Alvar Aalto – who preferred an organic approach to his work, using laminated plywood instead of tubular steel – had a huge influence on a number of young American designers, including Charles Eames and Finnish-born Eero Saarinen, both of whom used plywood in the construction of their chairs. The American architect and designer George Nelson produced a book, *Tomorrow's House*, which became a bible for contemporary

5   **6**   **7**   **8**

5 Dale Chihuly blue Venetian glass vase, *c.*1991
6 Troika pottery rectangular-shaped vase, *c.*1970
7 Butterfly chair, designed by Jorge Haroy, Antonio Bonet, and Juan Kurchan, *c.*1940
8 Wedgwood bone china coffeepot, designed by Susie Cooper, *c.*1970

living. It showed how entire living environments could be created out of the latest ideas.

In Britain, the "Britain Can Make It" exhibition of 1946 paved the way for the Festival of Britain in 1951, where the concept of light, colour, space, and ease of living with open plan interiors was displayed for the first time. This concept began the transformation of the way people thought about their homes. The space race and atomic age had also begun, and both had an influence on design.

The Swinging Sixties and onward

The burgeoning youth culture of the 1950s was firmly in place by the 1960s. The music scene had a huge influence and touched every stratum of society, including those at the cutting edge of design, who used colourful pop art, psychedelia, and the various materials and advanced production techniques available to shape the taste of consumers. And the centre of this fashionable universe was Swinging London.

With the arrival of the 1970s came the stark reality of the energy crisis, increased social unrest, and union confrontation with the government of the day. The Italian design group of Studio Alchimia came into being in 1976, producing furniture with a laminated plastic surface; however, such was its expense that it never became mainstream. The same can be said for the offbeat designs that emanated from the Italian Memphis design group, founded in 1981, which has achieved iconic status in recent years, especially through the work of Ettore Sottsass Jr.

The post-war decades still offer a wealth of collecting opportunities to the new or would-be collector, although prices have escalated for classic 1950s, 1960s, and 1970s design.

Furniture

The beginnings of modern furniture go back to the 19th century, with developments in industrialization and the bentwood furniture of the German Thonet brothers. Further inspiration was provided by the Germans Marcel Breuer, whose 1920s' tubular-steel designs are still made today, and Ludwig Mies van der Rohe, who coined the term "less is more".

After 1945, the advances in technology that applied to laminated wood and plastics provided designers with wider horizons. The clean lines of Scandinavian furniture had the advantage of being both radical and modern. The Danes led the way, courtesy of such designers as Hans Wegner and Arne Jacobsen, both of whom combined traditional materials with elegant form and ergonomic considerations.

In the United States, the husband and wife collaboration of Charles and Ray Eames designed laminated and fibreglass seating. In Britain, Robin and Lucienne Day and Ernest Race gained recognition as the most influential furniture designers. By the 1960s, the firms of G-Plan and Ercol found wide appeal with their Danish-inspired designs using teak and mahogany frames. Terence Conran opened the first Habitat shop in 1964, providing well-designed furniture at affordable prices.

In the 1970s and 1980s the Italian design studios of Alchimia and the Memphis group produced furniture that challenged traditional design but at prices that made their efforts elitist. In recent decades, Habitat and IKEA have provided good design for the masses, but their collectability remains to be seen.

American fibreglass and tubular steel Shell chair, designed by Charles and Ray Eames, manufactured by Zenith Plastics and Herman Miller. *c.*1955, size unavailable, £400/$680

American walnut coffee table, designed by Sam Maloof. *c.*1965, 153cm (60in) long, £4,500/$7,650

American upholstered easy chair and ottoman, designed by Warren Platner, manufactured by Knoll. *c.*1966, 99cm (39in) high, £950/$1,615

American lounge chair and ottoman, by Charles and Ray Eames, manufactured by Herman Miller. *c.*1960, size unavailable, £2,250/$3,825

Pair of American walnut spindle-back chairs, designed by Sam Maloof. *c.*1965, 94cm (37in) high, £4,400/$7,500

Danish fibreglass and upholstered Egg chair, designed by Arne Jacobsen, manufactured by Fritz Hansen. *c.*1965, size unavailable, £750/$1,275

Italian fibreglass and upholstered-leather Elda lounge chair, designed by Joe Colombo. *c.*1966, size unavailable, £1,000/$1,700

Danish steel and rope Flag Halyard chair, designed by Hans Wegner and manufactured by Getama. *c.*1950, 81cm (31¾in) high, £1,300/$2,200

Oak dining table and dining chairs

Frank Lloyd Wright designed this oak dining table with a set of eight upholstered dining chairs, which were commissioned by Benjamin Adelman for his residence in Phoenix, Arizona. This suite was designed in Wright's later years, yet it still manages to encapsulate his ability to remain inventive and contemporary – whatever the decade. *c.1951, table 244cm (96in) long, £30,000/$51,000*

The chairs are of a solid construction reminiscent of Wright's formative years with the Prairie School.

The cushions are covered with a fabric in a contemporary abstract pattern.

The construction of the chairs incorporates a central upright panel support.

The table has splayed "V"-shaped upright panel supports at each end.

The backrest panels are pierced with a geometrical design that adds to the inherent sculptural property of each chair.

American birch buffet, designed by Eliel Saarinen, manufactured by Johnson Furniture Co. *c.*1950, 183cm (72in) long, £640/$1,090

American rosewood and chromed steel dining table, designed by Florence Knoll for Knoll. *c.*1965, 244cm (96in) long, £1,200/$2,050

Upholstered plywood and steel frame Corona chair, designed by Paul Volther, manufactured by Erik Jorgensen. *c.*1965, 94cm (37in) high, £1,300/$2,200

Ceramics

The mass-produced ceramics of the post-war years mirrored an era of growing affluence, which encouraged a new informality in society and the rediscovery of the art of home entertainment. In Staffordshire, the firms of Midwinter and James Broadhurst and Sons benefited from the talents of freelance and in-house designers that included Jessie Tait, David Queensberry, and Terence Conran, with the name of Kathie Winkle being synonymous with Broadhurst. Wedgwood retailed the modernist ware of Keith Murray and the printed designs of the late Eric Ravilious. Poole pottery provided the 1950s market with its stylish Free-form range

of decorative vases, as well as its streamline tableware. In the early 1960s, the firm introduced its distinctive Delphis range, using a vibrant orange glaze with abstract decoration.

There was a growing appreciation for the work of the craftsman potter, and the St Ives pottery of Bernard Leach is recognized as the most influential. In London, the work of (Dame) Lucie Rie and Hans Coper found no shortage of buyers who appreciated the sculptural quality of their individual pots complemented with adventurous glazes. Studio pottery was provided on a grand scale by the Cornish Troika pottery, which operated from 1963 until 1983.

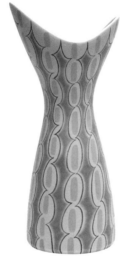

Wedgwood creamware Liverpool-shaped lemonade jug and a pair of matching beakers, decorated with the "Garden Implements" pattern, designed by Eric Ravilious. c.1939, size unavailable, £750/$1,275

Poole pottery Free-form vase (shape 724), with the "Bamboo" pattern, designed by Alfred Read and Guy Sydenham. c.1958, 35.5cm (14in), £300/$510

Troika pottery mask, modelled in low relief with a stylized face. c.1970, 25.5cm (10in) high, £2,500/$4,250

Zsolnay pottery green-lustred glazed figure of a stylized dog. c.1970, 16.5cm (6½in) high, £150/$255

Rosenthal elliptical-shaped Studio Line porcelain vase, with gilt trailed on an irregular grey ground. c.1975, 15cm (5⅞in) high, £80/$135

Poole pottery circular charger, designed by Terry Frost. c.1990–2000, 41cm (16⅛in) diameter, £150/$255

Glass

After 1945, the strongest influence in glass design came from Scandinavia. During the 1940s the architect-designer Alvar Aalto introduced organic shapes. Other Finnish designers, including Tapio Wirkkala and Timo Sarpaneva, continued the trend for smooth streamline designs in subtle colours. The Swedish firms of Orrefors and Kosta offered a wide range of abstract glass, including the work of Sven Palmqvist and Vicke Lindstrand, and in Denmark, Holmegaard made the mass-produced blue and smoky grey vases of Per Lutken.

With the advent of the 1960s, Venetian glass regained popularity, with firms such as Venini, Vistosi, Salviatti and Barovier, and Tosa providing asymmetrical forms in strong colours. The Venini Co. employed the innovative designer Fulvio Bianconi, whose Handkerchief vase was adapted and mass-produced worldwide. Several Venetian and other glass-makers used the *sommerso* technique, where two or more translucent colours are sandwiched into slender, smooth forms.

In mid-1960s Britain, the Whitefriars glassworks introduced a colourful range of textured abstract shapes designed by Geoffrey Baxter. His most distinctive works are the Drunken Bricklayer and Bark vases. In recent years, the large-scale work of the American glass-maker Dale Chihuly, who uses blown tubes and double-bubble shapes, has enjoyed international fame.

Venini *Fazzoletto* (Handkerchief) vase, with white latticino canes, designed by Fulvio Bianconi. *c.*1955, 23.5cm (9¼in) high, £500/$850

Whitefriars orange Drunken Bricklayer vase and green Banjo vase, designed by Geoffrey Baxter. Respectively 1967–77 and 1967–73, Bricklayer vase 32.5cm (12¾in) high, £520/$885 and £1,200/$2,050

Seguso two-handled red glass vase, with internal white spiral canes and clear handles spiralled in cobalt. *c.*1955, 36cm (14⅛in) high, £2,000/$3,400

Two Seguso *sommerso* glass ewers, the red and clear ewer with a foot, designed by Flavio Poli. *c.*1965, red and clear ewer 30cm (11⅛in) high, £300/$510 and £250/$425

Fucina Degli Angeli black glass vase, with intaglio carved and enamelled circus characters, designed by Jean Cocteau. *c.*1965, 19cm (7½in) high, £2,000/$3,400

Orrefors Graal "Aquarium" vase, designed by Edvard Hald. *c.*1957, 14cm (5½in) high, £300/$510

Teddy Bears, Dolls, and Toys

1

2

3

4

1 German teddy bear, by Bing, *c*.1907
2 French C.I.J. P2 Alfa Romeo tinplate racing car, *c*.1928
3 German all-bisque doll, by Kestner, *c*.1910
4 German painted wooden Noah's Ark with animals, *c*.1890

Of all the collecting areas open to the enthusiast, the teddy bear, doll, and toy market is unquestionably the most poignant. There are no end of antiques and collectables that manage to thrill, but only toys, dolls, and teddies have the magic to actually make you smile.

Teddies and dolls

Who would have dreamed 25 years ago that the major auction houses would devote sales entirely to teddy bears, attracting buyers from all over the world, prepared to part with huge sums of money for a coveted Steiff bear? The best bisque dolls also sell for heart-stopping sums these days, on a level with the best porcelain, silver, and furniture.

Originally, in 17th-century Europe, doll sellers plied their humble dolls from markets or put them on trays and sold them on the street. In the 18th century, the carved wooden dolls became highly prized, and they began to be produced and attired in the latest fashion. Since then wood, papier-mâché, and bisque dolls have been an established part of the marketplace, and collectors have now turned their attention to dolls made during the second half of the 20th century, including Barbie, Sasha, and other thoroughly modern misses.

The new nostaglia for toys

Children have always valued their toys, but as playthings and companions to be loved, abused, and discarded, according to mood and whim. It is adults who have elevated them to the display cabinet. The interest in old toys began roughly 60 years ago, but dedicated collectors were few, motivated by a love of the craftsmanship, enjoying the best of German tinplate toy production, or the

5 6 7 8

5 German black bisque-head character "squeeze toy", c.1910
6 British ¾in-scale Burrell traction engine, by Bassett-Lowke, c.1950
7 Pair of British Mickey and Minnie Mouse soft toy figures, c.1930
8 British Tri-ang Magic saloon car, c.1935

detail of trains scaled down from the noisy, hissing monsters that had enthralled them as children. They met to swap and share their pieces with little thought for commercial gain.

In the 1970s, a general fascination with the past and a passion for collecting began. Soon, toy departments were established in the major auction houses and top examples escalated in price.

Where to begin

It may have become a serious business, but collecting teddy bears, dolls, and toys is still a lot of fun. Some of the most established areas are difficult for the novice collector to enter because prices are high, but there is plenty of scope, even among pieces that are well over 100 years old.

Always buy the best example that you can afford and buy only what you like – values can go down as well as up so make sure you'll enjoy it. Sit in on one or two general toy sales at an auction before you begin to buy and keep notes of the prices paid. It is one of the best ways to get a feel for this volatile and constantly changing field.

You can concentrate on more modern toys, perhaps objects that remind you of the magic moments during your own childhood, or items that are currently being produced and are not yet appreciated. It really is a case of following your own instincts while not totally letting go of the child within. This is a collecting area dominated not only by the appeal of the inherent nostalgia of a bygone age, but equally by the pursuit of the unwrapped and unused toy. Such a toy qualifies as being "mint and boxed" and is sadly destined to be nothing more than a collector's prize.

Bears: Where to begin

A bear is more than the sum of its parts, but scrutinizing the parts is a good way to ascertain the date, country of origin, authenticity, condition, and even manufacturer. First, look at the fabric. Original old bears (pre-1930) are usually made of wool mohair. After 1930, new materials were introduced such as cotton and silk plush, and later in the 1950s, nylon and other synthetic fabrics. Next, try to determine what stuffing has been used. You can do this by assessing the bear's weight. If it is light, it is probably stuffed with kapok, a type of silky fibre from the seeds of a tropical tree, possibly mixed with wood wool, or excelsior, wood shavings used for packing. Heavier bears that are crunchy to the touch are probably stuffed with wood wool. After about 1940 new, lighter synthetic stuffing materials were used, and later on, lightweight foam.

The next areas of scrutiny are the ears, eyes, and nose. The ears should be correctly positioned. You'll only know for certain if they are correct by comparing them to similar bears or pictures of similar bears that you know to be genuine. Check the bear's head for signs of where different ears might once have been stitched,

in which case, the present ones are replacements. The eyes should also be scrutinized. If the bear was made before 1914, it should have boot-button eyes (black wooden eyes with metal loops on the back). However, during the 1920s, glass eyes became the norm, and plastic was sometimes used from the 1950s. Look closely at the nose stitching because this is a good way to identify a bear's maker. Each company tended to have its own distinctive type of stitching. Most noses were made of silk thread; black wool noses are probably replacements. Keep in mind that replacement ears, eyes, or nose do not make a bear unbuyable (or unsaleable), but any alterations should be reflected in the price.

Another area requiring attention is the paw pads. If these are original on earlier bears they will be of felt, or perhaps cotton; bears made in the 1940s and later may have plush or leather pads; ultrasuede has been used from the 1970s. Again, pads are often replaced and as long as they are sympathetic to the originals, they should not detract too much from the value.

You may also find more concrete evidence of the maker, and possibly even the date, on a label. These may be embroidered tags attached to the fur, or metal tags, usually on the ear or arm. Some bears, especially early ones, had no tags at all or only flimsy paper ones that have long parted from the bear. Always check that the bear itself seems consistent with the maker whose name appears on any label – the label may have been added at a later date.

Condition is important to price. If the bear is dressed, always look under the clothes to make sure they are not concealing any defects. Never attempt any restoration yourself, but instead seek specialist advice to ensure that the bear is restored in materials and details sympathetic to the original. If you do decide to have a bear restored, remember that the work may change its character.

Caring for a teddy bear

The simplest and most effective areas of professional restoration include restuffing and replacement pads or eyes, or nose restitching. However, you can clean your bear yourself. Start by brushing or vacuuming it (with the nozzle covered) in order to remove any bugs or dust. Then, using a small brush, apply a solution of very mild detergent for wool and cool water to the fur. Use as little solution as possible, being careful not to saturate the fur. Remove the foam with a dry cloth; you may also need to use a damp cloth afterward. Rinse the cloth in water and keep dabbing the fur until you have removed all the soap. Finally, allow it to dry naturally before combing the fur with a fine metal comb.

German teddy bear and British Chiltern "Tingaling" teddy bear, the former attributed to Herman, *c.*1935; the latter, *c.*1953

Teddy Bears

The United States lays claim to be the birthplace of the teddy bear after one was reputedly made by Morris Michtom to commemorate the incident in 1902 when Teddy Roosevelt declined to shoot a bear on a hunting trip. Important American makers include Michtom's Ideal Toy and Novelty Co., Gund, Knickerbocker, Bruin, Aetna, and the Character Toy Co.

German bears are made to a high standard and Germany is home to the most famous bear maker of all, Margarete Steiff, who produced jointed bears from 1902. Steiff bears have their trademark on a button in the ear. Other well-known German makers include Bing, who made mechanical bears, and Schuco, who made miniatures and novelties.

When teddy bear mania arrived in Britain, existing toy manufacturers began to produce their own versions, and the banning of German imports with the beginning of World War I led to an increase in the number of British makers. These include Chad Valley, Chiltern, Farnell, and Deans. After the World War II, British bears became plumper with short legs and a fat face, and synthetic fibres replaced Yorkshire mohair plush.

Although the teddy bear is a relative newcomer, its popularity has never waned and collectors today can pay serious money for an early and rare model when offered in good condition.

German Bears

Steiff teddy bear, with apricot mohair, five black stitched claws, and a cone-shaped nose. *c.*1905, 71cm (28in) high, £10,000/$17,000

Steiff teddy bear, with white mohair and a blank button to left ear. *c.*1905–07, 24cm (9½in) high, £1,700/$2,900

Steiff teddy bear, with golden brown mohair (with re-covered paw pads and wear to legs). *c.*1909, 58.5cm (23in) high, £1,800/$3,050

Steiff teddy bear, with light brown mohair (slight wear and some bald patches). *c.*1909, 64cm (25in) high, £3,400/$5,800

Steiff teddy bear, with cinnamon mohair, wearing a green velvet smoking jacket (some wear and paw pads re-covered in leather). *c.*1909, 41cm (16⅛in) high, £450/$765

German Bears

Bing mechanical Walking teddy bear.
c.1910, 28cm (11in) high, £1,000/$1,700

Bing Hanging Somersault teddy bear.
c.1910, 33cm (13in) high, £1,600/$2,700

Steiff teddy bear, with black mohair (upper paw pads re-covered and hole to nose). c.1912, 33cm (13in) high, £7,500/$12,750

Steiff teddy bear

This early Steiff teddy bear has a letter of provenance, explaining its ownership, along with a photograph of the bear with its original owner. The chocolate brown mohair is almost like new, with no trace of the wear associated with bears of this vintage. The bear's provenance and condition increases its value.
c.1909, 33cm (13in),
£4,200/$7,150

The ears are small, cupped, and set wide apart, suggesting that this is an early bear.

This bear's eyes are of boot-button type, a pre-World War I feature.

The left ear is fitted with a small white metal button embossed "Steiff".

The nose displays horizontal stitching joined below by an upturned Y-shaped mouth.

The paws feature four black stitched claws; earlier examples dating from 1905 feature five claws.

Bing teddy bear, with golden brown mohair and glass eyes. c.1925, 46cm (18in) high, £600/$1,020

Schuco Yes-No teddy bear, with movable head, bright gold mohair, and round feet with rayon pads. c.1920, 28cm (11in) high, £400/$680

Steiff Dickie bear, with chocolate brown mohair. *c.*1935, 32cm (12⅝in) high, £500/$850

Steiff Original teddy bear, with light brown mohair. *c.*1950, 70cm (27½in) high, £1,200/$2,050

Steiff Original teddy bear, with faded brown mohair. *c.*1952, 64cm (25in) high, £1,200/$2,050

British Bears

J.K. Farnell teddy bear, with bright gold mohair and glass eyes. *c.*1920, 41cm (16⅛in) high, £1,300/$2,200

J.K. Farnell teddy bear, with beige mohair with amber glass eyes. *c.*1920, 46cm (18in) high, £950/$1,615

Deans Rag Book Co. teddy bear, with pink mohair and silvered metal button in left ear (faded from the original bright pink). *c.*1930, 30cm (11⅞in) high, £500/$850

Teddy purse, with light brown mohair, boot-button eyes, swivel head, and stands on all fours. *c.*1925, 18cm (7in) long, £420/$715

J.K. Farnell teddy bear, with light brown mohair and glass eyes (eyes broken; lower paw pads re-covered). *c.*1920, 59cm (23in) high, £1,900/$3,250

British Bears

Chiltern Hugmee teddy bear, with golden mohair and orange glass eyes. *c.*1930, 69cm (27in) high, £480/$815

Chiltern Hugmee teddy bear, with golden mohair and amber glass eyes. *c.*1930, 66cm (26in) high, £800/$1,360

Chiltern teddy bear, with golden mohair and clear glass eyes. *c.*1930, 53cm (21in) high, £500/$850

J.K. Farnell teddy bear

This J.K Farnell Alpha teddy bear has white mohair and dark amber glass eyes. It has been suggested that the model for Winnie the Pooh was based upon the Alpha bear, which was first marketed in the early 1920s. John Kirby Farnell established a soft toy company, which upon his death in 1897 was carried on by his son and daughter, Henry and Agnes Farnell. By the end of the 1930s, the company had expanded and had showrooms in London, Paris, and New York. *c.1930, 71cm (28in) high, £2,500/$4,250*

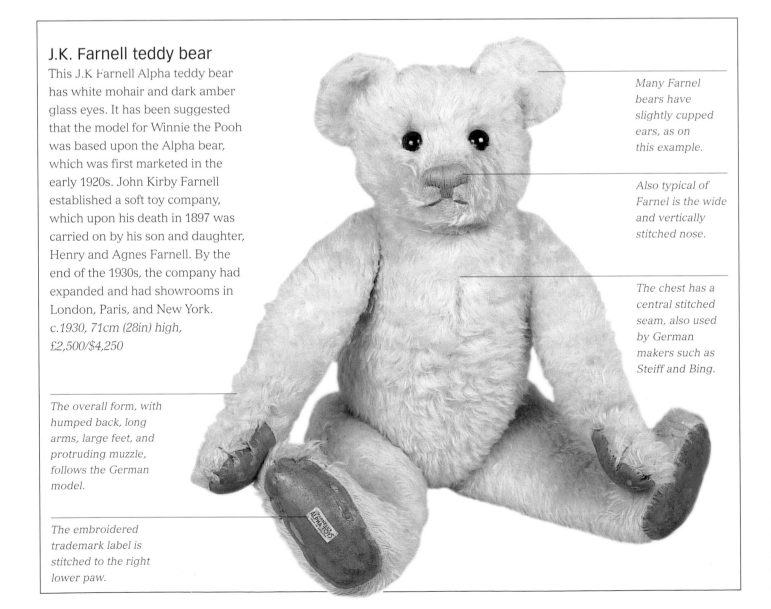

Many Farnel bears have slightly cupped ears, as on this example.

Also typical of Farnel is the wide and vertically stitched nose.

The chest has a central stitched seam, also used by German makers such as Steiff and Bing.

The overall form, with humped back, long arms, large feet, and protruding muzzle, follows the German model.

The embroidered trademark label is stitched to the right lower paw.

Invicta Toys golden teddy bear, with long bright gold mohair and large glass eyes. *c.*1950, 66cm (26in) high, £300/$510

Merrythought Cheeky Bear teddy bear, with golden mohair and orange glass eyes. *c.*1950, 36cm (14⅛in) high, £200/$340

Pedigree teddy bear, with gold mohair and glass eyes. *c.*1950, 46cm (18in) high, £300/$510

American and Other Bears

American Columbia Roosevelt teddy bear, with gold mohair, composition mouth, and glass eyes. *c.*1907, 46cm (18in) high, £2,000/$3,400

American Art Novelty Co. Patriotic teddy bear, with red, white, and blue mohair, collar, and sash. *c.*1908, 41cm (16⅛in) high, £1,500/$2,550

American Knickerbocker teddy bear, with rich brown mohair and typical triangular head with large ears. *c.*1930, 43cm (17in) high, £400/$680

French Fadap teddy bear, with cotton plush fabric. *c.*1930, 58cm (23in) high, £350/$595

Irish Tara Laughing teddy bear, with gold mohair and typical small semicircular ears. *c.*1953, 36cm (14⅛in) high, £150/$255

Australian Barton Waugh teddy bear, with gold mohair and typical square-shaped head. *c.*1953, 41cm (16⅛in) high, £250/$425

Dolls: Where to begin

It is important to gain an understanding of the development of doll-making and the history of fashion before embarking upon building a collection. Early dolls were wooden or partly wooden and unmarked. Large numbers are known to have been made by peasants from the Grödnertal region in Germany, hence these are referred to as Grödnertals. They are usually painted and intricately carved. However, quality deteriorated and dolls made after the early 19th century were more crudely carved.

There are several types of wax dolls' heads or shoulder-heads. In the 17th and 18th centuries, solid wax with carved details was common. In the 19th century, poured wax became more prevalent; these appealing dolls have glass eyes, painted faces, and real hair. Wax-over-composition, a less-expensive type developed in the early 19th century, was common in Britain and Germany.

The best way to date china and parian dolls (both with ceramic heads, but parian dolls' heads, made to imitate marble, were untinted) is to become familiar with the hairstyles of the period, which doll-makers faithfully copied. Fashion dolls, which had bisque heads (an unglazed porcelain that has been fired once, then tinted and fired again), were made mostly in France between *c*.1860 and 1890, with a wardrobe of elaborate and detailed costumes and a body that could be arranged in different poses.

Bisque was first used to make dolls' heads in the late 19th and early 20th centuries, replacing porcelain and china. The French produced huge quantities of high-quality dolls of all types, often depicting young girls, known as bébés, with idealized expressions.

Important French makers include Jumeau, Bru, Gaultier, and Steiner. They reigned until the Germans, especially with their "character" dolls and babies which had lifelike expressions, provided competition. Leading manufacturers include Heubach, Armand Marseille, Simon & Halbig, and Kämmer & Reinhardt.

Many dolls carry mould numbers, and the rarer the number, the more sought after the doll. The quality and degree of facial details also affect the price, as does the colour of the bisque – generally the paler the better. Bisque dolls represent the largest collecting area, the best fetching as much as £100,000/$170,000, but many lovely dolls can still be bought for as little as £100/$170.

Dolls: 20thC

At the beginning of the 20th century, dolls began to be made in a variety of new materials, especially celluloid, composition, and plastic, but they were also produced in fabrics such as stockinet and felt. French and German manufacturers continued to make dolls and adapted to the new media, especially celluloid. Some manufacturers even brought out new versions of dolls in celluloid made in moulds previously used for bisque dolls.

American manufacturers steadily increased in prominence, making dolls in all media. New York was the most important production area, with companies such as E.I. Horsman, the Ideal Novelty & Toy Co. (which made the first ever Shirley Temple doll), and the Acme Toy Co. However, the biggest impact was made with Barbie, probably the most successful selling doll ever, which was introduced in 1959 by the American firm Mattel.

Bisque-head dolls, with four by the German makers Simon & Halbig, Kley, and Hahn & Kestner, all *c*.1910, and a French bisque-head doll by Tete Jumeau, *c*.1895 (second from left)

Dolls

The rarest dolls that you are likely to find are those produced in the 18th century in carved wood covered in a thin layer of gesso (plaster) and with facial details that often include glass eyes, painted rosebud lips, and rouged cheeks. When dressed in their original clothes, early dolls are considered the ultimate acquisition among collectors. However, most people are willing to collect the bisque-head dolls produced in France and Germany during the late 19th and early 20th centuries. The French fashion dolls from the 1870s by makers such as Bru and Jumeau are considered to be the finest ever made, but they must be in their original clothes.

German makers in the Sonnenberg region of Thuringia gave the French doll-makers competition. Probably the best-known maker was Armand Marseille, who despite the name was Russian. His output continued into the early 20th century. The introduction of lifelike "character" dolls brought the German makers huge success, as did the introduction of sleeping eyes in 1914, which close when the doll is horizontal. Flirty eyes also move side to side.

Bisque-head dolls were made until the 1930s, by which time cheaper, less fragile materials such as composition, fabric, celluloid, and plastic became the normal choice.

French Bisque-Head Dolls

Bisque shoulder-head fashion doll, with fixed blue glass eyes, painted smiling mouth, and blonde ringlet wig, attributed to Bru Jeune & Cie. c.1875, 43cm (17in) high, £1,800/$3,050

Jumeau almond-eye bisque-head doll, with brown glass paperweight eyes, closed mouth, pierced ears, and blonde mohair wig. c.1885, 28cm (11in) high, £4,300/$7,300

Jumeau swivel bisque-head fashion doll, with large blue-grey glass eyes, closed mouth, blonde wig, and original clothes. c.1865, 36cm (14⅛in) high, £1,000/$1,700

Tete Jumeau bébé bisque-head doll, with fixed blue glass paperweight eyes, closed mouth, and brown mohair wig. c.1890, 48cm (19in) high, £750/$1,275

Jules Nicolas Steiner bébé bisque-head doll, with fixed blue glass paperweight eyes, open mouth with upper teeth, and blonde mohair wig. c.1890, 56cm (22in) high, £1,200/$2,050

French Bisque-Head Dolls

Jumeau bébé

This portrait bébé bisque-head doll, has fixed blue glass eyes, a closed mouth, and sheepskin wig. It is from the golden age of French bébé production – from 1860 to the late 1890s – and was originally priced for the luxury market. Pierre François Jumeau is known to have produced the first bébé (child doll) in 1855, prior to introducing his series of portrait bébés during the 1870s, which were allegedly based upon real-life models. *c.1880, 33cm (13in) high, £4,600/$7,800*

The fixed blue glass eyes incorporate paperweight white spiral inlay and are painted with long black eyelashes beneath paler, long, feathered eyebrows.

The pate of the head has a cork infill onto which the sheepskin wig has been nailed. This method is peculiar to French dolls.

The earliest examples – such as this one – have pale complexions, closed mouths featuring outlined lips, and ears pierced for earrings.

The composition body on this doll is fitted with wooden ball joints and fixed wrists. Later examples have articulated wrists.

The body is stamped in blue with the maker's mark of "Jumeau, medaille D'or, Paris".

German Bisque-Head Dolls

Gebrüder Kuhnlenz No. 34 black bisque-head doll, with fixed brown glass eyes, open mouth, and black mohair wig. *c.1910, 43cm (17in) high, £950/$1,615*

Simon & Halbig/K & R No. 117N bisque-head doll, with flirty blue glass eyes, open mouth, and blonde wig. *c.1910, size unavailable, £550/$935*

Simon & Halbig No. 1428 bisque-head character doll, with weighted blue glass eyes, open/closed mouth, and blonde mohair wig. *c.1910, 33cm (13in) high, £580/$985*

Kämmer & Reinhardt No. 117 bisque-head character doll, with weighted brown glass eyes, open mouth, four upper teeth, and brown mohair wig. *c.*1910, 100cm (39½in) high, £3,000/$5,100

Armand Marseille No. 241 bisque-head googly-eyed doll, with weighted blue glass side-glancing eyes, smiling mouth, and brown mohair wig. *c.*1915, 29cm (11⅛in) high, £1,200/$2,050

Gebrüder Heubach No. 10532 bisque-head character doll, with weighted blue glass eyes, open mouth with upper teeth, and long brown wig. *c.*1910, 76cm (30in) high, £550/$935

Other Dolls

George II wooden doll, carved and overlaid in gesso, with painted features, nailed wig, original dress, and various accessories. *c.*1740, 36cm (14⅛in) high, £2,900/$4,900

Georgian wooden doll, carved and overlaid in gesso, with painted features (black pupil-less eyes and rouged cheeks), and brown real hair wig. *c.*1800, 71cm (28in) high, £1,650/$2,800

German Grödnertal wooden doll and papier-mâché doll, both with painted features and original clothes. Respectively *c.*1820 and *c.*1830, tallest 24cm (9½in) high, £450/$765 and £280/$475

English poured-wax shoulder-head doll, with blue glass bead eyes, painted mouth, short brown hair, and original clothes and accessories. *c.*1855, 18cm (7in) high, £420/$715

German wax-over-composition shoulder-head doll, with fixed blue glass eyes, painted mouth, blonde wig, and original clothes. *c.*1870, 56cm (22in) high, £620/$1,055

Pair of Italian Lenci felt dolls of a young boy and girl, with side-glancing blue eyes and original clothes. *c.*1930, 43cm (17in) high, £1,300/$2,200

Toys: Where to begin

A toy can sometimes reflect the technical achievements, fashion, and social events of its time. For a simple illustration of the point, look no further than a tinplate car, a diecast train engine, or a battery-operated robot. A toy can also act as a reminder of a gentler bygone age, when the nursery was the one room in the house where children might be heard as well as seen. Some collectors feel drawn to a particular period in toy manufacture such as German tinplate toys of the early 20th century or plastic toys from the last 20 years. Once you choose the area in which you want to collect, learn about it before beginning a collection.

Condition

Because many toys were made comparatively recently and in large numbers, condition is the most important aspect for collectors. A list of abbreviations is commonly used among dealers and collectors to describe the various states in which toys can be found. These abbreviations and their descriptions of condition apply to the surface of the toy – usually the state of the paintwork and any transfers or lettering on the surface. Similar classifications apply to the boxes that contained them. Any other defects should be listed separately. Starting with the most desirable condition, here is the list:

M = Mint. As if it had just left the factory.
E = Excellent. Almost as good as mint but with a very few minor scratches or tiny chips to the paintwork.
E–G = Excellent to Good. Better than good but not quite good enough to be called excellent.

G = Good. Has been played with but was well looked after and is still in good condition.
F = Fair. Rather worn but still attractive to collectors.
P = Poor. Ranges from still slightly collectable to an item in pieces.

Serious collectors of toys usually aspire to own pieces in mint condition, but they often have to settle for less because of either scarcity or price. You should look for a piece that is as close to its original condition as possible – in fact, the less restoration a toy has undergone, the better. Original paintwork is particularly desirable, but it may not always be possible to find the most ideal examples within a reasonable price range. Therefore, it is quite acceptable to buy restored examples, providing the seller is not trying to pass them off as original and the work has been done well. Scrupulous restorers and collectors will mark the underside of an object so that when the piece is passed on, the restoration is recognized and the potential for deception is greatly reduced.

An enthusiast whose main interest is in the development of a particular toy manufacturer or of a specific type of toy can use a collection of restored toys to tell a story. However, in the marketplace, these toys will always be placed in the same classification as those in poor condition.

The packaging

If a toy was boxed when it left the factory, then the survival of that box is of enormous importance to the collector. The pinnacle is to find a toy "mint in mint box" – a rarity in the market and beyond the reach of the average buyer. Nevertheless, boxes are worth mentioning because they are of such interest and can represent the greater part of the value of an item. Collectors who enjoy researching their subject use boxes to tell them which companies were buying from the manufacturers, repacking the goods, and selling them to retailers at a particular point in the toy's history.

Some toys, particularly Dinky vehicles, arrived from the wholesaler in large trade boxes instead of in individual boxes. Surviving wholesale boxes with their contents are valuable. If buying modern toys as a long-term investment, never remove them from the box. If you want to handle the toy inside, buy two!

Rare set of Britains fusiliers,
marching with a mounted officer,
*c.*1893

Wooden Toys

It can be difficult to determine whether a carved wooden toy was homemade or produced by a factory. Simple spinning tops, push-along animals, and the bigger rocking horses, wheelbarrows, and toboggans were produced by fathers for their children and by professional toy-makers. Few pre-18th century examples have survived the ravages of time and woodworm, but wooden toys continued to be made into the 19th century, and examples from this period are now valued as much for their folk art appeal as for their ability to amuse and entertain. The development of the lithographic process of printing was also enormously helpful to toy-makers, who combined wood and paper to produce colourfully decorated ships, forts, nests of boxes, building blocks, and theatres.

Beware of reproduction pieces. Wooden toys are easy to fake and many modern Far Eastern imports have caused disappointment in recent years. You might be able to identify a wooden toy that has been faked to appear older than it is. An example that is painted with regular, sparsely applied brush strokes and has no gloss left on it may be a fake. When a toy has been played with, the knocks and scratches will be irregular and more prominent in areas where the toy would have received the most handling.

British wooden chromolithographed toy theatre, with a working curtain, side boxes, orchestra pit, and a selection of cut-out characters. *c.*1860, 46cm (18in) high, £120/$205

German painted wooden Noah's Ark, with approximately 100 pairs of painted and carved wooden animals and 8 members of Noah's family. *c.*1880, 33cm (13in) high, £1,500/$2,550

British carved wooden pull-along horse on wheels, gessoed and painted as a dapple grey horse. *c.*1895, 38cm (15in) high, £190/$325

British doll's mansion No. 24, with its contents, by G. & J. Lines. *c.*1909, 84cm (33in) high, £1,550/$2,650

British spring rocking horse, with King George V royal cypher saddle cloth, by F.H. Ayres. *c.*1911, 128cm (50½in) high, £5,000/$8,500

British wooden and metal pedal locomotive, with black painted boiler, brass pipe work, and rubber wheels, by G. & J. Lines. *c.*1910, 135cm (53in) long, £1,250/$2,125

Tinplate Toys

The 1851 Great Exhibition in London provided one of the earliest venues for the display of tinplate toys. These early pieces were handmade by tinsmiths, but in the following years mass-production techniques ensured that tinplate toys became more affordable. Germany was the major centre of manufacture, in particular the region of Nuremberg, and the country held the monopoly in the field into the 20th century. These mass-produced tinplate toys, often with a clockwork mechanism, became the favourite playthings of children all over Europe and the United States.

German companies such as Lehmann, Schuco, and Märklin made tinplate toys of every description in vast quantities. The firm of the Frenchman Georges Carette was also based in Nuremberg, and his model cars, dating from 1900 to 1914, are among the finest tinplate toys made. They are well detailed and hand-painted. His fellow countrymen were also tinplate makers but preferred to hand solder the joints instead of using the clips found in German toys.

Tinplate production declined during World War I, and after 1918 it was the British companies such as Meccano, Hornby, and Lines Brothers that prospered, as well as Marx in the United States. After World War II, Japan dominated the market and by the mid-1960s, most German manufacturers had gone out of business.

German tinplate horse-drawn fire pump, hand-painted. *c*.1885, 54cm (21¼in) long, £1,100/$1,870

Hessmobil flywheel-driven two-seater open tourer, with the original composition chauffeur, lithographed in green with red and gold lining. *c*.1908, 22cm (8⅝in) long, £800/$1,360

Carette tinplate clockwork limousine, with a chauffeur and hand-painted coachwork (missing one head lamp). *c*.1911, 32cm (12⅝in) long, £1,200/$2,050

Lehmann tinplate EPL683 Halloh cyclist, with gyroscope mechanism. *c*.1925, 53cm (21in) long, £1,100/$1,870

German man on a sledge tinplate toy, probably by Distler. *c*.1925, 11cm (4¼in) long, £220/$375

Lehmann clockwork tinplate EPL773 Masuyama rickshaw. *c*.1927–30, size unavailable, £480/$815

Gebrüder Bing tinplate clockwork Tonneau

The Nuremberg company of Gebrüder Bing was founded in 1863, initially as a wholesale company prior to starting its own toy production in 1879. It produced hand-painted tinplate model cars of high quality that were accurate in their detail from 1902 until 1906. After this time, it introduced lithographed tinplate cars. However, the quality had deteriorated and was not as good as that found in earlier models. One example of the features that can be found in this Gebrüder Bing four seat, rear-entrance Tonneau is that it has automatic steering.
c.1904, 24cm (9½in) long, £6,200/$10,550

The detail here is entirely hand-painted in red with yellow lining, indicating an early production.

The nickel-plated handbrake, steering wheel, and head lamps reflect the high quality of the model.

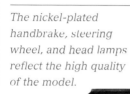

The automatic steering mechanism allows the car to travel five different routes.

The excellent condition of the model, its original head lamps, and its white rubber tyres all enhance its value.

This early model has plain wheels with thin spokes and rims – later examples have thicker spokes.

French C.I.J. P2 Alfa Romeo tinplate racing car, with orange paintwork. *c.1928, 53cm (21in) long, £1,600/$2,700*

Carr's steam wagon biscuit tin. *c.1929, 20cm (7⅞in) long, £1,500/$2,550*

German clockwork pressed-tinplate street vendor, with Mickey Mouse toy. *c.1935, 16.5cm (6½in) high, £350/$595*

Diecast and Lead Toys

Although toy soldiers and military figures, along with their vehicles, weapons, and animals, dominated the lead-toy market, many representations of a more peaceful existence, including zoos, circuses, and farms, were also produced. These figures were made of solid lead until 1893, when William Britain of the Britains Company, founded in Britain, developed the hollow-cast lead figure. Completely rounded figures with a hollow centre were created by pouring lead alloy into an engraved mould, and they required only half the metal of their solid predecessors so they were less expensive to produce. The innovation seriously challenged imports from the Continent, and although other companies adopted the process, Britains continued to dominate the market.

The earliest diecast toys, formed in a metal mould under pressure, were also made of lead, but in 1934 a safer magnesium and zinc based alloy known as mazac was developed, and it is still used to manufacture diecast toys today. Most are in the form of cars, trucks, and aircraft, and these have been made in such huge numbers that most boys growing up at any time during the past 60 years had several of them to play with at any one time. Pre-war boxed sets are rare because most boys bought vehicles individually wrapped.

Britains set No. 96 York and Lancaster regiment and set No. 113 East Yorkshire regiment, both in their original boxes. *c.*1940, size unavailable, £190/$325 and £230/$390

Set of Britains 12th Lancers, with only the lid of the original box. *c.*1894, size unavailable, £1,850/$3,150

Britains Royal Garrison Artillery, with special painted detail added to the uniforms and accessories. *c.*1938, size unavailable £1,600/$2,700

Bassett-Lowke Princess Coronation-class "Duchess of Montrose" engine and tender (the vehicle behind the engine), in British Railways green livery. *c.*1955, size unavailable, £1,600/$2,700

Bassett-Lowke "Flying Scotsman engine" and tender, in British Railways blue lined livery. *c.*1955, size unavailable, £1,100/$1,870

Bassett-Lowke 2-6-4 tank engine, in British Railways black livery. 1955, size unavailable, £950/$1,615

Minic 24M Luton transport van, with its original box. 1930s, size unavailable, £170/$290

Minic 23M tip lorry (or garbage truck), with its original box. 1930s, size unavailable, £130/$220

Dinky 514 "Spratts" Guy Van, with its original box. 1950s, size unavailable, £380/$645

Dinky 25b covered wagon, 2nd type. 1930s, size unavailable, £320/$545

Dinky 934 Leyland Octopus wagon, with its original box. 1956–64, size unavailable, £220/$375

Dinky No. 156 Rover 75, with its original box. 1954–59, size unavailable, £140/$240

Corgi 204m Rover 90 saloon, with its original box. 1956–61, size unavailable, £230/$390

Diecast and Lead Toys

Dinky No. 514 Weetabix Guy Van

The Dinky Weetabix Guy Van is the most desirable and valuable of six advertising vans with the number 514, including Lyons Swiss Rolls, Spratts Dog Food, Slumberland Beds, Golden Shred Marmalade, and Ever-Ready Batteries. *c.1952–54, size unavailable, £1,000/$1,700*

There are two wheel types. This early one sports ridged convex hubs; later types have a grooved flat hub. Both types are desirable.

Dinky produced very few yellow vehicles. The paint was applied thinly and scratches easily, so pristine examples are rare.

The original box is important and adds £300–£350/$510–$595 to the value. The orange and grey illustrated label on the blue box features the Guy Van.

The value of this model has varied over the past 30 years: collectors paid on average £1,500/$2,550 in the 1970s; £1,800/$3,050 in the 1980s; but only £1,000/$1,700 in 2005.

Corgi 227 Morris Mini-Cooper, a competition model, with its original box. 1962–65, size unavailable, £220/$375

Matchbox 53a Aston Martin DB2-4, with its original box. 1958–62, size unavailable, £320/$545

Matchbox 11a "Esso" ERF tanker, with original box. 1955–58, size unavailable, £850/$1,445

Tri-ang Spot-On 104 MG sports car, with original box. Introduced 1959, size unavailable, £130/$220

Tri-ang Spot-On 118 BMW Isetta, with original box. Introduced 1960, size unavailable, £95/$160

Robots

Science fiction really began in the early 20th century, due to H.G. Wells and his book *War of the Worlds,* followed by the late 1930s space hero Flash Gordon, who could always command the cheers of the children attending the cinema every Saturday morning. However, it wasn't until the post-war years and the advent of the space race that the imaginations of children, fostered by such characters as *Eagle* comic's Dan Dare, began the role play of earthmen versus little green men. The 1956 film *Forbidden Planet* introduced Robbie the Robot, after which the mania for robots escalated.

The Japanese were quick to perceive the potential market and during the 1950s and 1960s they unleashed onto the western market an incredible variety of clockwork and mostly battery-powered robots and spacemen. Early examples were made of printed tinplate, but by the 1960s, plastic began to dominate the market. The biggest problem was that at the time batteries allowed for only a couple of days' playtime, after which the robot was either manhandled or ignored. The buyers today pay serious money for 1950s and early 1960s models, but as with so many toys, having the original cardboard box is of paramount importance.

Nomura battery-operated Earth Man, with its original box. *c.*1958, size unavailable, £400/$680

Japanese Horikawa battery-operated Rotate-O-Matic Super Astronaut, with its original box. *c.*1965, size unavailable, £200/$340

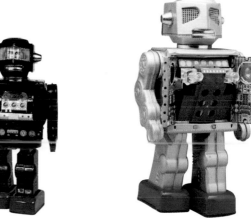

Japanese Horikawa battery-operated "Attacking Martian" Robot, with its original box. *c.*1965, size unavailable, £220/$375

Japanese Horikawa battery-operated Gear Robot, with its original box. *c.*1965, size unavailable, £200/$340

Japanese Alps battery-operated Television Spaceman Robot, with its original box. *c.*1965, size unavailable, £180/$305

Louis Marx battery-operated BBC *Dr Who* television series Dalek, with its original box. *c.*1965, size unavailable, £300/$510

Collectables

1   2   3   4

1 Art Nouveau theatre poster, featuring Sarah Bernhardt in the role of Gismonda, *c*.1895
2 Tabletop gramophone, with "morning glory" painted horn, *c*.1915
3 Olympic torch and a Royal Naval Athletics Club vest, 1948
4 French limestone water fountain, *c*.1925

The antiques marketplace I began working in over 35 years ago has undergone such radical shifts in attitude that it doesn't appear to be the same world that I fell into all those many years ago. However, the business is far better off without some of the mindless prejudice I often encountered back then, when the word "Victoriana" was often accompanied with a derisory shake of the head – and as for Art Deco, well let's not even go there. Meanwhile, between then and now there has been an evolving and continuous re-evaluation of areas that used to be considered unimportant in collecting terms. This process has been helped by the growing media interest in collecting, with new magazines, television programmes, and reference books devoted to the subject multiplying rapidly every year. We now live in a truly global marketplace courtesy of the internet that allows you to browse the auction, dealers' and collectors' sites anywhere worldwide, whether in Newcastle or New York.

Today, it is no longer considered valid only to consider collecting objects that fit strictly within the term "antique", indicating something that is over a hundred years old. The major auction houses and dealers now take seriously entire categories of pieces produced as late as the 1950s and 1960s to almost the present day. If you had suggested to an expert in the field of antiques at the beginning of the 1970s that the memorabilia of the rock and pop industry would be making serious money at auction a mere twenty years later, your comments would have met with a polite smile. Yet this has come about, and more besides.

Time was when collectors who chose a subject outside conventional bounds were considered eccentric. This is no longer the case. To announce a devoted interest in airline cutlery or beer mats

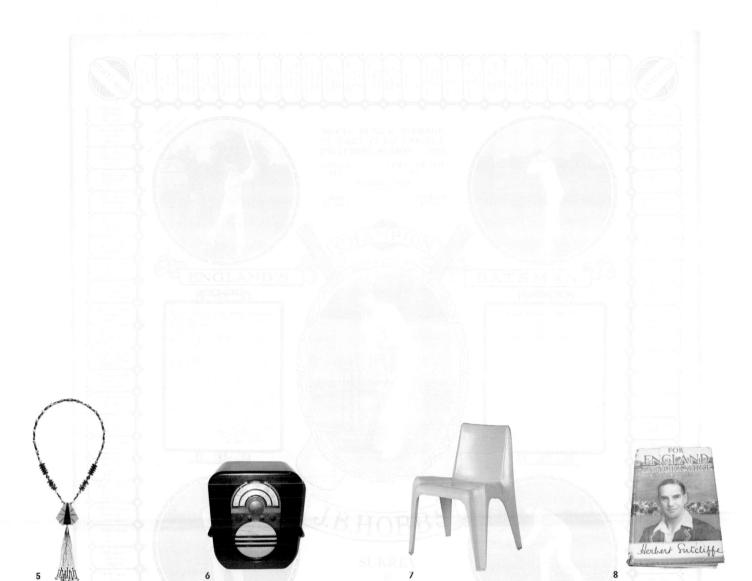

5 French Art Deco plastic necklace, with tasselled pendant, c.1930
6 British Bakelite Ecko A.C.T. 96 radio, c.1935
7 German Bofinger plastic stacking chair, designed by Helmut Batzner, c.1966
8 Signed hardback copy of *For England and Yorkshire*, by Herbert Sutcliffe, c.1950

scarcely excites comment these days, and many a happy hour is spent pursuing objects that may never be worth a great deal of money but bring a good deal of pleasure, especially to those on a strict budget. In fact, one of the most attractive aspects of collecting within some of the categories on the following pages is that so many things are still affordable. Certain types of cinema posters can still be bought inexpensively, as can costume jewellery, sports programmes, and memorabilia.

Collectables of the future

As we move forward into the new century much thought is going into what will become collectable in the future. A good tip is to seek out objects that were the first of their kind in a particular area. Over twenty years ago I suggested the Japanese battery-operated space toys of the 1950s and 1960s,

which reflected the excitement the post-war space race, would be the future collectable – if only I had had the common sense to buy a few at the time.

Progressing laterally, the first electronic calculators, disposable cameras, and mobile (cell) telephones could be important antiques of the future, just as the first one-piece moulded plastic furniture and tableware are being seriously collected today. With the ongoing interest in vintage fashion it could pay to think twice before throwing away that Jasper Conran dress or the Mulberry sports jacket. The same might be said for empty perfume bottles that once contained essences retailed by Jean-Paul Gaultier or Issey Miyake. Never forget that the throwaway of today has an uncanny knack of becoming the collectable of tomorrow. Concentrate on respected, well-known designers and manufacturers and you may be on to an appreciating asset.

Mechanical Music

Musical mechanisms were first fitted in Swiss clocks and automata in the 17th century. The musical box, powered by clockwork or operated by a handle, came into being in its own right in the 18th century. It has a rotating cylinder that produces sound when raised pins pluck a row of fine steel teeth that form a comblike metal plate. By the 19th century the musical box was established as an affordable form of entertainment. As techniques improved, seven or eight tunes could be set on one cylinder. Earlier boxes with a wooden inlaid flap or glass top are in demand, and rare types with special effects or features that improve the sound are prized.

The first phonograph that used a rotating cylinder and needles to record and play the human voice was produced by Thomas Edison in the 1870s. Ten years later, Alexander Graham Bell developed the grapho-phone using wax cylinders. About the same time, the gramophone was also introduced, and with it, flat discs, a great innovation. At first, hand-cranking made the speed of the records difficult to regulate, but the development of a clockwork mechanism overcame the early problems. By the 1920s, electrical recording had been introduced and the world of mechanical music began to take on a new dimension.

Swiss Nicole Frères key-wind cylinder musical box, playing four airs, with a rosewood case. 1855, cylinder 21cm (8¼in) long, box 37.5cm (14¾in) long, £1,200/$2,050

Swiss Drums, Bells, and Castanets visible musical box, playing ten airs, with a rosewood case, probably by Baker Troll. 1885, cylinder 33cm (13in) long, box 61cm (24in) long, £1,000/$1,700

Polyphon-style 104P penny-in-the-slot upright disc musical box, with a carved walnut cabinet and 40 sheet metal discs included. 1895, disc 50cm (19½in) diameter, box 78cm (30¾in) wide, £4,500/$7,650

Polyphon-style musical box, with a walnut case and 18 sheet metal discs (mechanism damaged). 1895, disc 20.5cm (8in) diameter, box 25.5cm (10in) wide, £240/$410

Edison Red Gem model K phonograph, with black painted horn and oak case. 1899, 25.5cm (10in) wide, £360/$610

EMG model XB gramophone, with an electric motor, oak case, and Davey papier-mâché horn. 1920, case 53cm (21in) wide, £2,700/$4,600

Automata

The earliest automata date from the 18th century and often feature animals and birds made in precious metal. Late 18th century examples that are typical of the ambassadorial gifts of the time can be found in Britain at the Bowes Museum in County Durham, which boasts a silver swan with moving neck, and at Waddesdon Manor in Buckinghamshire, which is home to a magnificent elephant with flapping ears.

The golden age of automata occurred in the late 19th and early 20th centuries, with many of the top makers working in Paris. Such makers included Gaston Decamps, Gustave Vichy, Léopold Lambert, J. Phalibois, and Fernand Martin.

Regarded at the time as parlour pieces, automata were a great source of entertainment and amusement. They were made mainly for adults and had mechanical movements (sometimes incorporating music), which, when wound, caused rabbits to rise up out of cabbages or dolls to dance, or operated dancing sailors and rolling waves, fiddling monkeys, and magicians who were able to remove their own heads.

Simpler types of automata included clockwork swimming and walking dolls and, after Thomas Edison produced the miniature phonograph, sophisticated French dolls that could talk and sing by means of a wax cylinder hidden in the body.

French Turkish smoker automaton, with a hookah and sipping from a coffee cup, by Léopold Lambert. *c.*1890, 53cm (21in) high, £3,000/$5,100

French *polichinelle* (Punch) on a velocipede automaton, with legs that alternately lift as the vehicle is ridden, by Alexandra Nicolas Theroude. *c.*1860, 28cm (11in) long, £4,000/$6,800

French whippet automaton, with a turning head and legs that move to give forward motion, by Roullet & Decamps. *c.*1910, 26cm (10¼in) high, £620/$1,055

French peasant and pig automaton, with the pig making head, shoulder, and foot movements when fed by Paddy the peasant, with integral music box, by Antoine and Gustave Vichy. *c.*1900, 76cm (30in) high, £8,800/$14,950

French coin-operated village panorama automaton, in a glazed cabinet (converted from original clockwork mechanism to electric power). *c.*1880, 102cm x 94cm (40in x 37in), £300/$510

French musical automaton of a waltzing couple, by Gustave Vichy. *c.*1880, 33cm (13in) high, £3,000/$5,100

Posters

The illustrated poster began to gain prominence from about 1880, as manufacturers began to understand the enormous benefits that could be gained from pictorial advertising. This was an age that had new and exciting merchandise to sell, such as bicycles, corsets, and cigarette papers, and these products often lent themselves magnificently to the skill and imagination of such artists as Henri de Toulouse Lautrec, Jules Chéret, and Alphonse Mucha.

The lithographic printing process, which was introduced in the 1840s, revolutionized the art of poster-making. The new technique involved the use of a flat stone onto which a design was drawn in wax crayon, which acted as a resist.

The stone was then washed with a powerful acid, which ate away the areas that were unprotected by the wax. The remaining raised design was then inked, and the poster was printed from it. The stones were thick enough to be rubbed down and used again.

After World War I, the fantasy maidens and music hall girls of Toulouse Lautrec and Chéret disappeared, when the modern age heralded another revolution in poster design. The preoccupation with speed and new, fast, comfortable methods of transport, such as the train, the ocean liner, and the airplane, were reflected in the work of designers such as A.M. Cassandre and Paul Colin.

Jules Chéret "Exposition des Maîtres Japonais". 1890, 83.5cm x 121.5cm (32¾in x 47¾in), £460/$780

Henri Thiriet "Omega" advertising poster. 1897, 138cm x 97.5cm (54¼in x 38¼in), £1,000/$1,700

Jules Chéret "Bigarreau Mugnier" advertising poster. 1895, 241cm x 82cm (94¾in x 32¼in), £1,000/$1,700

Eugène Grasset "Marque Georges Richard Cycles et Automobiles" advertising poster. 1899, 105.5cm x 145.5cm (41½in x 57¼in), £850/$1,445

Alphonse Mucha "Cassan Fils" advertising poster. 1896, 163cm x 60cm (64in x 23½in), £2,800/$4,750

F. Coulet "Salle de L'Étoile" advertising poster.
1900, 159cm x 117cm (62½in x 46in), £450/$765

Alphonse Mucha poster
The Czech artist Mucha produced this "Lorenzaccio" poster for "Theatre de la Renaissance", one of a series of dramatic theatrical posters commissioned in the 1890s by the French actress Sarah Bernhardt, who is depicted here. *1896, 201.5cm x 70cm (79¼in x 27½in), £4,000/$6,800*

The meditative pose and dark colour hints at the theatrical role. The grotesque beast adds a powerful Gothic element to the composition.

Mucha often includes architectural detail such as lettered mosaic, sometimes enhanced with gilt. The subject overlapping the architectural detail creates a three-dimensional effect.

Mucha includes the name of the printer F. Champenois at the base of his posters. Mucha's signature is included at the bottom right.

Alphonse Mucha "Biscuits Lefèvre-Utile" advertising poster and calendar. 1897, 61cm x 45cm (24in x 17¾in), £1,500/$2,550

Anonymous "Cie Gle. Transatlantique" travel poster. 1925, 98.5cm x 69.5cm (38¾in x 27¼in), £340/$580

Roger de Valerio "Citroen" advertising poster. 1920, 119.5cm x 161cm (47in x 63¼in), £680/$1,155

Architectural Antiques

There was a time when such items as Victorian fireplaces and mantelpieces, cast-iron jardinières, wrought iron gates, and garden seating were available in great quantity at low prices. However, with the passion we now have for recreating the past, all these objects have acquired value. Architectural salvage has become big business and collectors are prepared to pay large sums of money for the right piece.

One of the main reasons for buying these objects is to install them in older houses and gardens that have had a series of "improvements" during the 1950s and 1960s and are now being passionately restored to their original glory.

Buyers are paying not only for the craftsmanship of the past, but also for the age and wear. The genuine patina of a section of oak panelling, the original paint on a garden seat, the moss and lichen on a stone urn, and the original chains and drops of a chandelier are all desirable qualities in this market.

The Coalbrookdale ironworks in Britain produced the cast iron garden furniture, ornamental gates and hallstands that are most sought after today. However, wrought iron gates incorporating elaborate designs can often be found at reasonable prices, which are usually lower than that of a modern replacement.

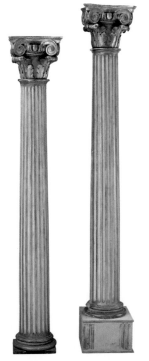

Large French Baroque stone trough, with an everted top rim. 17th–18th century, 188cm (74in) long, £1,700/$2,900

French Baroque limestone fireplace surround. *c.*1680, 270cm (106in) high, £4,000/$6,800

French cast iron pump. *c.*1850, 97cm (38in) high, £600/$1,020

Italian Vicenza stone capital, carved as a Corinthian capital with scrolling acanthus. *c.*1900, 43cm (17in) high, £550/$935

Pair of British cast iron two-handled garden urns, with Neoclassical decoration. *c.*1875, 61cm (24in) high, £700/$1,190

Pair of Louis XVI painted and parcel-gilt columns and a single pedestal. *c.*1785, without pedestal 183cm (72in) high, £3,000/$5,100

Italian Neoclassical urn

The sculpture studios found in Naples, Florence, Rome, and other major Italian cities produced all types of decorative architectural and garden statuary such as this urn with its cover. These studios are probably better known for their classical, historical, and literary subjects, as well as the commissioned portraits of wealthy European travellers who undertook "the Grand Tour" during the 18th and 19th centuries.

c.1875, 73cm (28¾in) high, £2,000/$3,400

The surface of this urn and its cover shows evidence of being orginal garden statuary. If colourful lichens are present, they often enhance value and should not be removed.

The way in which the stylized floral swags are carved indicates a late 19th century production.

More often than not architectural objects are unsigned. If present, signatures add value.

The socle base has evidence of damage, which lowers the value in comparison with a perfect example. However, most buyers prefer repairs on an older piece rather than modern replacements.

Two similar Italian Renaissance-style carved marble jardinières, with associated stands. *c.*1880, 75cm (29½in) and 70cm (27½in) long, £2,500/$4,250 (for the pair)

One of a pair of Louis XV-style giltwood doors, incorporating antique elements. 1880s, 308cm (121in) high, £2,200/$3,750 (for the pair)

French Baroque stone and iron wellhead. 17th–18th century, 210cm (82½in) high, £2,750/$4,675

Kitchenware

Along with "kitchenware", the term "domestic bygones" encompasses items as varied as copper saucepans, pewter jugs, dairy equipment, and wooden carpet beaters. However, few individual collections include examples of every type of object that contributed to the running of a household. Many collectors of metalware, for example, would not dream of buying treen (small domestic wooden objects) and a collector of jelly moulds would not necessarily seek out copper warming pans or smoothing irons.

Collectors in the United States were probably the first to appreciate what is often considered folk art, attaching significance to the mundane but often beautifully made objects that tell us so much about how ordinary people went about their daily lives.

The skill of the maker and the years of hard use so often evident in these pieces are now thoroughly appreciated by collectors. Although kitchenware has grown in popularity in recent times, it is still a collecting area where there is plenty of scope to buy items at affordable prices. However, there are specialized areas such as early treen and Cornishware (blue and white-banded pottery storage jars) that have seen a rapid escalation in prices.

Cast iron and wood egg stand.
c.1830, size unavailable, £250/$425

Kenrick quarter-pint cast iron pestle and mortar. c.1880, size unavailable, £90/$155

Carved wooden butter dish and knife, with a Staffordshire "Willow" pattern inset dish. c.1895, size unavailable, £60/$100

Two cast iron box-type coffee grinders, the larger by Baldwin, the other by Kenrick. c.1860, sizes unavailable, £100/$170 and £80/$135

Copper jelly mould, by Benham and Froud. c.1880, 18cm (7in) high, £350/$595

Various buff stoneware storage jars and covers, with applied and embossed ribbon labels. 1880–1920, sizes unavailable, £15–£35/$25–$60 each

Swedish enamelled four-pint teakettle. *c.*1935, size unavailable, £20/$35

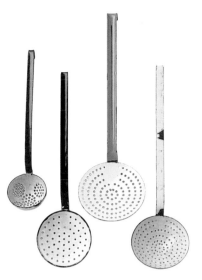

Three American enamelled skimmer/strainers and a straining ladle. Respectively, 1900, 1870, 1930, and 1910, sizes unavailable, £15–£40/$25–$70 each

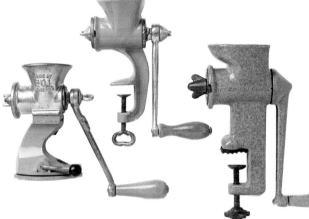

Three enamelled mincers or grinders. 1930s–50s, sizes unavailable, £15–£20/$25–$35 each

Various aluminium measuring jugs. *c.*1920s, sizes unavailable, £10/$17 each

Painted pine kitchen cupboard/food safe. *c.*1935, size unavailable, £75/$130

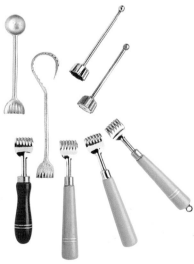

Selection of butter curlers and two butter pat makers. 1920s–50s, sizes unavailable, £5–£10/$9–$17 each

Cornishware storage jars and covers, by T.G. Green. *c.*1930, sizes unavailable, £30–£60/$55–$100 each

Costume Jewellery

Jewellery made from coloured glass and base metals was produced as early as the 18th century. In the late 19th and early 20th centuries, glass beads and fake pearls were fashioned into pieces that were considered grossly inferior to those with real gems. However, this changed during the 1920s and "costume jewellery" became popular with the liberated post-war woman, who now wore more informal clothes and wanted casual jewellery to match. Parisian couturiers, including Poiret, Molyneux, Patou, Schiaparelli, and Chanel, began to produce stylish costume jewellery that complemented their clothes. In 1927, *Vogue* magazine stated,

"Fashion has decided that all we need ask of an ornament is to adorn us, and that neither our complexions nor our gems are to be natural."

During the 1930s, the focus of design switched to the United States, where costume jewellery was designed by top names, manufactured on a massive scale, and had a great following. The best pieces by designers such as Haskell and Chanel have gone up consistently in price over the last ten years and will probably continue to do so, whereas examples by certain 1960s designers such as Paco Rabanne are still affordable and may prove a good investment.

Art Nouveau insect brooch, with paste ruby, citrine, and a later emerald pendant inset in an alloy metal mount. *c.*1890, 7cm (2¾in) high, £225/$380

Bakelite "crib toy" necklace, with sailor pendant. *c.*1945, pendant 5.5cm (2⅛in) high, £200/$340

Coro Art Deco silver and paste necklace. *c.*1937, 42cm (16½in) diameter, £175/$300

Art Deco Cartier-style Tutti-Frutti type flower basket brooch. *c.*1925, 5.5cm (2⅛in) high, £225/$380

Enamelled butterfly brooch, with a large square-cut imitation amethyst. *c.*1935, 7.5cm (2⅜in) wide, £180/$305

Josef of Hollywood hoop necklace. *c.*1945, 45cm (17¾in) diameter, £550/$935

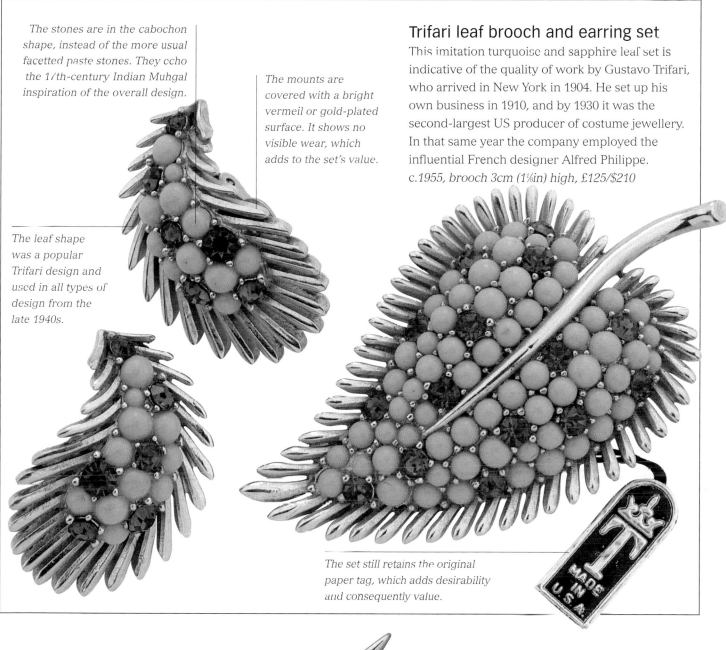

The stones are in the cabochon shape, instead of the more usual facetted paste stones. They echo the 17th-century Indian Muhgal inspiration of the overall design.

The mounts are covered with a bright vermeil or gold-plated surface. It shows no visible wear, which adds to the set's value.

The leaf shape was a popular Trifari design and used in all types of design from the late 1940s.

Trifari leaf brooch and earring set

This imitation turquoise and sapphire leaf set is indicative of the quality of work by Gustavo Trifari, who arrived in New York in 1904. He set up his own business in 1910, and by 1930 it was the second-largest US producer of costume jewellery. In that same year the company employed the influential French designer Alfred Philippe. *c.1955, brooch 3cm (1⅛in) high, £125/$210*

The set still retains the original paper tag, which adds desirability and consequently value.

Marcel Boucher wheat-sheaf brooch, with a *pavé* setting of rhinestones in a rhodium-plated mount. *c.*1940, 11cm (4¼in) high, £200/$340

Black Bakelite penguin brooch, inset with diamante. *c.*1935, 6.5cm (2½in) high, £45/$75

Floral necklace and earrings, with paste topaz, by Henkel & Grosse for Christian Dior. *c.*1964, necklace 42cm (16½in) diameter, £480/$815

Sporting Memorabilia

In recent years, memorabilia relating to a huge range of sporting events and activities has become big business. However, most people who have an interest in collecting concentrate on just one, or possibly two, areas. In each category, the most expensive pieces are usually clothing or equipment known to have belonged to a famous sports personality, and the least expensive are pamphlets, programmes, and tickets relating to specific events. Whether your passion is for football, golf, fishing, baseball, rugby, tennis, or billiards, you will find no shortage of objects.

The bigger the sport is internationally, such as cricket, football (or soccer), and golf, the greater the number of

collectors there will be, compensated for by the volume of memorabilia produced. Baseball, for example, is primarily collected in the United States, so if you find baseball material outside North America it is likely to be under-appreciated.

Most football (soccer) programmes are usually affordable, but exceptionally rare examples can fetch phenomenal sums if they commemorate a special sporting event. The world record price for a football (soccer) programme is £7,130/$12,120, paid for one printed for the 1889 Cup Final between Preston North End and Wolverhampton Wanderers, when Preston became the first club ever to win the League and the Cup in the same year.

Large, smooth gutty golf ball (unused). *c*.1850, size unavailable, £5,000/$8,500

Silvertown gutty golf ball, moulded and mesh lined (retaining 95 percent of its original paint). *c*.1890, size unavailable, £500/$850

Feather golf ball (with a split seam). Early 19th century, 4.5cm (1¾in) diameter, £1,000/$1,700

Silver vesta case, inset with a colour enamel plaque depicting a golfer in full swing. *c*.1905, size unavailable, £480/$815

Monochrome print of the celebrated golfer "Old Tom Morris". *c*.1910, 34cm x 22cm (13⅜in x 8⅝in), £50/$85

Silver rectangular presentation dish, with a colour enamelled plaque titled "The 19th Hole" in the centre and engraved "Neasden Golf Club". Birmingham hallmarks for 1916, size unavailable, £750/$1,275

Royal Doulton rack plate, colour printed with an episode from Charles Crombie's *Illustrated Rules of Golf*. *c*.1910, size unavailable, £100/$170

Carlton Ware tobacco jar and metal cover, printed and hand coloured with a golf scene titled "Far and Sure". *c*.1900, size unavailable, £170/$290

Royal Doulton pottery vase, with an elliptical panel colour printed with a golf scenario titled "Is a caddie always necessary?", after Charles Dana Gibson. *c*.1910, 9cm (3½in) high, £180/$305

1930 World Cup gold medal

This gold medal was presented to José Nasazzi, captain of the Uruguay team, during the "Glorious Period" of football at the River Plate, from the early 1920s to the mid-1930s, when the team won three South American Championships, two World Olympic Championships (later recognized as World Cups), and the first World Cup Championship, held in 1930. *1930, 2cm x 3.5cm (¾in x 1⅜in), £23,000/$39,100*

The medal was cast in Paris from pure gold. It appears that only one gold medal was cast for presentation to the winning captain, making this medal exceptionally rare and highly important.

The obverse features the Jules Rimet trophy, incorporating the winged figure holding olive branches emblematic of peace, beneath the inscription "Coupe Du Monde".

The reverse bears the inscription "José Nasazzi, Capitan" within a victor's laurel crown, cast in low relief, and the date "Juillet 1930", beneath the match venue "Montevideo".

The stylized medal was designed by the French sculptor Abel Lafleur, who worked in the popular contemporary style recognized today as Art Deco.

Royal Doulton Morrisian Ware pottery vase, printed with a cavalier golfer in full swing. *c*.1905, 22cm (8⅝in) high, £580/$985

Hardback edition of the book *Golf Courses on the G.W.R.* *c*.1923, size unavailable, £550/$935

Sporting Memorabilia

Pottery point-of-sale figure (used to promote a product in a shop), inscribed "Superorma, The New Tailoring". *c.*1930, 33cm (13in) high, £250/$425

Brass figural ashtray, mounted with a bramble golf-ball head golfer, designed by John Hassall. *c.*1925, 14.5cm (5⅝in) high, £150/$255

Silver-plated figure of a golfer, modelled in full swing, by W. Zwick. *c.*1910, 29cm (11½in) high, £800/$1,360

Point-of-sale figures of Dunlop Man, Silver King Man, and Bromford Man. *c.*1930s, sizes unavailable, £200/$340, £6,000/$10,200, and £750/$1,275

Large Royal Doulton The Golfer character jug. *c.*1970, size unavailable, £60/$100

Autographed cricket bat, from the 1954–55 Ashes test series, with signatures from 17 English and 13 Australian players. *c.*1955, size unavailable, £400/$680

Autographed 1948 Ashes test series team sheet, with 18 signatures, including the captain Don Bradman. 1948, size unavailable, £440/$750

Autographed cricket bat, signed by Jack Hobbs, used to achieve 211 runs in the test match series against South Africa held in June 1924 at Lords. *c.*1924, size unavailable, £15,000/$25,500

Limited-edition colour print, depicting Geoff Hurst scoring his hat trick and final goal in the 1966 World Cup at Wembley, signed by Geoff Hurst. *c.*1966, size unavailable, £210/$360

Newcastle United 1926–27 1st Division championship shirt, worn by Hughie Gallacher. *c.*1926, size unavailable, £7,600/$12,900

2005 Ashes test series cricket stump, used in Nottingham, 25th–29th August, when England recorded a three-wicket victory, with letter of authenticity. 2005, size unavailable, £850/$1,445

Silver-plated boxing belt, won in 1909 by John Broughton Meal (1886–1965) of Huddersfield, cased. *c.*1909, size unavailable, £400/$680

Gilbert rugby ball, signed by 26 members of the 2003 England World Cup Squad. *c.*2003, size unavailable, £130/$220

Muhammad Ali vs Henry Cooper programme, for the World Heavyweight Championship held on 21st May 1966 at the Arsenal Stadium, Highbury, London. 1966, size unavailable, £160/$270

Everlast boxing glove, signed by Muhammad Ali, with certificate of authenticity. Late 20th century, size unavailable, £500/$850

Original Oxford University athletics meet programme, for the 6th May 1954 one-mile run by Roger Bannister in 3 minutes and 59.4 seconds, signed by Roger Bannister. 1954, size unavailable, £440/$750

Plastics

To supplement the dwindling supplies of luxury materials, such as tortoiseshell, ivory, horn, lacquer, shellac, and amber, plastics were developed during the second half of the 19th century. The introduction of Bakelite between World Wars I and II widened the scope for designers such as Wells Coates, who were keen to exploit the malleability of the material, with inventive shapes applied to radio and telephone design.

By the 1930s various plastics were being used to make everything from basic household goods to the most startling, innovative, state-of-the-art furniture, model cars, scientific and medical equipment, and jewellery. However, plastics suffered an image problem after World War II. The explosion in production, sometimes at the expense of design and quality, meant that plastic goods were seen as downmarket. The designers who long appreciated the scope offered by plastics fought back, with the result that some of the most exciting and well-crafted objects have been made in plastic. During the 1960s, Italian and Danish furniture designers explored the possibilities of injection-moulded thermoplastic, where the powdered plastic was heated to a malleable state when subjected to intense pressure. Verner Panton's one piece, brightly coloured stacking chair, produced in 1970, resulted from this technology. Still made today, the early examples sought by collectors have thicker bodies.

Red and white "Chicpack" cosmetic box, with a screw-twist lid. *c*.1935, 7cm (2¾in) wide, £45/$75

Simulated streaked amber Scottie dog comb. *c*.1935, 14cm (5½in) wide, £35/$60

Black cat ring stand, on a circular red base. *c*.1930, 8.5cm (3¼in) wide, £110/$190

Simulated mother-of-pearl lady's cigarette case, featuring a hand at the clasp. *c*.1935, 8cm x 9cm (3in x 3½in), £195/$330

Horse head brooch, in simulated lapis, with a stylized gilt-metal mane. *c*.1935, 5.5cm (2⅛in) high, £45/$75

Bakelite simulated red-brown lacquer, organically shaped atomizer. *c.*1925, 16.5cm (6½in) high, £195/$330

GPO 232 Chinese red telephone

This particular telephone model is referred to as a hand combination set, with the hearing and speaking devices combined in one hand-held section. It was introduced in 1937 and made into the late 1950s. It was also produced in ivory, jade green, and the more standard black.
c.1955, 23cm (9in) wide, £500/$850

Always check for a solid colour, because some black telephones have been sprayed to emulate the more desirable and expensive red and green versions.

The original handset cable is normally in a colour that matches the set.

The "cheese drawer" slides out to reveal a telephone exchange card.

Examples that retain their original printed number discs are more desirable.

Ecko A22 Bakelite radio, by E.K. Colc Ltd. *c.*1945, size unavailable, £470/$800

Clear plastic tiara, inset with diamante. *c.*1935, 5cm (2in) high, £195/$330

Bakelite "Golden Arrow" model car, by Automobiles Geographical Ltd. *c.*1930, 42.5cm (16¾in) long, £500/$850

Index

Acknowledgments

The author would like to thank the following for their assistance in producing this book: Jeanette and Malcolm Hayhurst; Linda B.; David Rago; B.B.C. Worldwide; Greta Johnson; Kneale Chapman; Roland Whitehead; Ryk Barnett; Leigh Edwards; Frances Godden; Michelle Gonsalves; Josephine Olley; Julian Roup; Leigh and Rachel Gotch; James and Sally Stratton; Frank Maraschiello; Christi Clark; John Sandon; Fergus Gambon; Susan Newell; Colin Sheaf; Anthony Du Boulay; Mark Oliver; Natalie Evison; Johanna Rhodes; Michael Moorcroft; Lorraine Turner; Beth Atwood; Gareth Williams; Sue Lunt and the Decorative Arts Department at The Walker Art Gallery, Liverpool; Muir Hewitt; Nick Jones; John Clarke; Beverley Adams; L. Adams; Beth Meyer; The Trustees of the Wedgwood Museum, Barlaston, Stoke-on-Trent, Staffordshire

Picture credits